What the Bible Really Says:

Casting New Light on the Book of Books

What the Bible Really Says:

Casting New Light on the Book of Books

MANFRED BARTHEL

Translated and adapted by Mark Howson

William Morrow and Company, Inc.
New York   1982

Library of Congress Cataloging in Publication Data

Howson, Mark.
    What the Bible really says.

    Translation and adaptation of: Was wirklich in
der Bibel steht / Manfred Barthel.
    Bibliography: p.
    Includes index.
    1. Bible—Criticism, interpretation, etc.
I. Barthel, Manfred, 1924–   Was wirklich in
der Bibel steht.   II. Title.
BS514.2.H6813   220.6   81-18679
ISBN 0-688-00821-6   AACR2

Printed in the United States of America

First Edition

1 2 3 4 5 6 7 8 9 10

BOOK DESIGN BY MICHAEL MAUCERI

CONTENTS

I
THE BOOK OF THE BIBLE

PAPYRUS AND PARCHMENT   17
PAPER AND PRINTING: THE RAW MATERIALS OF
   LUTHER'S REFORMATION   22

II
THE OLD TESTAMENT

Introduction   27

The Creation Myths   33

   THE TWOFOLD CREATION   33
   THE SEARCH FOR PARADISE   37
   THE TREE OF KNOWLEDGE; OR, WHAT'S WRONG WITH
      THIS PICTURE?   40
   ZIUSUDRA'S ARK   44
   WHY THE TOWER OF BABEL WAS NOT ONE OF THE
      SEVEN WONDERS OF THE WORLD   56

The Dream of the Promised Land   63

   THE MYSTERY OF ABRAHAM   63
   JOSEPH; OR, UP FROM SLAVERY   87
   MOSES   104

The Conquest of Canaan   129

THE BOOK OF JOSHUA: MYTHOLOGY OR MILITARY
    HISTORY?   129
THE BOOK OF JUDGES: HISTORY WRITTEN IN BLOOD   138
THE BOOK OF RUTH: A GOOD MAN IS HARD TO FIND   155
FIRST AND SECOND SAMUEL; OR, THE KINGMAKER OF
    CANAAN   159

Splendor and Majesty: The Legacy of Solomon   174

THE FIRST BOOK OF KINGS: CONCERNING DAVID AND
    ABISHAG, BATHSHEBA AND ADONIJAH, SOLOMON,
    AND MANY OTHERS   174
THE SECOND BOOK OF KINGS: THE BEGINNING OF THE
    END   194
THE BOOK OF EZRA AND THE BOOK OF NEHEMIAH:
    THE RESTORATION OF JERUSALEM   230

*Ripping Yarns: The Apocryphal Books of Tobit and Judith,
and the Book of Esther*   234

TOBIAS, THE DREAMER   235
JUDITH, THE HEROINE   236
ESTHER, THE QUEEN   238

*Rebellion and Resurrection: The First and Second Books of
the Maccabees*   241

The Poetic Books   248

THE BOOK OF JOB: REASONING WITH GOD   248
THE PSALMS: PLAY SKILLFULLY WITH A LOUD NOISE   252
THE BOOK OF PROVERBS: THE WISE SHALL INHERIT
    GLORY   255
THE BOOK OF ECCLESIASTES: KOHELET THE FATALIST 258
THE SONG OF SOLOMON: I HAVE COMPARED THEE, O
    MY LOVE . . .   261
ECCLESIASTICUS AND THE WISDOM OF SOLOMON:
    FROM PROVERBS TO PLATO   262
THE PROPHETS   265

Contents

III
THE ESSENES: THE CHILDREN OF LIGHT AND THE TEACHER OF RIGHTEOUSNESS

IV
THE NEW TESTAMENT

Jesus: The Man from Galilee   298

Jesus and His Disciples   313

The Gospel According to Saint Matthew   318

The Gospel According to Saint Mark   328

The Gospel According to Saint Luke   337

The Gospel According to Saint John and the Book of Revelation   345

    REVELATION   353

V
THE LAST DAYS OF JESUS

VI
THE APOSTLE PAUL

APPENDICES

Miracles Performed by Jesus   390

Parables of Jesus   392

Historical—Biblical Chronology   394

Selected Bibliography   397

Index   401

In the beginning was the word.

—John 1:1

PART I

THE BOOK OF
THE BIBLE

*My favorite book? You're going to laugh—
it's the Bible.*

—Bertolt Brecht

"Our ultimate purpose in reading the Bible is to make us better men and women." Thus wrote the philosopher Immanuel Kant almost two hundred years ago.

If Kant's reasoning is still valid today—and who are we to contradict him?—that means that in one year alone at least 9,280,222 men and women set out on this particular path to self-improvement; or at any rate, taking 1978 as an example, over nine million copies of the Book of Books were distributed throughout 150 different countries.

The Bible—in 286 different languages—can be found on bookshelves all around the globe. The Japanese alone, though fewer than 1 percent of them are professing Christians, have bought more than 150 million Bibles in the past few years. In West Germany the Bible, as a category in itself, is outsold only by atlases and cookbooks. The ordinary consumer seems to get a lot more use out of the latter, however; out of every hundred Bible owners only fifteen are actually Bible readers. The Good Book seems rapidly to be achieving the status of a piece of bookshelf bric-a-brac, or at best an attractive bookend.

Still, a copy of the Bible is not hard to come by in most ordinary, worldly contexts. You can pick one up at the supermarket. You can slip one from your hotel-room drawer into your luggage without suffering any particular pangs of guilt. The spoken Word is widely available on records and cassettes;

some cornflakes boxes in America are adorned with scriptural texts; and in one Black Forest spa you can put a five-mark piece in a vending-machine slot and wait for the machine to disgorge your vacationer's pocket Gospel. All this does not change the essential fact that though virtually no other book has been as widely disseminated as the Bible, it remains a book that comparatively few readers seem to be willing to crack—in short, a best-seller that no one reads.

This curious state of affairs has inspired a whole series of new translations, all trying their best to make the venerable, familiar words of the Gospels keep pace with the "living language." This may not be the right way to go about it, though; as new revisions and translations multiply, more and more questions are being raised about the linguistic accuracy of scriptural verses that we have been familiar, if not always comfortable, with since childhood.

Because we no longer look to the Bible as the model for our everyday conduct, but only as a monument of our literary language, the gulf between the Bible and its readers threatens to grow wider with time. Ever since the linguists and philologists began toiling in this particular vineyard, the Book of Books has increasingly become approachable only after an extensive course of study—twelve semesters at least—in theology and the sister disciplines.

What's to be done about this? Should we just put our *Good News* or Anchor Bibles back on the shelf and regretfully agree with the poet Ricarda Huth, who writes, "There can be no doubt that Luther's German Bible* has a beauty that no other translation could ever hope to match. Luther's language is the language of a true believer as well as a great poet; his words have

---

* The German Bible appeared in 1537 and has since become the authoritative standard of the German written language, perhaps even more influential than the Authorized Version has been in English.

12

a gritty, expressive power which has never been equaled. No other translation has the same strong, sweet pungency, which evokes the landscape of the Holy Land and the wondrous works of the Lord, and makes the soul rejoice"?

With all due respect to Ricarda Huth, however, we should bear in mind that the mighty Luther based his translation on a Hebrew edition of the Old Testament prepared by Gershon ben Moshe Soncino, which was published in Brescia in 1494 (barely forty years earlier), and that Luther was writing for his contemporaries and relying on the knowledge that was available to him at that time. He had no original texts to work from, and he was obviously innocent of all the new techniques and discoveries in the realms of archaeology and textual criticism that have since done so much to change our conception of the biblical world.

It is true that the power of Luther's language has never been surpassed, and that the King James Version contains some of the finest passages of English prose, but many words have taken on different meanings since these translations were written, and many historical ambiguities have been clarified to a degree that was hardly possible in the sixteenth century. For example, in Genesis 24:2, Luther refers to a remarkable gesture that is associated with the taking of an oath. Abraham says to his "eldest servant," "Put, I pray thee, thy hand under my thigh, and I will make thee swear by the Lord." But this description of an oath-taking ceremony has no parallel in any known culture, past or present, and in fact is simply not the way it must have been.

Luther interpreted this passage to mean that the eldest servant grasped Abraham's thigh. More recent archaeological research has made it clear that in cultures in which the phallus was sacred, it was customary for a man to put his hand over his own genitals when he was swearing a solemn oath. (The similarity between our words *testify* or *testament* and *testicles* is not just a linguistic coincidence.) This is the ceremonial gesture that the author of the original text had in mind, but for us the translator's mistaken reading, "Put thy hand under my thigh," is still in the Authorized Version. Luther's text is identical to the 1611 King James Version in this respect, and most subsequent versions of the Bible in German and English have perpetuated the misunderstanding.

Such things may not seem important to Fundamentalist readers; the Bible is the literal embodiment of their faith, and it will not lose one iota of its real meaning, even if not a single verse of the Holy Writ can be corroborated by independent historical investigation. On the other hand—apart from all considerations of the ultimate truth of the Bible—it is also clear that the account the Bible gives of actual events is indelibly colored by the historical context of the events, so deeply embedded, if you will, in the common clay of the archaeological record that their particular meaning can be uncovered only if we resort to the most recent scholarly findings, including the discovery and decipherment of parallel ancient texts. Our new translations should not try to modernize the language of the Bible, but they can and must clear away the accumulated dust and rubble that prevent us from finding our way to a clear understanding of the actual meaning of the text.

Obviously, this is no easy task. After all, the Bible is really a kind of anthology, an assortment of incredible stylistic diversity—songs, chronicles, riddles, fables, proverbs, and revelations—which makes the epithet "Book of Books" very apt in a strictly literal sense.

We must also bear in mind that the contents of these various books were brought together over a period of some fifteen hundred years. The earliest writings date from about 1200 B.C. and the latest from around A.D. 150, about the same span of time that separates *Beowulf* from Günter Grass. And on top of that, at least in the case of the Old Testament, most of the recorded events had already become immemorial traditions by the time they were finally written down. These were stories told around the campfires and in the tents of nomadic tribes, stories that were lavishly embroidered upon, transmitted solely by word of mouth for generations, until they were set down in writing by whoever felt inclined to do so—certainly not by their original authors, who were long dead by then.

Even so, these original texts of the Bible were not the texts that the scholars who produced our modern translations had in front of them. The Latin manuscripts of the Bible from which our modern versions are derived date from about A.D. 1000; by then Charlemagne had been dead for 186 years, the Vikings had long since settled down in Normandy, and the Venetian fleet already ruled the Adriatic.

How many scribal errors and mistranslations crept in, in this span of a thousand years or more? Surprisingly few, in fact, though we have known this for certain only since the early 1950s when the first of the Dead Sea Scrolls were successfully unrolled and deciphered. The scrolls, originally copied between about 150 B.C. and A.D. 70, contain, among various other things, Hebrew versions of several books of the Old Testament that are almost identical to the later Latin and Greek translations. That is to say that no significant variations had been introduced in the written transmission of the Old Testament for more than two thousand years—sixty generations! We have the Masoretes to thank for this—a school of pious, pragmatic Jewish scholars who appointed themselves guardians of the purity of the Old Testament in about A.D. 100. The Masoretes were perfectionists. For example, they painstakingly reckoned the number of verses (5,845), words (79,856), and letters (400,945) in the first five books of Moses.

Thus, if the original text is letter-perfect, we can feel fairly secure about our translations, noting that words often change meanings over the centuries. For example, Luther uses the word *Dirne* (the equivalent of "handmaiden" or "serving woman" in the King James). In modern German, *Dirne* has come to mean "prostitute," in much the same way perhaps that the "loose woman" referred to in Deuteronomy was originally, and quite literally, "unattached" (or "a stranger" in some versions) and hardly the disreputable hussy that the phrase conjurs up today.

It is not the inevitable change in the meaning of actual words but the conscious process of selection (and rejection) of canonical and "apocryphal" texts that gives rise to all the different Bibles we have to choose from. For instance, "the Bible" is not just the Bible, because the Word of God exists in both Protestant and Catholic versions; and the Protestant and Jewish versions are a good deal thinner, by all of seven books, than the Catholic version. The Protestant Book of Daniel has twelve chapters; the Catholic, fourteen. The charming story of Susanna and the Elders (one of the so-called Additions to Daniel) has been left out of the Protestant Bible altogether!

The final selection process for the Old Testament was settled as early as A.D. 90, at the Council of Jamnia. Since the Council of Laodicea (A.D. 363), presided over by Pope Liberius, the New Testament has contained four canonical Gospels, but we know that originally there were at least eighty! In 1960 Professor Pines of the Hebrew University of Jerusalem published fragments of an early Christian text that mentions an original Hebrew account of the life and teachings of Jesus, a Gospel prototype as it were, no trace of which has ever been discovered. But the Middle East may hold in store many more literary surprises. For example, the discovery in 1946 of an early Coptic manuscript which purports to be the Gospel of Saint Thomas, one of the so-called Gnostic Gospels, has touched off a considerable amount of scholarly controversy in recent years. In fact, every year brings fresh evidence to light—and raises fresh questions and uncertainties—that will compel us to reappraise our present ideas of what really "belongs" in the Bible and of how this selection process was (or should have been) made.

These are the sorts of questions, then, that we should try to answer in the near future. What we really require is an "ecumenical" edition of the Old Testament that would be acceptable to all faiths, and one of the New Testament acceptable to Protestants and Catholics alike. Current Bibles differ not only quantitatively (on the "canonical versus apocryphal" question) but qualitatively as well (in the interpretation of many disputed or ambiguous passages in the texts that are acknowledged by all).

This goal has been pursued for several decades in German-speaking countries: a translation of the Bible that would bring the bishops of Austria, Germany, and Switzerland as well as the Protestant Pentecostal Brotherhood into the same fold. But with so many different flocks involved, it is hardly surprising that by the end of 1979 only a handful of copies of this new "ecumenical" edition of the New Testament had come off the presses.

A press report that appeared in March 1978 should make it clear just how much more painstaking work still must be done before the project is completed. Since 1977 six biblical scholars from five different countries working under the auspices of the International Bible Society in Stuttgart have been trying to produce a definitive reading for more than three thousand disputed passages in the Old Testament. A lot more water will have rolled down the Jordan before a consensus can be reached on all three thousand, though—especially because a unanimous vote is hardly the same thing as a clear understanding of what the actual text of a particularly knotty passage was originally intended to mean. And so it seems that our modern editions of the Bible, like their predecessors, make for stimulating, even exciting reading, but—perhaps unlike earlier readers—we can no longer allow the Bible to remain a book with seven seals.

Papyrus and Parchment

The earliest surviving copies of the Old Testament are not

17

books at all but scrolls made of leather, parchment, or papyrus. The longest of the Dead Sea Scrolls found at Qumran, the site of the cave where a Bedouin shepherd boy discovered this remarkable cache in 1947, is over twenty-five feet long.

The papyrus itself was attached at both ends to wooden rods, so that the scroll could be rolled and unrolled—always toward the right, because the Hebrew alphabet is read from left to right. The great men of antiquity were often represented in paintings and sculpture holding a scroll—always in their right hand—simply to indicate that they knew how to read. In fact, this was no mean accomplishment, because a scroll could be read only straight through; skimming ahead or flipping back to check a reference or to find a particular passage out of context was virtually impossible. The context was (and is) all-important in ancient Hebrew, because in the written form of verbs there is no distinction between the past, present, and future tenses; the tense can be deduced only from the meaning of the entire sentence.

This is because in the earliest Hebrew texts, as in Egyptian and several other ancient languages, only the consonants were written down. So when a reader came across the word written KSR "break", he would simply have to decide for himself whether the three characters were intended to mean "he breaks," "he broke," or even—with the addition of a single stroke of the pen—"he allowed someone to escape."

An even greater potential for confusion exists where numbers are concerned, because there were no Hebrew numerals; numbers were represented by Hebrew letters, a fact that provides a fertile field for misreadings and misinterpretations (many of which are still with us). Bear in mind that the Old Testament was not drafted in some Prussian chancellery but dictated, so to speak (often with a lapse of several centuries between the spoken and written word), by Oriental storytellers. Thus the specific numbers that are mentioned in the Bible—like the "sacred" seven or forty—were often chosen purely for symbolic effect.

*   *   *

The first five books of Moses (the Pentateuch) were first set down in writing during the age of the Kings (around the ninth and tenth centuries B.C.). The first pre-Christian translation of the Old Testament was the famous Septuagint, prepared at the behest of the king of Egypt or perhaps the director of the great Library of Alexandria, during the third and second centuries B.C., and written in Greek, which was still the common language of the Mediterranean world.

The name Septuagint (Latin for "seventy") refers to the legend in which the high priest of the Temple in Jerusalem chose six famous scholars from each of the twelve tribes of Israel. When the seventy-two chosen translators convened on an island in the Nile delta, each finished his own translation of the entire text in exactly seventy-two days. And when all seventy-two versions were finally compared, they were found to be absolutely identical, word for word.

The Septuagint was written on sheets of papyrus, which are called *chartēs* in Greek and *carta* in Latin (from which our own words *card*, *chart*, and *charter* are derived).

If you should ever find yourself in Cairo, you can still watch papyrus being made, on a converted Nile steamer that is now permanently at anchor at the Papyrus Institute (3 Avenue of the Nile, Giza-Orman). The technique has not changed in four thousand years, though the price appears to have been rising steadily over the last few millennia—a single sheet of papyrus, thirty by forty centimeters (about twelve by eighteen inches), costs about two hundred dollars. In ancient times papyrus was hardly cheap, and many surviving papyrus fragments show signs of having been recycled many times over; either the original writing was scrubbed off or the rough reverse side of the sheet was used.

The papyrus plant is a kind of reed which grows to a height of about ten feet. Only the pith is used in the manufacture of papyrus sheets. It is cut into thin strips, which are pounded flat, laid out in two overlapping layers, one perpendicular to the other, and then pressed together. The sap of the papyrus plant serves as an adhesive that binds the two layers into a single sheet. To keep the ink from bleeding into the fibrous weave of the papyrus, the sheet is sprinkled with a mixture of flour, water, and vinegar, and one side of the sheet is burnished with a flat stone to provide a smooth writing surface. In ancient times papyrus was manufactured in several different grades, each with a different name, from deluxe, tinted, scribal-grade writing papyrus to ordinary wrapping papyrus.

Papyrus, in all its forms, was a staple of the Egyptian export trade. The manufacturers were quick to exploit their monopoly by deliberately limiting production in order to drive up the price—another age-old tradition that is still carried on today, though on a much wider scale. The Egyptians, however, finally went too far in their efforts to play off the supply against the demand. Ptolemy V, who bore the resounding throne name Epiphanes ("manifestation of the god"), slapped a prohibitively high export duty on papyrus, though he did this not out of acquisitiveness but out of sheer national pride. It so happened that the citizens of Pergamon in Asia Minor were planning to endow a library which they hoped would eventually rival the great Library of Alexandria. Their presumption so deeply offended the haughty Epiphanes that he decided to price the Pergamians out of the market (this was about 200 B.C.) and cut off the supply of papyrus at the source.

As it turned out, the resourceful Greeks of Asia Minor managed to circumvent the Egyptian papyrus embargo by inventing a far superior writing material, which was appropriately named after the city of Pergamon—their word *pergamnos*, after a series of linguistic mutations (medieval Latin *per-*

caminum, French *parchemin*), emerged as *parchment*. The process of parchment-making began with an undressed animal skin—the most expensive grades were made from the skins of unborn calves—which was first scraped and cleaned to remove the flesh and hair, and then treated with lime. Like papyrus, a sheet of parchment could be "erased," either by scrubbing or, if the ink had a metallic base, by rubbing with pumice stone. A sheet of parchment that has been "recycled" in this way is called a *palimpsest*, and because present-day scholars are generally more interested in the original (but usually almost illegible) text that lies beneath, special photographic techniques have been developed that make it possible to restore the faint traces of the original text.

At first parchment books were not bound but simply folded into consecutive sheets like a newspaper; *codex* (plural, *codices*) is the technical term for an unbound parchment manuscript of this kind. With the decline of secular learning under the late Roman Empire, monasteries became the parchment industry's principal customers. The monks' elaborate handwritten illuminated Bibles often had bindings adorned with jewels or silver inlay. Whole teams of copyists and artisans worked for decades to produce these treasures, which are almost beyond the reach of even the wealthiest collectors today. The medieval "Poor Men's Bibles" command scarcely less impressive prices at today's art auctions; the name is misleading, because these were not cheap popular editions but lavishly illustrated volumes in which Bible stories were told in pictures for the benefit of pious but illiterate patrons. "Rainbow Bibles" were so called because different-colored paper was used to indicate the different manuscript sources of the text.

Paper—the invention that has done more to change our world than any other, including gunpowder—was already known, to the Chinese at any rate, by the first century A.D. It was a good five hundred years before this discovery spread to the Middle East, thanks to Chinese prisoners of war who had fallen into the hands of the Arabs. The Arabs in turn introduced paper into Europe—along with a great many other useful innovations—and it was in Europe that paper and printing (also invented if not perfected by the Chinese) came together and helped to turn a theological controversy involving a handful of monkish scholars into an international religious revolution.

Paper and Printing: The Raw Materials
of Luther's Reformation

It is certainly true that Luther's efforts to reform the Church would have remained an intramural dispute between Luther (and a few like-minded German monks) and the Vatican had not the technological development of paper-making and movable type come to fruition in Luther's lifetime. As long as Luther's "open letters" stayed on parchment, they were read only in the scholar's study; but as soon as they appeared in print, his ideas immediately became a topic of passionate discussion in the tavern and marketplace as well.

It is important, however (to step back about fifty years), to put the accomplishments of the first European printer in their proper perspective. In the 1450s Johannes Gensfleisch ("Gooseflesh"), who wisely preferred to be known professionally as Gutenberg, printed an edition of only 200 copies of his celebrated Bible— 165 on paper, 35 on parchment. Even in Gutenberg's time, his Bibles were selling at a truly extortionate price; a copy on parchment cost 42 gulden (as a basis for comparison, a yoke of oxen sold for only 6 gulden). Today, of course, when one of the 22 extant Gutenberg Bibles changes hands, the sums involved are quite a bit more impressive. In 1970 a complete Gutenberg Bible was offered for sale in New York; the winning bid was just under $250,000. Today a single page from a Gutenberg Bible can fetch a price of up to $10,000. In 1978 the city of Mainz decided to acquire one of three two-volume Gutenberg Bibles printed in Mainz in 1455. To be competitive within the New York art market, they were obliged to raise over $2 million before their long-lost civic treasure was restored to them. (A printed book that dates from before 1500 is called an *incunabulum* [plural, *incunabula*, from the Latin word for "cradle"]; only a few tens of thousands of them exist.)

The Gutenberg Museum in Mainz boasts a collection of thirteen "first editions" with footnotes and marginal annotations that scholars are fairly certain were printed in Gutenberg's workshop, perhaps even by the master himself. The most valuable collection of rare and costly editions of the Bible in the entire world can be found in the Württemberg State Library in Stuttgart.

But it is in a more remote corner of Germany, in the Benedictine cloister at Beuron (a famous pilgrimage center in Swabia, on the Upper Danube), that the real work of preservation and restoration—not just of old, rare manuscripts but of the living words of the Old Testament—has become an ongoing scholarly enterprise. At Beuron visitors are politely but firmly turned away at the abbey's massive gates, because it is here that the panel of philologists and Protestant and Catholic theologians mentioned earlier in this chapter are patiently sifting through all the existing textual variants of the Old Testament. As the work goes on, it becomes increasingly clear how little of our prevailing picture of the Bible actually dates from biblical times. In fact, the scholars assembled at the Beuron abbey might best be likened to the restorers of Old Master canvases in museums and galleries, who painstakingly remove the accumulated varnish, overpainting, and inauthentic additions and adornments of many centuries to reveal the painter's original conception in very nearly its original freshness. The biblical scholars and archaeologists of today can help point the way, not to an entirely new interpretation, but to a more direct understanding of the original text of the Bible. Though it was written more than two thousand years ago, it can have as much meaning for us in our time as if the ink were hardly dry on the first copy of the manuscript.

The Bible was written to be read, as it once was and as it can certainly be again. The barriers to our understanding of the text that have been erected by reverential piety, and perhaps more seriously by hairsplitting scholarship, are not insurmountable. The Bible does not deserve, any more than other literary classics, to degenerate into a neglected quarry that is only occasionally plundered for the odd quotation. The way our grandmothers chose their Bible text for the day—by opening the family Bible at random, stabbing the page with a knitting needle, and dutifully reading the verse that chance had selected—no longer seems adequate. We must find our own way into this book as intelligent, open-minded adults; and as we read, we must remember that though many believe this book to be the Word of God, the actual words we read were assembled and selected by mortal men.

Let there be light . . .

—GENESIS 1:3

PART II

THE OLD TESTAMENT

The impulse to discard the Old Testament in the second century was a mistaken one that was correctly repudiated by the early Church; retaining it in the sixteenth century was an act dictated by fate which the Reformation was not yet capable of resisting; but preserving it, since the nineteenth century, has simply been the result of spiritual paralysis and ecclesiastical inertia.

—ADOLF HARNACK

Introduction

"In the beginning God created the heaven and the earth": these are the first words in the Old Testament, to be sure, but they are not necessarily the oldest. The idea that the present sequence of chapter and verse in the Old Testament reflects the chronological sequence in which they were composed is simply wrong, one of many misconceptions that stand between us and a real appreciation of the text.

To begin with, even the word *testament* seems a misnomer—at least in its modern sense, as reflected in the phrase "last will and testament." In fact, *testament* actually refers to the old and the new covenants (or dispensations) that God has made with man. The first covenant was announced to Moses on Mount Sinai; the second was established when God sent his "only begotten Son," Jesus Christ, into the world. Clearly, then, the division of the Bible into the Old and New Testaments is primarily a theological distinction.

In the Old Testament God has many names—six in the Hebrew texts alone—though this is not surprising in a work that is the compilation of the writings of many, many authors over a span of many generations. The most common name (which appears exactly 6,832 times, by the way) is Yahweh, which was written *YHWH*. YHWH was thought to be the actual name of God, which pious Jews could not even speak out loud without committing sacrilege. (The correct translation of the word is still in doubt, though it most probably means "he who calls into being.") And so, to remind the reader that YHWH was not to be spoken out loud, the word *adonai* ("lord") was written below it in the manuscript. From the third century B.C. on, the scribes simply wrote the Hebrew vowel signs for the word *adonai*, namely A-O-I, underneath the unpronounceable tetragrammaton YHWH. Later, uninitiated Gentile readers mistakenly combined the consonants of *YHWH* with the vowels of *adonai* to produce *Jehovah*. At this point, however, that seems to be a mistake that is long past correcting, as the Jehovah's Witnesses would certainly be the first to point out.

The third of the six Hebrew names of God is Elohim. It occurs some 3,350 times and is reminiscent of the Arabic *Allah*, as well as the Semitic *El* ("divinity"), which is also to be found in the word *Israel*. We translate *Elohim* as "the Almighty," and a variant of this, El Eliyon, gives us the fourth name as well.

The fifth, which is used least frequently (301 times), is Shaddai, the meaning of which is somewhat obscure; perhaps it originally meant "he who lives on the mountaintops." The sixth name is familiar to us from the Psalms and perhaps from the text of the mass and many other liturgical pieces—Lord Sabaoth, "Lord of Hosts." The God of the Old Testament has as many attributes as he does names. He is ruthless, wrathful, vengeful, jealous, peace-loving—but above all, he is almighty.

From a Christian standpoint, the decisive change came when the Old Testament Yahweh became the Greek *kyrios* ("lord") of the New. As the great theologian Adolf Deisler has pointed out, "The Bible in which God was called Jahweh was the Bible of a single nation; the Bible in which God was called *kyrios* was the Bible of the world."

It was originally as Yahweh that this formidable deity set himself apart from the myriad rival gods and goddesses of neighboring peoples in the ancient Near East—at the same time that the chronicles and heroic legends of those peoples were being absorbed into the early writings of the Old Testament.

The original source of those borrowed tales was the Fertile Crescent, a term that describes the belt of rich, arable land that extended roughly from the Nile valley in the west to Damascus in the north and down to Ur and Babylon in the southeast. The term Fertile Crescent also evokes the incredible intellectual productivity of the ancient peoples of Mesopotamia, who lived between the Tigris and the Euphrates rivers. It was there that mathematics, astronomy, medicine, and many more of civilization's great intellectual advances were first investigated systematically and preserved in writing. Writing itself, one of mankind's greatest achievements, was also invented there, more than five thousand years ago.

The Old Testament is a product of this tradition, following and incorporating the many legacies of even more ancient cultures—the Creation myth, the story of the Flood, and most important, the idea of monotheism, the belief in one God. Sometimes this fidelity to the tradition even extends to outright plagiarism. Here is just one example.

29

Thou alone hast created the world according to Thy wishes, with men and their herds and flocks, together with all wild creatures that are on the earth and that go upon the rivers and that soar through the air above us on their wings.

How splendid are all the works of Thy mind, Thou Lord of Eternity. On earth all things are accomplished at a nod of Thy head, for Thou art the Creator. Thou alone art life, for man lives but through Thee.

It is easy enough to recognize this as a psalm, but it is not from the Old Testament. This is the "Hymn to the Sun," written by the Egyptian pharaoh Akhenaten, who took the throne about 1330 B.C.; his fame has been somewhat eclipsed over the centuries by that of his consort, who bore the felicitous name "The Beautiful One Approaches," or in ancient Egyptian, Nefertiti.

In fact, the Old Testament equivalent of Akhenaten's "Hymn to the Sun" can be found in Psalm 104:

Who laid the foundations of the earth, that it should not be removed for ever. . . .

He sendeth the springs into the valleys, which run among the hills.

They give drink to every beast of the field: the wild asses quench their thirst.

By them shall the fowls of the heaven have their habitation, which sing among the branches. . . .

He causeth the grass to grow for the cattle, and herb for the service of man: that he may bring forth food out of the earth. . . .

Thou sendest forth thy spirit, they are created: and thou renewest the face of the earth.

The glory of the LORD shall endure for ever. . . .

I will sing unto the LORD as long as I live. . . .

—VERSES 5, 10–12, 14, 30, 31, 33

30

The similarity between the psalm and Akhenaten's hymn is no accident. The compilers of the Old Testament had no scruples about incorporating other people's songs or heroic sagas into their anthology (as long as they met their rather strict doctrinal standards, of course).

For centuries, however, a person's life was at stake even to hint that so much as a single verse of the Old Testament might have been lifted from some alien tradition. The Bible was proclaimed to be the Word of God, and God clearly doesn't need to consult any secondary sources, because he himself is the Primary Source. . . . Then the pendulum swung wildly in the other direction. Parallels between the Old Testament and more ancient texts had been identified, and so the originality of the Old Testament as a whole was thrown open to serious question. Freud was probably the most stalwart champion of this point of view, but books are still published today in which it is announced with tremendous fanfare (accompanied by an undertone of malicious scholarly gloating) that monotheism, long thought to have originated with Moses, was actually already established some centuries earlier as the state religion of the Egyptian New Kingdom during the brief reign of Akhenaten. Unfortunately, the effect of the fanfare is marred by a single discordant note: Akhenaten's god, Aten, cannot really be considered a forerunner of the God of the Old Testament. Aten was the sun, a nature god, who was represented in the form of the solar disk. The God of the Old Testament is a transcendental deity who cannot even be conceived of in any material or corporeal form; he can be known to us only through his works, which is to say the heavens and the earth.

Archaeology has unearthed the Old Testament's literary predecessors and thus disproved the idea that the Old Testament is a unique, unprecedented, and unified expression of God's Word. In many cases the investigation of ancient sites has verified passages in the Old Testament that had previously been dismissed as myth and legend. The names of kings and cities that were as fully encrusted with legendary associations as Arthur or Camelot have been transformed into historical realities, and a great many surprises are still in store for us in the future: a mere 5 percent of the known sites that date from biblical times have thus far been disturbed by the archaeologist's spade.

But the cheering news that archaeology can confirm the historical authenticity of some passages in the Old Testament has unfortunately led to the astonishing conclusion that everything in the Old Testament *must* be verified scientifically—if not by archaeology, then by physics or astronomy. And when archaeological verification becomes the acid test for biblical authenticity, if a particular passage then fails the test, we are meant to doubt not only the biblical description, but also the very existence of the event.

For the moment, however, it should be enough for us to realize that the soundings and burrowings of the archaeologists can help us achieve a better understanding of the Bible, which means that we have both a great deal to learn and a great deal to forget. The churches will have to realize that not every word of the Bible was necessarily dictated by the Almighty. Archaeologists will also have to stop assuming that discrepancies between their findings and a biblical account discredit the Bible, for scholars of the second millennium A.D. (as well as scribes of the first millennium B.C.) have been known to misinterpret their data and make mistakes. And Bible readers would do well to distinguish between purely religious writings—which can still be profitably compared with material from other contemporary traditions—and straightforward historical narrative, because the Bible contains a great deal of both.

Philo, the Jewish historian and philosopher who lived in Alexandria around the time of Jesus (A.D. 30), maintained that "Everything that is in the Old Testament is true, and everything that is true is in the Old Testament." A comforting thought, but today we have to look a bit further than that. The modern interpretation of the Bible, for example, starts with the premise that everything in the Book of Genesis from the Creation up to the construction of the Tower of Babel is quite simply a parable in which the authors were trying to make comprehensible the unfathomable workings of the Lord.

The Creation Myths

The Twofold Creation

The unsuspecting reader is already confronted with a puzzling problem in the first two chapters of Genesis: two consecutive and mutually contradictory accounts of the Creation. In the first account God creates the heavens, the oceans, and the earth, and man is the final event on the program; in the second we are simply told that "the Lord God planted a garden eastward in Eden," and a man is the first living creature to be brought into being.

This seems to be a fairly glaring inconsistency, to say the least. But we can also regard it as a stroke of luck that two different accounts by different authors have been kept separate from each other and not collated into a single narrative, as is unfortunately the case with the story of Noah and the Flood. This provides us with an excellent opportunity to compare the different literary treatments of the Creation story.

The second author's style is dry and matter-of-fact, rather like that of a small-town journalist of the old who-what-when-where school. But our first author is clearly a romantic, drunk on the sound of his own words, who has tried to use concrete, highly specific imagery to make the reader feel that he was actually present at such an awesome and inexplicable event as the Creation. Thus, we should propose a posthumous vote of thanks to those long-dead scribes who had the good sense and good taste to realize that these different accounts were the products of two entirely different literary temperaments and that they should be appreciated as such.

We also have reason to be grateful to the nineteenth-century linguist and biblical scholar Julius Wellhausen, who demonstrated in a showpiece of philological detective work that the present text of the Bible was the work of many different hands and was compiled over the course of many centuries. Although self-evident today, in 1880 that was a very audacious proposition, which naturally was greeted by a storm of indignant controversy. More specifically, Wellhausen demonstrated that the second Creation story (the garden eastward of Eden) is a great deal older than the first; he fixed the date of the earlier account at about the ninth century B.C. and the later one at about the sixth century B.C. For us, both dates may seem to be, as the phrase has it, "lost in the mists of antiquity," but let us choose two comparable periods from our era, say the year 1500 (when, for example, roughly 88 percent of the globe was *terra incognita* as far as Western Europe was concerned) and the year 1800 (by which time fully 82 percent of the globe had been explored and charted). Why should we not assume that the three centuries that intervened between the two Creation accounts in Genesis witnessed a similarly dramatic expansion of man's spiritual, technical, and economic (as well as geographical) horizons?

At any rate, literary historians were overjoyed by Wellhausen's discoveries, which enabled them to file both Creation stories in their proper historical pigeonholes. Then the natural scientists entered the discussion, and with boundless confidence in the power of science to unravel even the knottiest problem, they proceeded to pick apart the Creation stories in Genesis, sentence by sentence, until nothing was left that had not been thoroughly debunked. *The world was created in seven days? Preposterous!* Quite true, of course, though this contention is explicit in only the first (chronologically the later) account in Genesis: "And on the seventh day God ended his work which he had made." This is the first appearance in the Bible of the mystical number seven, which figures prominently in the heroic tales of the Babylonians and still enjoys widespread currency in our own popular mythology. The Israelites paraded for seven days around the walls of Jericho, and seven priests sounded the ram's-horn trumpets that brought down the walls. The menorah (the Jewish ritual candelabrum) has seven branches; and Christians have their seven sacraments, seven deadly sins, and seven cardinal virtues; and—if all goes well—there is seventh heaven. The ancients spoke of the Seven Wonders of the World and the seven sages of Greece; the Brave Little Tailor slew his seven at one blow; and the seventh son of a seventh son is said to be born with a special gift for prophecy, even if it is only second sight.

No one has the definitive explanation as to why it was seven and not six or eight or any other number that signified completion or totality. The seven heavenly bodies (the sun and moon plus the five known planets) of antiquity may have provided the original metaphor, but this, like so much else, is only speculation.

And what does all this have to do with the seven days of Creation? In fact, the brash skeptics of the 1880s were quickly brought to heel by their colleagues in the ancient Near Eastern language faculties, who were able to supply a simple and highly practical explanation for what was "obviously" nothing more than a mystical exercise in absurdity. The text of Genesis goes on to say: "And God blessed the seventh day, and sanctified it: because that in it he had rested from all his work which God created and made." The philologists concluded from this, in light of Wellhausen's evidence for the multiple authorship of Genesis, that this specific reference to God's resting after his labors on the seventh day of Creation was in fact a later interpolation. This immemorial and highly distinguished precedent was intended to reinforce the religious prohibition against any kind of secular activity on the Sabbath. The priests of a later era had revised the original text of the Creation story in order to invest this ritual law with the force and solemnity of the will of the Almighty. That kind of retroactive tampering with history is hardly unusual; historians of every age have tended to tincture their accounts of distant events and peoples with a dose of whatever they feel will do their contemporary readers a bit of good. Tacitus, for example, probably would not have lavished so much praise on the Germans if he had not felt that his decadent fellow Romans might stand to profit from their example of uncomplicated barbarian virtue.

In our own century the rationalists' campaign to discredit the biblical account of the Creation has lost a great deal of momentum. Contemporary scientific theories of the origin of the universe are not necessarily incompatible with the Book of Genesis. Even the Big Bang, the catastrophic cosmic event that many scientists believe resulted in the formation of our present universe some twenty billion years ago, implies a definite first day in the history of the universe, just as in the biblical account of the Creation. Werner Heisinger, one of the most prestigious physicists of this century, has observed, "At the beginning of all these developments there must have been a primal creative agency at work." Or, in other words, the Holy Spirit did not fall from the sky; it was present from the very beginning, implicit in the act of creation itself.

And the LORD *God planted a garden eastward in Eden.*

—GENESIS 2:8

36

The Old Testament

The Search for Paradise

The idea of an earthly paradise is as old as humanity; certainly it was already part of the common cultural heritage of the Fertile Crescent by 3000 B.C., perhaps even earlier, as recent inscriptions from the early Semitic site of Ebla, near Aleppo, would suggest. The word *paradise* itself—derived from the Persian *pardes*, which means nothing more than "park" or "garden"— never occurs in the Old Testament, which speaks only of Gan Eden, the Garden of Eden. The first evidence of this prebiblical paradise was discovered by English archaeologist George Smith. He had deciphered some Assyrian cuneiform tablets which contained, along with the usual lists of kings and their conquests, and digests of legal codes, several texts of a purely literary character, including descriptions of the Assyrian version of the earthly paradise. These, however, turned out to be mere trifles in comparison with Smith's later discoveries.

As Smith continued translating the hoard of clay tablets he had unearthed in the library of Assurbanipal at Nineveh, he discovered that the Assyrian texts were based on an earlier literary model; and that the idea of the Garden of Eden, even the word *eden* itself, was originally Sumerian. In the Sumerian language, however, *eden* simply meant "plain" or "steppe"; the Sumerian paradise was actually called Tilmun, a happy land that was "pure, bright, and fair, where the lion does not make his kill nor the wolf carry off the sheep," enriched by the sun god with "the sweet waters of the ground"—or at least until its only human inhabitant, Enki, fell under the curse of the gods of Sumer.

All this has a genuine biblical ring; Smith had uncovered the prototype of the Old Testament's Garden of Eden. In Genesis 2:10–14 even the location of the earthly paradise is fixed with almost mathematical exactitude:

> *And a river went out of Eden to water the garden; and from thence it was parted, and became into four heads.*
>
> *The name of the first is Pison: that is it which compasseth the whole land of Havilah, where there is gold;*
>
> *And the gold of that land is good: there is bdellium and the onyx stone [soham].*
>
> *And the name of the second river is Gihon: the same is it that compasseth the whole land of Ethiopia.*
>
> *And the name of the third river is Hiddekel: that is it which goeth toward the east of Assyria. And the fourth river is Euphrates.*

There are many puzzling references in this passage, notably "bdellium," presumably the resin of the balsam shrub, which, like the resin we are more familiar with, consists of tiny golden grains. The true meaning of the Hebrew word *soham* in verse 12, which the King James panel rather arbitrarily translated as "onyx stone," is still something of a mystery; *soham* may be nothing more than a scribal error for *sohar*, "gleam" or "luster," which could apply equally well to onyx, carnelian, or a variety of other semiprecious stones.

The profusion and apparent precision of the place names in the preceding passage have tempted a great many learned men to try to find their way back to the Garden. Before the crusading impulse finally died out in the sixteenth century, hundreds of thousands set off for the East to reclaim the earthly paradise with the sword; the irony of this must not have been as apparent to the late medieval mind as it is to ours today. The scholars and commentators stuck closer to home for the most part, poring over the tantalizing Genesis text, rummaging through nonbiblical descriptions of the Garden of Eden, spinning all sorts of ingenious philological conjectures. The wildest of these involved the elusive river Pison. Some believed it to be the Indus, which would have put the land of Havilah somewhere in northwestern

India; others could "prove" that the Pison had once flowed through the Wadi el-Rauma, a dried-up watercourse in the Arabian desert; and still others boldly equated the Pison with the Nile and the Gihon with the Ganges.

All in all, more than eighty learned theories identified the "true" location of the Garden of Eden, some of them illustrated with detailed maps, like Herbinius's highly imaginative production of 1678. Even Columbus noted in his journal after he had first sighted the mouth of the Orinoco, "This river must flow through Paradise." This was not intended as a metaphorical appreciation of the lush beauty of the landscape but as a serious geographical observation. This theory does not seem to have found widespread acceptance, even along the Orinoco, and the search for Gan Eden still goes on today. One recent expedition has proposed the more plausible site of Hor, in Iraq, where the waters of the Tigris and the Euphrates meet in the marshy delta of the Shatt-al-Arab. This region is about four thousand square miles in area, which makes it about twice the size of the state of Delaware. Hor is inhabited by some 100,000 so-called Marsh Arabs who call themselves Madan. They live on artificial islands rising out of the shallow waters of the delta. Their spacious communal dwellings, with roofs rising as high as thirty feet, are made of great mats woven of marsh reeds. The patterns of the weave, identical with the designs incised on Sumerian cylinder seals, represent a tradition of craftsmanship that has apparently persisted for some five thousand years. The Madan, though highly conservative in this respect at least, were pioneers in the development of prefabricated housing and the principles of planned obsolescence; their reed longhouses are dismantled every ten years and reassembled from scratch. Where the Madan will find themselves in a decade or so is another question. The battlefront in the Iraqi-Iranian war is only a few tens of miles to the east; perhaps even more critically, the reed platforms of the Madan float in a brackish lake of bitumen, which usually indicates the presence of substantial deposits of petroleum. The first oil rigs have already gone up in the marshlands, and the Madan may not be able to linger for many more years in Paradise.

But the question of where and what the biblical Gan Eden really was is not one that any number of expeditions can answer. The Genesis authors' description of the earthly paradise is not a travelogue but an allegory of the original harmony that prevailed between the natural world and its earliest human inhabitants. Martin Luther recognized this and, as usual, disposed of the whole vexing question bluntly and succinctly: "It may be that it was so that God made such a garden or fixed the bounds of such a country, but it is my understanding, and I would be well pleased if others would also have it so, that this country or garden may have been the whole world."

And out of the ground made the LORD God to grow every tree that is pleasant to the sight . . .

—GENESIS 2:9

The Tree of Knowledge; or, What's Wrong with This Picture?

Everyone knows how the story goes: Eve, seduced by the serpent, picked an apple from the tree of knowledge, offered it to Adam, and . . . Actually, with the great advances in education in recent years, most of us are probably aware that the fruit of the tree was not necessarily an apple, according to the Bible at least; some scholars insist that it was most likely a banana.

Why, then, did Dürer, Cranach, Holbein, and so many Old Masters insist on showing Eve reaching for an apple? They had been misled, not by the serpent but by the Greeks. Just a few centuries after the Book of Genesis was written, Greek vase painters were decorating their kraters and amphoras with the motif of a tree laden with golden apples and guarded by a baleful serpent—an illustration of the myth of the Garden of the Hesperides, who were the four daughters of Atlas and Nyx. Nyx was a formidable figure in her own right; as the goddess of sleep, she had the power to overcome both gods and men with drowsiness. Atlas was a Titan who had tried unsuccessfully to storm the citadel of the gods on Mount Olympus and was accordingly sentenced to a perpetual term of hard labor—bearing the vault of the heavens on his shoulders (not the globe of the earth yet, because the Greeks were not aware that the earth was round). He was also obliged, in partnership with a dragon, to keep watch over the golden apples in the garden of his daughters, the nymphs of the Hesperides, in the far west of the world. It was the theft of three of those apples that would be the first of the labors of Hercules.

Thus, it seems that the apples painted by Dürer and the others were not biblically inspired but cribbed from a Grecian urn. The expression "Adam's apple" (*Adamsapfel, pomme d'Adam*), on the other hand, originated in Germany during the Middle Ages, and the pleasing notion that the fateful bite had stuck in Adam's throat was adopted into several Western European languages. And here we might safely leave the subject of Grecian apples and the biblical tree of knowledge, were it not for the existence of another unsettling archaeological find from the ancient Near East—in this case a four-thousand-year-old Sumerian cylinder seal. This in itself was hardly unusual, for these matchbook-size cylinders, carved from semiprecious stones, have turned up by the thousands in Mesopotamia. Originally they were worn around the neck on a chain and engraved with their owner's personal seal, which could conveniently be impressed into an unfired clay jar as a mark of ownership or a wet clay tablet as a signature, the forerunner of the signet ring or the modern bureaucrat's rubber stamp.

This particular cylinder seal, however, which is currently on display in the British Museum, was quite unusual in its design: a tree flanked by male and female figures. The woman is reaching out toward the tree, which is guarded by a serpent. Archaeologists have dubbed the seal the "Temptation Cylinder Seal." Thus neither the Greeks nor the Hebrews were the first to tell the story of a magical tree with tempting fruit; and the guardian serpent of the tree had played an important symbolic role in earlier Near Eastern religions. Originally, though, the serpent was a symbol of fertility, and it was in the Old Testament that he was cast in the villain's role for the first time.

Another important difference exists between Genesis and the earlier versions of the story: the inhabitants of the Sumerian paradise, Tilmun, were gods and goddesses rather than men and women, though these immortals had all the typical flaws and frailties that are ostensibly reserved for humans (the name Adam itself appears in Sumerian mythology as Adamah, which means "clay," "clod of dirt"). And while we are on the subject, I should mention one final linguistic curiosity. The Bible refers to the "tree of the knowledge of good and evil," and the Latin for "good and evil" is bonum et malum. Malus in Latin also means "apple." Medieval theologians, who had a particular fondness for such neatly worked-out verbal allegories, went so far as to explain that the apple was actually so called because it had been the original cause of evil's coming into the world.

But what was the unpardonable sin that Adam and Eve committed? They disobeyed God's command, inasmuch as they ignored an explicit prohibition against eating the fruit of the tree. But is this a serious enough infraction to merit such severe punishment (among other things, Adam is told, "In the sweat of thy face shalt thou eat bread, till thou return unto the ground")? Clearly they must have done something truly awful—but what exactly?

The real nature of the offense has been subject to various

interpretations over the centuries, changing to suit the mores of each different era. In the Middle Ages it was thought to have been the sin of gluttony; then later, when the need to curb somewhat different appetites was felt to be paramount, original sin was redefined as sexual desire, which Eve had awakened in her susceptible mate. But curiously enough, the Bible makes no mention of this, which seems incredible by modern lights, because sex is surely one of the most pressing of all human concerns. On the contrary, in fact, the Bible states explicitly, "And they were both naked, the man and his wife, and were not ashamed" (Genesis 2:25). And it was only after the Fall that the fig leaf, the beloved accessory of moral zealots of every age, first came to hang in its accustomed place.

Actually it does not require any great subtlety of interpretation to discover what crime Adam and Eve committed, because the Bible makes this quite clear: "For God doth know that in the day ye eat thereof, then your eyes shall be opened, and ye shall be as gods, knowing good and evil" (Genesis 3:5). If the serpent were speaking today, he would probably simply say, "God knows, if you eat the fruit, you'll lose your innocence." Today, could we still by any chance have any of our innocence left to lose? The nineteenth-century Romantic novelist Heinrich von Kleist addressed the question of the loss of innocence in this brief passage from his essay "On the Marionette Theater":

> *Once three years ago I went bathing with a young man whose entire bearing was suffused with a wonderful grace. . . . As it happened, we had both recently seen the statue of the boy taking a splinter from his foot in Paris. . . . The young man happened to glance at his reflection in a large mirror just as he was putting his foot up on the stool to dry it off and was at once reminded of this statue. He smiled and told me of the discovery he had made.*
>
> *In fact I too had noticed this and, either as a kind of test of his self-assurance or as a mild salutory reproof to his vanity, I*

laughed and replied that he must be subject to hallucinations.

He blushed and raised his foot again to show me the same gesture, which he had made so effortlessly before, but this second attempt miscarried badly. In some perplexity he raised his foot a third, a fourth, finally a tenth time—in vain! He found himself quite unable to carry it off again.

From that day, even from that moment, on, an incomprehensible change seemed to come over him. He began to spend his days in front of the mirror, and all his charms deserted him, one by one. Some irreparable and inexplicable force seemed to have gripped him in a mesh of iron with the intent of stifling the free and easy play of his movements, and after a year had passed, there was not a trace of the grace and vivacity that had once made him the cynosure of so many delighted eyes.

And what are we to conclude from all this? Neither the geologists nor the archaeologists, nor even the philologists, can help us find our way back to Paradise. And if we appeal to the poets, we are left with the choice between Jean Paul's rueful aphorism, "Memory is the only paradise that we can never be driven out of," and Peter Bamm's pessimistic prophecy, "World history began with Paradise lost, and the splitting of the atom may well have been the beginning of the end." Or we may simply prefer to stick with Luther—"But it is my understanding, and I would be well pleased if others would also have it so, that this country or garden may have been the whole world."

And the flood was forty days upon the earth . . .

—Genesis 7:17

Ziusudra's Ark

As mentioned earlier, the biblical story of the Flood, like the Creation story, incorporates two independent and often inconsistent accounts of the same event, though unfortunately in this case these have been patched together into a single composite text that is accordingly often redundant and self-contradictory. But for all its defects as a work of literature, the story of the Flood at least seems to have preserved a substantial kernel of historical truth. Confirmation of this first came to light, most inappropriately, in the parched wasteland of what is now northern Iraq. Here, at the site of the Assyrian royal city of Nineveh, over a century ago, the indefatigable George Smith discovered (among thousands of others) twelve clay tablets inscribed with the text of a long heroic poem that has come to be called, after its principal character, *The Epic of Gilgamesh.*

Today, if you look over the vast expanse of ruined Nineveh on the outskirts of the modern city of Mosul, you might imagine that only a madman, and a hopelessly optimistic madman at that, would consider sifting through the dust and debris of so many centuries in the hope of turning up the odd clay tablet. In 1873, when Smith first set to work, the task must have seemed all the more hopeless, but Smith was undaunted, and as we shall see, he had everything to gain in the circumstances.

George Smith was an engraver by trade and an amateur Assyriologist who had published several papers that earned him a certain reputation in the scholarly community, and later an assistant curatorship of the Assyrian collection in the British Museum. The story of Smith's subsequent career might have been written by Horatio Alger. He began by translating some Assyrian texts, which predated the Bible and which described the creation of the world and a universal deluge. At that time *The Epic of Gilgamesh* had been recovered only in fragmentary form, and Smith's articles repeatedly stressed the misfortune that both archaeology and world literature had suffered—more than half of the text was still unaccounted for and might even be irretrievably lost.

The London *Daily Telegraph* took Smith's words as a

challenge and offered a prize of a thousand guineas—the equivalent of over twenty-five thousand dollars in contemporary purchasing power—to the eventual discoverer of the missing tablets. The editors congratulated themselves on the brilliance of this gesture—the announcement made a tremendous sensation, and of course no one came forward to claim the prize. It was not long, however, before Smith picked up the gauntlet, packed his trunks, and set out for Nineveh.

Nineveh was hardly a virgin site by this time; it had already been systematically excavated by such celebrated archaeologists as Paul-Émile Botta, a French consular official who was already on the scene, and the English scholar-diplomat Sir Austen Henry Layard, the great pioneer of scientific archaeology in Mesopotamia. Both Botta and Layard had come up dry, at least as far as *Gilgamesh* was concerned. Smith then found the twelve missing tablets; the complete text of *Gilgamesh* was restored, and both Smith and world literature were richer for it.

The Flood is described in the eleventh tablet, almost exactly as it is in the Bible, and whenever Genesis departs from the Babylonian * original, the narrative is invariably less compelling and the imagery less concrete. Understandably so, for *Gilgamesh* was composed about 2500 B.C., and the biblical account of the Flood was written down about nineteen centuries later and thus—assuming that there actually was such a flood—was that much further removed in time from the event itself, about the same amount of time that separates Antony and Cleopatra from Hiroshima, for example. Scholars have since deciphered and dated three great epics from the intervening Babylonian-Akkadian period which describe a universal deluge, though there is

---

* The Assyrians, for all their faults, had great reverence for the literary classics of the Babylonians, whom they had supplanted as rulers of Mesopotamia, and of their even more distant precursors, the Sumerians, in much the same way that the Romans were at such pains to imitate and preserve the art and literature of the Greeks.

still a gap of several centuries between them. All this remained in the realm of epic poetry rather than "real" history until the discovery of Sumerian king lists which divided Sumerian history into two periods: before and after the Great Flood. Thus, the chronicles and heroic epics of the Sumerians and their cultural heirs, the Babylonians, Akkadians, and Assyrians, all seem to regard the Great Flood as the primary event of their history. But is there any independent physical evidence of this? Indeed there is, of a sort.

The eminent British archaeologist Sir Charles Leonard Woolley was firmly convinced that the extensive deposits of mud and silt that were uncovered by his excavations at Ur furnished sufficient proof of the reality of the Flood. Woolley's claims were picked up by the international press and, like the discovery of King Tut's tomb, became one of the great popular sensations of the 1920s. Today, however, scholars believe that Woolley had actually come upon the traces of a purely "local" inundation, though it did involve a considerable area—about one hundred miles wide and four hundred miles long. There was another serious flaw in Woolley's theory; the chronology was all wrong. Woolley's mud samples were about four thousand years old, but according to the Sumerian king lists, Ziusudra, the earliest of the semilegendary heroes of the Great Flood, reigned during the first predynastic period, over a thousand years earlier.

Subsequent excavations at Uruk and Lagash have turned up similar deposits that settled during the same period; these deposits do appear to be the legacy of a serious flood that may have devastated an entire region. Still, it was hardly a global catastrophe on the scale described by the Book of Genesis. In the atomic age it is easy enough to imagine such a catastrophe, but what did the ancient Mesopotamians mean when they wrote of a great flood that had engulfed the entire world? For them, presumably, the whole world was the region they had traveled over and seen with their own eyes, and during a "local" inundation of the kind that overwhelmed the city of Ur four thousand years ago, its inhabitants could easily believe that the whole world was underwater.

Does this mean, then, that all the Mesopotamian tales of the Great Flood were simply artistically enhanced recollections of one or more of these regional disasters? We might be satisfied with this explanation were it not for the similar accounts of a universal deluge from virtually every culture on earth—and it seems unlikely that word of even the most disastrous flood in Mesopotamia could have reached Australia or the Amazon four thousand years ago. For several decades scholars very sensibly decided to ignore this embarrassing surplus of data while they concentrated on wrangling about the chronology: Did the Flood actually engulf the earth, or selected portions of it, four thousand years ago?

Finally, it was the geologists who intervened decisively by announcing that both sides were wrong in this dispute; the philologists and prehistorians were taking the narrow, parochial view and neglecting the big picture. As the geologists explained it, the earth's axis had shifted many times, most recently between about 8000 and 15,000 B.C., and the obvious consequence must have been a dramatic change in climate, worldwide. (At this point the philologists and prehistorians began to take notice.) First of all, the polar ice caps, suddenly transposed to the temperate zone, would start to melt, and the level of the oceans would rise accordingly. Second, erupting volcanoes would fill the skies with clouds of dust and ash, and this in turn would cause torrential rainstorms. Thus, all the continents would be exposed to the full fury of what the Bible calls in another context the waters above and below the earth.

Geologists, meteorologists, and physicists agreed that such a primeval catastrophe must have occurred, with results essentially as described; and historians and anthropologists were prepared to testify that natural upheavals on a much smaller scale had been preserved in mankind's collective memory for many centuries, if not millennia. Even without the help of the Book of Genesis, science would eventually have arrived at the conclusion that a universal deluge, perhaps a whole series of them, had overwhelmed the earth in prehistoric times. Today no one seriously disputes this, though the biblical assertion that all the high hills and mountains lay beneath so many cubits of water may still be explained best by the scribe's and poet's natural tendency to improve on a good story.

And, of course, according to Genesis we have the patriarch Noah to thank for the survival of the human race and our fellow creatures. The dimensions of Noah's ark, laid out according to God's specifications, are recorded in Genesis 6:15. To begin with, "the length of the ark shall be three hundred cubits, the breadth of it fifty cubits, and the height of it thirty cubits." A cubit was defined as the distance between the point of a man's elbow and the tip of his middle finger, which in practice seems to have been standardized at 17.72 inches, though another common linear unit was the royal cubit, 20.72 inches—perhaps kings had longer arms or fingers. If we take the average of these two as a safe value for the cubit, the ark must have been about 480 feet long, 80 feet wide, and 48 feet high (or roughly the same size as the typical Hilton hotel laid on end).

The fact that the Bible supplies detailed specifications for the construction of such an enormous vessel has naturally provoked a great deal of curious speculation. The first edition of the *Encyclopaedia Britannica*, which appeared between 1768 and 1771, printed an elaborate cutaway plan of the ark, accompanied by a long technical discussion of the layout, seaworthiness ("pitched within and without"—that is, the wooden planks of the ark were caulked with bitumen to make them watertight), and carrying capacity of the vessel (whose total tonnage, the *Britannica* soberly informed its readers, must easily have exceeded that of Saint Paul's Cathedral). The actual number of cabins and the arrangement of the stalls for the livestock remained a topic of learned controversy well into the nineteenth century, though one practical-minded Victorian critic finally balked at the suggestion that the ark may have had as many as four hundred or even two hundred compartments:

> *Pelletier speaks of only 72 compartments, viz., 36 for the fowls and as many again for the beasts. His conclusion was based on the following reasoning: If we imagine a greater number, e.g. 333 or 400, then each of the eight persons aboard would have been responsible for cleaning and maintaining 37, 41, or even 50 compartments every day, which in his view was patently impossible.*

The Epic of Gilgamesh, at least, is more informative on this point; in it we are told explicitly that the ark built by the hero's ancestor, Utnapishtim (acting on the instructions of the god Ea, "the friend of mankind") consisted of "seven stories and nine chambers [in each story]," and so Pelletier's inspired hunch that the ark could have had no more than seventy-two compartments seems to be borne out by the only available evidence.

> *And he went into the ark with his sons, and his wife, and his wife's sons, before the waters of the flood. "All that I had, I caused to be put on board, the seed of many kinds of living creatures. I brought into the ship my family and all my kindred, herds and flocks of the fields, wild beasts of the fields . . ."*

This too, is *Gilgamesh,* not Genesis, though all the familiar elements of the story are there, along with a few extra refinements that seem to have been lost in transmission over nineteen hundred years. Utnapishtim sails off with a considerable retinue, for example, not just his immediate family and the animals but "all the artisans of the city" and a navigator, plus a cargo of jewels and treasure. And when the waters finally subside (after a poetic catalog of the destruction wrought by the Flood that sounds remarkably realistic), he sends out a dove, a raven, *and* a sparrow to search for dry land.

Even so, Utnapishtim does not merit the title as the first of the great legendary navigators; an even earlier Sumerian epic has since been discovered in which the god Eki warns the hero Ziusudra that the gods intend to send a flood to destroy the world. Ziusudra very sensibly begins to build an ark.

The legend introduces an interesting complication at this point, however. Eki has sworn an oath to his fellow gods that he will not speak a word of this to any mortal man. Thus, to warn Ziusudra he is forced to resort to a ruse; he addresses himself not to Ziusudra but to the wall of Ziusudra's house. He says nothing directly to his human protégé except:

> *Take yourself to the wall to my left. Through the wall I will speak to you. Heed well my commands, and follow my counsel.*

And so it is the wall and not Eki that transmits the crucial message:

> *O Ziusudra, man of Shurrupak,*
> *Pull down your house,*
> *And build a boat.*
> *Disdain your kingdom,*
> *Forsake your goods,*
> *And save your life.*

The terse, almost telegraphic style of this five-thousand-year-old tale of suspense, with its clandestine meetings and cryptic secret messages, provides a surprising and perhaps refreshing contrast to the unhurried rhetorical solemnity of the Lord's conversations with Noah in the Book of Genesis. But the most serious discrepancy between the various Sumerian epics and the biblical story of the Flood concerns the exact location of the ark's final resting place:

And the ark rested in the seventh month, on the seventeenth day of the month, upon the mountains of Ararat.

—GENESIS 8:4

Whereas *The Epic of Gilgamesh* tells us:

For a fifth day and a sixth day the mountain of Nisir held up the ship and did not let it waver. When the seventh day came, I sent forth a dove and let it loose. The dove flew away and shortly returned; she had seen no resting place and so she came back.

Presumably the mountain of Nisir lies somewhere between the Tigris and Zab rivers in modern Iraq, though it is certainly not to be found on any modern map. Ararat, on the other hand, retains its ancient name. Hard to miss, its snowcapped twin peaks are clearly visible from three countries (Iran, Turkey, and Soviet Armenia), and the volcanic cone of Great Ararat, on the Turkish side of the border, rises to a height of slightly over seventeen thousand feet. This does not necessarily imply, as both Muslim and Armenian Christian tradition insists, that the timbers of Noah's ark are still preserved for eternity among the glacial ravines and fissures of Great Ararat. Nevertheless, expeditions have set out repeatedly over the past several centuries to seek the remains of the ark. Recently they have had to confine their search to the Turkish side of the border, a region infested with bandits. The nearest substantial settlement is Erzurum, a city of nearly 200,000 inhabitants, but from there the intrepid ark hunter is faced with a long trek up the eastern branch of the Euphrates, which has its source among the peaks of the Ararat massif. Along the way at least he can count on finding lodgings for the night at a Turkish army outpost, for this whole region is a military zone, heavily patrolled and strewn with the latest in electronic listening devices tuned to pick up the slightest rumblings from the direction of the Soviet frontier. (And of course the Turkish authorities will want to satisfy themselves that the hunter has come to look for souvenirs of the ark and nothing more.)

A great many adventurers and amateur archaeologists have set out to find traces of the ark on Great Ararat, but they have come back with nothing much more impressive than a matchstick-sized splinter. So far none of these purported relics of the ark has been authenticated by the carbon-14 dating procedure, and no reputable university or archaeological institute has played any part whatsoever in mounting one of these expeditions. The reason for this is simple: there is actually no compelling reason to believe that Noah's ark landed on Great Ararat at all. The Bible speaks of "the mountains of Ararat," not "Mount Ararat." Conceivably this could refer to the twin peaks of Great and Little Ararat, but the best evidence is that Ararat was the biblical name for the ancient kingdom of Urartu, whose boundaries corresponded roughly to those of the Soviet republic of Armenia—which enlarges our prospective hunting ground from a single (or possibly double) mountain peak to an entire country approximately 11,500 square miles in area, all of which is largely inaccessible for political reasons.

But even granting all this, what if someday someone does happen to find—on Ararat, Nisir, or somewhere in Soviet Armenia—the debris of an ancient vessel that can be proved to be over five thousand years old? How would this enhance our understanding of the Bible? It wouldn't. The Flood and Noah's ark are not verifiable historical facts but episodes in a symbolic drama, whose real importance lies not in its presentation of past events but in its symbolic significance, whether the event "really happened" or not. The best illustration of this is the masterly way in which the authors of the Old Testament are able to enrich the traditional heroic tales of the ancient Near East with a new emotional content. For example, in the earliest of the Sumerian myths of the Flood the god Enlil unleashes the deluge on the world simply because the unaccustomed ruckus created by mankind has disturbed him in his sleep, and he begins to weep uncontrollably. In *The Epic of Gilgamesh* the gods as well as men are forced to take refuge from the Great Flood on the highest mountains. It is only in the Bible that the Flood is described as God's judgment on sinful mankind.

> *And* GOD *saw that the wickedness of man was great in the earth, and that every imagination of the thoughts of his heart was only evil continually.*

> —GENESIS 6:5

And only in the Bible is one man—Noah—deliberately chosen at the outset to be spared from annihilation, and thus the ark becomes the symbol of the promise of salvation that God holds out to man. (In contrast, the Sumerian heroes Ziusudra and Utnapishtim are warned of the coming deluge by their patron gods, but only after the decision to destroy mankind has already been made. In defiance of the other gods, this act seems motivated by friendship, more a personal favor than an act of salvation in the biblical sense.)

A second symbolic event completes the biblical story of the Flood—the appearance of the rainbow, the emblem of God's covenant with man:

> *I do set my bow in the cloud, and it shall be for a token of a covenant between me and the earth.*

> —GENESIS 9:13

This idea, completely new, has no equivalent in the Sumerian or any other myths. People of all cultures have looked on the spectral display of the rainbow as something inexplicable, something sent down by the gods; but no other culture has adopted the rainbow as the symbol of the ultimate reconciliation between God and man. In the Eddas, for example, the great medieval compilation of Norse mythology, the rainbow is said to be the bridge over which the gods come down to earth from Valhalla. To the Indians of Central America it is the bridge over which the spirits of the dead make their journey to the other world. In the Hindu Vedas it is the bow of the war god, Indra. Even today "rainbow dogs," which are seen to be sitting or lying down so that their backs appear to touch the end of the rainbow, are greatly prized by the Zulus, who are convinced the dogs must come down the rainbow from heaven. Anyone who can catch such a dog is thought to have powerful "medicine" and accordingly gains a great reputation as a sorcerer.

Not until the seventeenth century did René Descartes, the great French philosopher and mathematician, discover that the rainbow's colors are produced by the refraction of rays of sunlight as they pass through individual raindrops. We also know now that the center of a rainbow is always in the eye of the beholder, and as he or she moves forward, backward, or sideways, the rainbow appears to follow. We know all this, but it has not yet enabled us to discover the secret that lies behind the rainbow. We can give a plausible explanation for the bright colors that suddenly appear overhead, but we still have no idea what the arc "means." The idea of the rainbow as a bridge between heaven and earth, as a bond between God and man, seems to have a transcendent meaning that overshadows any possible scientific explanation, and for this definitive interpretation we must turn to the Bible.

> . . . *Go to, let us build a city and a tower,*
> *whose top may reach unto heaven. . . .*
>
> —GENESIS 11:4

Why the Tower of Babel Was Not One of the Seven Wonders of the World

We already know that the mystical number seven was the ancient symbol of completion and accomplishment, and so it seems clear enough why there were precisely seven wonders of the ancient world, rather than, say, eight, ten, or an even dozen—which is just as well, because most of us can probably name no more than four or so. This is certainly no disgrace, though; even the greatest authorities of antiquity were not always in agreement on exactly which temples, statues, or other awesome monuments really belonged on the list. The official list of the wonders that finally prevailed was originally compiled by the Greek poet Antipater in about 130 B.C. It included:

1. The Temple of Artemis (Diana) at Ephesus (compare chapter 29 of the Acts of the Apostles, as well as page 387 herein).

2. The pyramids at Giza—the only one of the seven wonders to have survived more or less intact. The Great Pyramid, even without its limestone cap, still rises to a height of 451 feet.

3. The gold-and-ivory statue of Zeus in the Temple of Zeus at Olympia.

4. The Pharos Lighthouse in the harbor of Alexandria—*faro* in Spanish and Portuguese, and *phare* in French, are still the everyday words for "lighthouse."

5. The Colossus of Rhodes—the gigantic statue of Apollo that straddled the island port, with one foot on each of the two projecting moles that sheltered the harbor. (Modern skeptics have claimed that the Colossus merely stood at the entrance to the harbor and that the traditional image of tall galleys sailing between its legs is no more than a picturesque invention.)

6. The Hanging Gardens of Babylon, built by King Nebuchadnezzar (more about them on page 228).

7. The Tomb of Masolus at Halicarnassus—the origin of our word *mausoleum*.

But the Tower of Babel does not figure on Antipater's list or on those of any of his competitors, which may be surprising, because it has always been thought of as the loftiest, most ambitious achievement of antiquity, and it has fired men's imaginations in a way that the Temple of Diana or the Tomb of Masolus certainly never did. You may have already guessed by now—in light of the failure of our last two armchair expeditions, the search for the primeval mud of the universal deluge and the petrified timbers of Noah's ark—that the Tower of Babel never really existed. Or, to be more accurate, that the tower that inspired the biblical story was not a particularly spectacular, or even noteworthy, architectural achievement.

The story of the Tower of Babel is really the last of the Creation myths in the Book of Genesis. Although it takes place in a "historical" setting (Babel is the biblical name for the city of Babylon), which suggests a kind of false continuity with the later historical accounts of the Babylonian Captivity and the writings of the later prophets, we should bear in mind that it has to be read, like the rest of the Book of Genesis, with more of an eye for its emotional truth than for archaeological accuracy. In other words, the story of the Tower of Babel is just that: a story. To be precise—for no account of Babel would be complete without a word or two of incomprehensible jargon—it is an etiology, a narrative that blends fact and imagination in an attempt to describe the cause (Greek *etios*) of some phenomenon, in this case how we came to speak many different languages.

Like the Flood, the Babylonian confusion of tongues is interpreted as a punishment sent by the Lord. The Flood, however, was meant to destroy "all flesh that moved upon the earth"; the confusion of tongues was intended only to chastise the human race. (Fortunately, God had already promised Noah, with the sign of the rainbow, that mankind would never again be destroyed outright.) The Hebrew word for "confusion" is *balal*, which furnished the authors of Genesis with a plausible pretext for setting this tale of divine retribution in the city that they called Babel. Its inhabitants called it Bab-ilu ("the gates of the Lord"), which the Greeks later turned into Babylon. (The English word *babble*, by the way, has nothing to do with Babel or *balal*; it is ultimately derived from the same root as *baby* and *barbarian*, the basic idea being that of someone who doesn't know how to talk properly.)

Babel is the first city to be mentioned by name in the Bible; it also became a synonym for "the archenemy," in both the Old and New Testaments, where *Babylon* is used as a code word for another hated oppressor, imperial Rome. But why has the story of the Tower of Babel, which takes up only the first ten sentences of chapter 11 of Genesis, always held such fascination for generations of philosophers, artists, and poets? Perhaps for the very reason that it is told with such masterly economy; a wealth of realistic detail is compressed into so very few words, and the story itself is narrated in a sparse, unconventional style that leaves all its extraordinary implications to the reader's imagination. The second sentence sets the scene simply and precisely:

> *And it came to pass, as they journeyed from the east, that they found a plain in the land of Shinar; and they dwelt there.*

—GENESIS 11:2

Shinar is the biblical name for Mesopotamia, though today we prefer to call it by its older name, the land of Sumer; and "they" are the Sumerians, originally a nomadic people who migrated from the east and settled in the delta of the Tigris and Euphrates around 3500 B.C. The plain of Shinar has been called by other names as well—Akkad, Chaldea. The modern name, Iraq, means "the land on the shoreline," and it is the alluvial silt deposited by the Tigris and the Euphrates that created this flat landscape, altered and reshaped it, sometimes almost beyond recognition. The two rivers now empty into the Persian Gulf almost a hundred miles to the east of where they did five thousand years ago.

Turning again to Babel—the next sentence reads:

And they said one to another, Go to, let us make brick, and burn them thoroughly. And they had brick for stone, and slime had they for morter.

—GENESIS 11:3

"Brick for stone"—because the land of Sumer was an alluvial floodplain, there was no stone, no timber, and no metal to speak of in the entire region. Sun-dried bricks were (and still are) the only naturally available building material. The recipe hasn't changed—wet clay is poured into a wooden mold, smoothed down, and baked dry in the sun or in a wood-fired kiln.

"Slime had they for morter"—*slime* is actually bitumen, or asphalt, so called because it can often be skimmed off the surface of a stagnant pool in this oil-rich country. In addition to filling in for "morter," it was also used to insulate a building's foundations against groundwater seepage, just as it is today. So, with all this building material ready at hand, the Sumerians set to work:

And they said, Go to, let us build a city and a tower, whose top may reach unto heaven; and let us make us a name, lest we be scattered abroad upon the face of the whole earth.

—GENESIS 11:4

"Make us a name"—Luther translates this as "for we would make us a monument," but both versions eloquently express the nomads' decision to put an end to their wanderings and to reunite their scattered nation within the walls of a permanent settlement. On the flat plains of the delta, a tower was both the architectural and spiritual center of every substantial city, not only in Babylon but at Ur, Uruk, Eridu, Assur, and many other ancient sites. The entire Mesopotamian plain is dotted with the crumbling foundations of these sun-baked brick towers, which we now call by their Akkadian name, ziggurats, which simply means "to rise high, to stand tall."

Why the Sumerians began to build such towers is unclear. They were not tombs; the Sumerians did not believe in life after death and had no need for monuments of that sort. That much is clear, but scholars over the centuries, like the megalomaniac builders of Shinar, have persisted in piling one theory upon another until the whole subject is, quite appropriately, buried in Babylonian confusion. Thus, the ziggurats may or may not have been refuges from rising floodwaters or wild animals, astronomical observatories like the pyramids of the Maya, or artificial mountains created by the Sumerians in imitation of the rugged terrain of their original homeland to the east—this does not even begin to exhaust the list of possibilities.

The earliest detailed account of what a ziggurat looked like was written by the Father of History himself, Herodotus, the insatiable Greek traveler and collector of curious facts of the fifth century B.C. We can be quite certain that the Babylonian tower that he describes so vividly was not the original Tower of Babel, which presumably rose and fell some three millennia before Herodotus visited Babylon in about 450 B.C. Nevertheless, he was quite impressed:

> In the middle of the sanctuary there is a walled tower fully a stadion [about six hundred feet] on each side. There is a second smaller tower built upon the first, a third built upon the second, and so on—eight towers in all, one built upon another. All these towers are joined by a staircase, and when one has climbed halfway to the top, there are benches to rest upon. On the topmost

tower is a great temple, and inside the temple is a wide couch with cushions and a golden table. The only ones who may pass the night there in the temple are those Babylonian women who have been selected by the god Marduk. . . .

But the most curious thing about this is that Herodotus could not possibly have seen the tower and the temple with his own eyes, because some thirty years earlier, in 482 B.C., the ziggurat was destroyed, once and for all, by Xerxes, the Great King of Persia. A century and a half later, Alexander the Great decided to rebuild it as the showplace of the capital of his world empire, but the impetus for his ambitious project died with him in 323 B.C.

The modern tourist who visits the ruins of Babylon will not find a trace of the vanished ziggurat, and only an enormous excavation, now filled with groundwater, marks the site of Alexander's ill-fated attempt to rebuild the Tower of Babel. With the flooding of the site, archaeologists have not been able to (and probably never will) uncover the tower's foundations. This has not discouraged scholars from attempting to calculate its original dimensions on the basis of comparisons with other, more accessible ziggurats. For example, M. André Parrot, chief curator of the French national museums, has asserted that the base of the bottom tower was a square, 91 meters (298.55 feet) on each side, and that the total height of the entire eight-story structure was exactly 91.5 meters (300.2 feet). We should be careful, however, not to overlook what is really important in the midst of this mathematical exactitude; it is often all too easy to get the decimals right and still miss the point.

The most impressive surviving descendant of the Tower of Babel is the ziggurat at Ur. The steps leading to the upper platform actually do seem to reach unto the heavens, or at least that is the impression one gets when one is standing at the base of the exterior staircase, more than 150 feet below. It almost seems as if the ziggurat had originally been conceived as a kind of monumental illustration of Jacob's vision of the heavenly ladder in Genesis 28:12:

And he dreamed, and behold a ladder set up on the earth, and the top of it reached to heaven; and behold the angels of God ascending and descending on it.

Now, the question of which particular ziggurat served as the prototype for the biblical Tower of Babel becomes secondary, at best, when we examine the real point of this highly sophisticated parable. God has punished man, we are told, by confounding the language of all the earth "that they may not understand one another's speech." In other words, he has substantially diminished the one human faculty that most clearly distinguishes mankind from the rest of the animal kingdom: the ability to communicate complex ideas through the medium of the spoken word. As Karl Jaspers has said, "Our ability to talk to one another is what makes us human." And the Babylonian confusion of tongues impaired our ability not only to understand each other's speech but to understand each other's thoughts as well. The imposition of this original language barrier brought prejudice and misunderstanding into the world.

Consider Talleyrand's famous epigram: "Man was given the gift of speech to make it easier for him to conceal his thoughts." What else is this but a cynical, or merely pragmatic, acknowledgment of the parable's implications? Apparently the price we had to pay—the confusion of our speech and dispersal over the face of the earth—was not enough to deter us from embarking on even more ambitious projects than the Tower of Babel, projects ambitious enough to justify the Lord's earlier forebodings: "and now nothing will be restrained from them, which they have imagined to do." The prerequisite for the raising of the tower was a common language—"the whole earth was of one language, and of one speech." Now the scientists and technologists have rediscovered this universal language in the figures and formulas that enabled them to rebuild buried ziggurats and make new towers to reach unto the heavens—the gantries and missile silos, ICBMs with thermonuclear warheads, the neutron bomb. The question now is whether we will restrain ourselves from doing what we have prepared ourselves for, including the annihilation of all life on this planet. We might do well to remember that the parable of Babel, the last of the Creation myths in the Book of Genesis, does not have the reassuring finale of the story of Noah's Flood: the Lord's explicit promise to spare the human race from destruction is not repeated, and in our present circumstances, perhaps we should regard this silence as slightly ominous.

The Dream of the Promised Land

Then Abraham fell upon his face, and laughed . . .

—GENESIS 17:17

The Mystery of Abraham

Abraham is the first historical figure who appears in the Old Testament. No scholar seriously doubts that there actually was such a person, even though there is not a simple piece of independent evidence to prove that he ever existed. What is more, the biblical account of Abraham's life is an inextricable tangle of history and myth; later embellishments and more ancient traditions eventually became firmly associated with the legends that gathered around Abraham, the forefather of his people, and around the formation of the Hebrew nation.

Abraham's original name, as the Bible tells us in Genesis

17:4–5, was Abram, and it was God himself who gave him the symbolic name of Abraham:

> *As for me, behold, my covenant is with thee, and thou shalt be a father of many nations.*
>
> *Neither shall thy name any more be called Abram, but thy name shall be Abraham; for a father of many nations have I made thee.*

Abraham means "father of the nations" in Hebrew (the King James scholars gloss this word as "father of multitudes"), and Abraham, the eternal wanderer, the homeless sojourner, became the symbolic representative of a people whose restless history so closely paralleled his own.

For Christians, Abraham is one of the central figures of the Old Testament. The Roman Catholic Church (and several translations of the Bible) have awarded him and his son Isaac and his grandson Jacob, the title of patriarch, which literally means "chief of the fathers' tribe." Abraham's family tree is laid out in great detail in the Book of Genesis: he was tenth in the direct line of descent from Noah, and the first man since Noah who talked directly with God. Later, in the Gospel According to Saint Matthew, the ancestry of Jesus is painstakingly traced back, through King David, all the way to Abraham. Luke is even more exhaustive in his genealogical research—all the way back to "Adam, which was the son of God." We need not necessarily take this as Gospel truth, at least in the usual sense; the Evangelists were simply trying to express that the lineage of Jesus Christ as the long-awaited Messiah must inevitably extend back to Abraham—that is, to the beginning of the political and spiritual history of the Jewish people. Abraham is also revered as one of the prophets of Islam, in a direct line of spiritual succession which includes Noah and Jesus and culminates, of course, in the life and teachings of Muhammad:

Whosoever has a fairer religion than he who has submissively turned his face toward Allah, then he is truly godly and follows the creed of Abraham, who believed in the one true faith, for Allah took Abraham to be his friend.

—THE HOLY KORAN, SURA 4, VERSE 124

When the first clay tablets bearing the name Abraham (Ibrahim) were discovered in Mesopotamia, scholars were convinced that they had finally found conclusive proof of the historical existence of the patriarch of Genesis. But when many more such tablets had come to light from several different cultures, dating from many different centuries, all inscribed with the name Ibrahim, this seemed like too much of a good thing. A paradox now faces the scientist—the archaeologist in this case; he finds himself confronted with such a wealth of inconclusive data that the archaeological discoveries of the last century have only deepened the mystery surrounding the "historical" Abraham. So much so, in fact, that by way of analogy we can imagine the plight of future historians, many millennia from now, who are fairly certain that there had once been an important historical figure called Alexander the Great; they are not quite certain whether he was a king of Macedon, a Renaissance pope, or the czar of Russia. As far as Abraham is concerned, we really have no idea when or where he lived or whether he was a king, a priest, or a nomad chieftain. As usual, though, there are several competing theories, each with a certain amount of evidence to support it:

Abraham lived . . . in Sumer, which is to say at some time during the second millennium B.C.

. . . in the kingdom of Mitanni, which would necessarily put Abraham somewhere between 1600 and 1400 B.C.

. . . in the kingdom of Ebla, which flourished during the third millennium B.C.

The first theory, at least, is borne out by the Book of Genesis:

And Terah took Abram his son, and Lot the son of Haran his son's son, and Sarai his daughter in law, his son Abram's wife; and they went forth with them from Ur of the Chaldees. . . .

—GENESIS 11:31

Chaldees, or Chaldeans, simply means "people of the plain," and Chaldea was none other than Sumer. Ur, the site of the impressive ruins of the ziggurat mentioned on pages 61–62, was in fact one of the principal cities of the Sumerians. The Bible occasionally mentions Chaldea or Shinar, but the name of Sumer, long since forgotten by biblical times, was rediscovered only in 1850 by the French archaeologist Jules Oppert. Biblical scholars had always assumed that Ur of the Chaldees must have been an oasis, where nomads pitched their goat's-hair tents by a convenient water hole and where, in the finest tent of all—with more pegs, rugs, pillows, and canopies than any other—the patriarch Abraham lived contentedly among his family and flocks. This vision of pastoral simplicity, enshrined in numerous woodcuts and steel engravings that hung in pious European homes, was rudely shattered in 1854, when the ruins of Ur were first excavated. It quickly became clear that this had been a royal city, not a shepherd's camp—a city of paved streets and closely packed stucco houses, most of them two stories tall and some with as many as ten rooms. Consequently, Abraham could hardly have been a nomadic chieftain; he must have been a prosperous citizen of one of the largest cities in the world.

Today it takes a certain effort for a visitor to the excavation site to imagine what this metropolis might have been like. Apart from the ziggurat, very little remains of the ancient city except the bricks of crumbling foundation walls; the excavation itself is only a brief interruption in the barren, featureless plain that stretches to the horizon.

Four thousand years ago this was rich, arable land. The city stood on the banks of the Euphrates, and all the surrounding countryside was laced with an elaborate filigree of irrigation canals. Since then the Euphrates has altered its meandering course by almost fifteen miles, and today the faint outlines of the Sumerian irrigation system are visible only from the air. Nowhere else in the ancient world were the destinies of cities so closely linked to those of their parent rivers as in Mesopotamia. Life sprang up where the water flowed; when the river shifted its course, the desert reclaimed the land. In this respect, at least, the story of the rise and fall of Ur is entirely typical.

The Chaldees of Ur seem to have been a clever, rich, and peace-loving race, judging by the evidence of the cuneiform tablets and bits of jewelry that they left behind—the latter of such delicate workmanship and such exquisite design that nineteenth-century archaeologists were astonished. Until then ancient artifacts of such quality were encountered only among the grave goods of the Egyptian pharaohs, and this jewelry was easily one thousand years older. The Sumerian cuneiform script of the tablets was deciphered, which allowed the men and women of Ur to speak again after a silence of almost five thousand years. Much of what they had to say has a refreshingly mundane and thus entirely modern ring to it. Included are proverbs such as "An open mouth just lets the sparrows fly in," or "Marry for pleasure; get divorced when you've thought it over"; commercial contracts in which, for example, an undertaker agrees to accept "seven pitchers of beer and 420 loaves of bread" for services rendered; and this home remedy for stomachache: "Pour strong beer over resin, heat it up, and mix this fluid with oil, then give it to the sufferer to drink."

But even after scholars had sifted through this buried treasure, still no trace of Abraham was to be found—no mention of him as a party to any of these contracts, no inventory of trade goods that bears his signature seal. Apart from the single biblical reference to "Ur of the Chaldees," there is no other evidence to connect Abraham with the royal city of Sumer. However, several lesser mysteries involving Abraham—biblical passages that had never been satisfactorily explained—could now be unraveled with the help of these newly deciphered Sumerian texts. For example, in Genesis 15:8, Abraham asks the Lord for a sign: "whereby shall I know that I shall inherit it [the land the Lord has promised him]?" The Lord replies with a series of detailed instructions, which Abraham faithfully carries out; he at least seems to know what's going on here, even if we are left completely in the dark.

> . . . *Take me an heifer of three years old, and a she goat of three years old, and a ram of three years old, and a turtledove, and a young pigeon.*
>
> *And he took unto him all these, and divided them in the midst, and laid each piece one against another: but the birds divided he not.*
>
> *And it came to pass that, when the sun went down, and it was dark, behold a smoking furnace, and a burning lamp that passed between those pieces.*
>
> *In the same day the* LORD *made a covenant with Abram. . . .*
>
> —GENESIS 15:9–10, 17–18

Cuneiform tablets from Ur and Mari describe a similar ritual, which was simply the way in which important contracts were solemnized in ancient Mesopotamia. The contract went into effect as soon as both parties had prepared a sacrifice in the manner described in Genesis and "passed between those pieces"—that is, they had to walk between the split carcasses of the sacrificed animals. This kind of circumstantial evidence might be taken as proof that Abraham—Abram, as he was then—really did live in the land of Sumer, circa 2000 B.C., if only we didn't have other evidence to suggest a rather different conclusion.

Let us take a closer look at Genesis 11: "And Terah took

Abram his son, and Lot the son of Haran . . . and they went forth with them from Ur of the Chaldees . . . and they came unto Haran, and dwelt there."

Haran can still be found—the city, that is, not Lot's father—in modern Turkey, near the Syrian border. In ancient days Haran was part of the kingdom of Mitanni, sometimes known as Huri, or the kingdom of the Hurrians, or Khurites, or Horites. (Modern archaeologists prefer to call them the Mitannians, and we would probably be well advised to do the same.) At any rate, the Mitannians were an Indo-European people who originally came from Asia and settled on the upper reaches of the Tigris and Euphrates in about the fourteenth century B.C. There they founded a kingdom, usually called Mitanni, which was originally the name of the Mitannians' ruling clan. "Founded" a kingdom is the kind of innocuous-sounding euphemism with which historians prefer to describe the conquests and other blood-drenched exploits of someone of whom they approve, and there is no doubt that the Mitannians were basically a likable people. Happiest when they were on horseback, they spent most of their time breeding, breaking, and training horses. Instead of epic poetry, they composed long treatises on dressage and other horsey topics.

The Mitannians seem also to have had a keen sense of the mounted aristocrat's natural superiority over their pedestrian subjects, which they expressed, among various other ways, by giving new names in their own language to the cities they conquered (a habit that persisted into our own times among various Indo-European "master races"). Just as our modern conquerors preferred Leopoldville to Kinshasa or Breslau to Wrocław, the Mitannians immediately renamed the ancient city of Nuzu (or Nuzi) as Guzur, which became the capital of Mitanni. (Haran, the dwelling place of Terah, Lot, and Abraham, kept its original name.)

Another foreign refugee who visited Mitanni was Sinuhe, an

Egyptian courtier who had fled from the pharaoh's displeasure to live an adventurous life of exile in various foreign parts. The *Tale of Sinuhe* includes a flattering description of Haran and its environs, where Sinuhe rested for some time in his wanderings: "It was a fruitful land. There were figs and more wine than water; it was also rich in honey, and olives were there in abundance. The branches hung heavy with fruit. The herds were numerous beyond counting. There were fields of barley and emmer [a kind of wheat with hard red kernels]." The people were well fed, Sinuhe goes on to say, famine was unknown, and commerce flourished. Haran stood at the junction of several caravan routes. There merchants could find lodgings in the huts and guest houses of the city, take care of business, and give their pack mules a few days' rest—a busy, cosmopolitan marketplace where something was always going on.

Haran is not recommended as a stopover for the modern tourist, however. The local farmers seem to resent the mild notoriety their ancestors brought upon them—perhaps because they are tired of notching their plowshares on potsherds and other fragments of ancient Haran—and any car that approaches is likely to be met with a hail of stones. Archaeologists have excavated the site, without finding anything of great interest. In fact, the most striking things about Haran, at least from an antiquarian standpoint, are the *tulli*, beehive-shaped houses of sun-dried brick, each with a tall, pointed dome. The design as well as the name has not changed in four thousand years. The dome collects rising hot air from the interior rooms, as well as smoke from the hearth fire, and then funnels it out a ventilation hole at its tip. Smaller ventilation holes along the sides of the dome let sunlight in. The floors below are covered with rugs and cushions. If, after all, Abraham did not live in a nomad's goat-hair tent or a Sumerian stucco townhouse, is it possible that he lived in a snug, air-conditioned beehive?

It seems very likely that he did. At least this has been the consensus among scholars since 1938, when a team of American archaeologists began to investigate the ruins of the Mitanni capital of Nuzu-Guzur and found a cache of four thousand clay tablets, their most important discovery. Not so impressive, perhaps, compared with the municipal archives of Mari that contained some twenty-three thousand tablets, these cuneiform texts nevertheless have told us quite a lot, not just about the manners and customs of the Mitannians but about the Book of Genesis as well.

First of all, it is clear that the Mitannians themselves were not simply a band of carefree horse fanciers; every aspect of their public and private lives was regulated by a rigid caste system, the details of which were codified and minutely described in the clay tablets found at Nuzu. Second, it seems that Abraham and the world he lived in were governed by a social and moral code that was virtually identical to that of the Mitannians. As described in the Book of Genesis, the social background of Abraham's early career, even in the most trifling details, seems to fit very neatly into the sort of legalistic, caste-ridden society that is described in the Mitanni tablets.

For example, in Genesis 15:2–3, Abraham plaintively asks the Lord, "What wilt thou give me, seeing I go childless, and the steward of my house is this Eliezer of Damascus? . . . to me thou hast given no seed: and, lo, one born in my house is mine heir." In other words, he seems to be saying that he has reluctantly named his steward, a superior sort of house slave, as his heir because he has no children of his own. And in fact, according to the Mitanni tablets, this was exactly the procedure—a childless couple were obliged to adopt a stranger as the heir to their estate.

But this is only the beginning. What are we to make of Abraham's instruction to his wife, Sarah, in Genesis 12:11–13?

And it came to pass, when he was come near to enter into

Egypt, that he said unto Sarai his wife, Behold now, I know that thou art a fair woman to look upon:

Therefore it shall come to pass, when the Egyptians shall see thee, that they shall say, This is his wife: and they will kill me, but they will save thee alive.

Say, I pray thee, thou art my sister: that it may be well with me for thy sake; and my soul shall live because of thee.

Strange goings-on indeed, even if Sarah actually was Abraham's half sister (in an earlier passage he explains that Sarah was "his sister, the daughter of my father but not of my mother," though some authorities have taken this to mean that she was his niece). At any rate, this strange decision to pass off his wife as his sister simply in order to save his own skin does not say too much for Abraham's moral fiber. Generations of Bible readers have searched, in vain, for an honorable, or even plausible, explanation of this incident. But not until the Mitanni legal tablets were deciphered was this matter finally sorted out—and Abraham exonerated, without a stain on his character.

In the Mitanni scheme of things, women's legal and social status was so much inferior to that of men that they were scarcely considered to be human—fair game, in other words, for lustful Egyptians and other predators. There was, however, one exception to this dreary rule: a man's sister was considered to be his social equal. Thus, for a man to acknowledge his wife as his sister actually amounted to a social promotion; his sister, as far as other men were concerned, was strictly taboo.

The lowly status of women in the Mitanni social order may also have some bearing on another curious episode in the Book of Genesis. When Lot was visited by two angels of the Lord, the men of Sodom "compassed the house round" and shouted out to him, "Where are the men which came in to thee this night? bring them out unto us, that we may know them." Lot decided to strike a bargain with them:

> *Behold now, I have two daughters which have not known man;*
> *let me, I pray you, bring them out unto you, and do ye to them as*
> *is good in your eyes. . . .*

> —GENESIS 19:8

It is a little hard for us to imagine how Lot could be so solicitous of his two visitors that he was willing to sacrifice his daughters to a howling mob on their behalf. But according to the Mitanni code, hospitality has the highest priority, whereas wives and daughters take a distant second place. Genesis 16:2 illustrates another example of the clash between Mitanni morality and our own; Sarah's suggestion to Abraham has always struck puritans as being scandalously indecent and rationalists as a flagrant violation of the laws of human nature:

> *Behold now, the LORD hath restrained me from bearing: I pray*
> *thee, go in unto my maid; it may be that I may obtain children by*
> *her. And Abram hearkened to the voice of Sarai.*

The result of Abraham's dalliance with his wife's maid, Hagar the Egyptian, was a child called Ishmael, who in Islamic tradition is the ancestor of the Arab people. The tomb of Hagar and Ishmael is one of the great pilgrimage sites of the holy city of Mecca. In any case, Sarah's proposal was, by Mitanni standards, neither indecent nor even unusual. A childless woman was expected to provide her husband with a surrogate wife, though the surrogate—even if she bore a child—could never replace her as mistress of the household (this is also borne out by the biblical account of Hagar's being driven into the wilderness).

In addition to the legal tablets, other Mitanni artifacts found in Nuzu have familiar, if less sensational, biblical associations. Gold jewelry, for example, included golden nose rings of the kind that Abraham's servant offered as Rebekah's bride price (the King James calls hers an "earring"), "of half a shekel weight."

73

Near the jewelry were found several sausage-shaped gold and silver rings which, because there was as yet no standardized coinage, were used for currency. "Coins" of smaller denominations could simply be cut off these rings in chunks of so many shekels' weight. (A shekel was a unit of weight, not value.) This was how Abraham paid for his family's sepulcher in the cave of Machpela:

> . . . *and Abraham weighed to Ephron the silver . . . four hundred shekels of silver, current* money *with the merchant.*
>
> —Genesis 23:16

The King James translators put the word *money* in italics to indicate that it does not appear in the original or that this reading is merely conjectural. Luther translates this phrase more literally as "according to the weight that is customary in trade." What does this mean exactly? Simply that Abraham paid out pure silver in the correct amount? Or perhaps that a shekel was not always a shekel? The latter, in fact—a shekel of silver was 16 grams, a shekel of gold 16.4 grams; at that time silver was scarcer and thus more valuable than gold.

To sum up, there appeared to be so many remarkable correlations between the legal tablets of Mitanni and the rather peculiar social standards that prevailed in Abraham's world that even the most enthusiastic partisans of the Ur-of-the-Chaldees theory were finally won over. Abraham must certainly have been a subject of the kingdom of Mitanni and a citizen of Haran. This implies, as mentioned earlier, that he lived about five hundred years later than was previously supposed—that is, about 1500 B.C.; the Mitannians managed to hold onto their empire for only a little over two hundred years before the Hittites displaced them, sometime after 1400 B.C.

And there the matter rested, at least until A.D. 1977, when a radically different chronology was proposed for the life of

Abraham—some thousand years earlier, well back into the third millennium B.C.—and an entirely new setting as well. Italian archaeologists had uncovered the ruins of the ancient city of Ebla, where they found extensive traces of a sophisticated urban culture in a region that had previously been dismissed as an arid, semidesert steppe that in ancient times was inhabited only by wandering tribes of nomads.

The site of the dig was a hill called Tel Mardiqu, some thirty miles from the modern Syrian city of Aleppo. Although Ebla is not mentioned in the Bible, scholars already knew the name from Sumerian inscriptions. No one had suspected, however, that Ebla had been a considerable power in its own right, a metropolis of some 250,000 inhabitants and the capital of a great Syrian empire.

Before 1977 archaeologists were convinced that no blank pages remained to be filled in concerning the history of the ancient Near East. The fifteen thousand clay tablets discovered in the royal enclosure at Ebla not only disproved this but cast into serious doubt all previous assumptions about cultural dispersion patterns and "the origins of civilization." Unfortunately, it seemed at first that none of these questions could be resolved for quite some time; the municipal archives of Ebla were written in unfamiliar characters, presumably in an unknown language. Even with a whole bank of computers and all the resources of modern cryptography, it would still take decades before scholars could begin to decipher these tablets or even to pick out a tentative phrase or two.

Fortunately, though, the scribes of Ebla had anticipated this problem five thousand years earlier—they had thoughtfully left a bilingual dictionary lying at the bottom of this enormous heap of clay tablets. This dictionary—the oldest in the world—was a simple list of words and phrases in the unknown language of Ebla together with their equivalents in Sumerian cuneiform script. Thus, the deciphering of the archives would require only a fair amount of patience and hard work, instead of a cybernetic miracle. Still, this was just the beginning. As Professor Giovanni Petinato, the archaeologist who found the key to the "Eblaite" language, has observed, "Reading many of the tablets is comparatively easy, but understanding them is quite a different matter."

Professor Petinato's interpretations of the Eblaite tablets have already come into conflict with several well-established archaeological truisms, and it seems that many of these, perhaps our entire conception of the early history of the Fertile Crescent, will have to be revised accordingly. For example, when Petinato announced that he had come across the word *Damascus* in one of the Eblaite tablets, a colleague from Damascus objected, "That's absolutely out of the question. Granted that Damascus is the world's oldest continuously inhabited city—still, we know that it simply did not exist before the second millennium B.C." A few weeks later the floor of a Damascus mosque was demolished in the course of routine renovation work—uncovering an arched vault below that dated from the *third* millennium B.C. Ebla was vindicated.

Professor Petinato and his colleagues have also come across a great many Eblaite literary texts—including a Creation story and an account of the Flood—which should be of interest to Old Testament scholars, because these are undoubtedly the earliest of their kind that have ever been discovered. Even more to the point, however: the Eblaite commercial transactions that have been deciphered so far refer to several ancient cities whose names were previously unknown—except in the Book of Genesis. The Eblaite tablets mentioned other cities as well—Admah, Zebo'im, Zoar, even Sodom and Gomorrah, all names from Abraham's world.

Professor Petinato even suggests the possibility that the Eblaite King Ebrum may be the "Eber" who, according to Genesis 11, was no less than Abraham's great-great-great-great-grandfather— and who may well have been the eponymous ancestor of the

Hebrews (which simply means that the word *Hebrew* is probably derived from *Eber*). If this is true, it seems to follow that Abraham was most likely an Eblaite as well.

Before leaping to this heady conclusion, we must bear two things in mind. First, it will be some time before scholars interpret the Eblaite tablets and the other intriguing discoveries from Tel Mardiqu, and arrive at a reasonable understanding of their real significance. At the moment, Ebla is still uncharted country, and Old Testament scholars and archaeologists will have very few landmarks to guide them in their search for the historical Abraham. Second, as mentioned at the beginning of this chapter, it is very difficult to separate this single strand of history from the formidable tangle of legend, myth, and pseudohistorical embroidery that surrounds it. By the time this story was finally written down in its present form, sometime after the return of the Jewish people from the Babylonian Exile, about 530 B.C., Abraham was no longer a distinct historical figure but a kind of anthology of all the moral virtues personified.

We have already seen how later scribes tampered with the original Hebrew Creation myth to provide retroactive justification for a religious practice—observance of the Sabbath—that was adopted only much later. The biblical account of the origin of ritual circumcision, which figures prominently in the story of Abraham, is another example of this technique labeled priestly "revisionism," or what scholars call "ahistorical accretion." According to Genesis 17:10, Abraham received a direct command from the Lord to the effect that ". . . every man child among you shall be circumcised." This incident is almost certainly a later interpolation, because circumcision was customarily practiced among almost all the peoples of ancient Mesopotamia. This was purely a hygienic precaution, like the later Hebraic and Islamic prohibition against pork because of the danger of trichinosis, and so it is hard to see why circumcision would have been adopted as a special token of the covenant between the Lord and the house of Abraham; almost everyone else would have been circumcised as well. Apparently it was much later, during the Babylonian Captivity, or about 580 B.C., that circumcision began to be regarded as a peculiarly Jewish custom, simply because it was no longer practiced among the Babylonians. And it was at this time that the Jewish priesthood began to elaborate this minor cultural peculiarity into the primary symbol of God's covenant with his Chosen People—even if it meant, for the sake of internal consistency, that Abraham had to be circumcised at the incongruous age of ninety-nine (Genesis 17:24).

Another suspicious passage can be found in Genesis 14:20, in which Abraham offers one-tenth of the recovered booty from the sack of Sodom—"and he gave him tithes of all"—to Melchizedek, king of Salem and "priest of the most high God" (Genesis 14:18). This was presumably added by the priests of the Temple, solely to back up their frequent requests for sacrificial offerings with a patriarchal precedent.

Several incidents in the story of Abraham seem to describe the customs and attitudes of a much earlier, more primitive period. The most famous of these is the story of Abraham and Isaac. The Lord commands Abraham to offer his only son as a sacrifice—certainly the sort of capricious, bloodthirsty behavior that we would normally associate with one of the more ferocious deities of ancient mythology. That is precisely the point; this episode was borrowed from a much older Sumerian legend, with the climactic scene heavily adapted to dramatize the ways in which the God of Abraham sets himself apart from all the other gods: by refusing the sacrifice in a last-minute display of clemency and benevolence.

Finally, putting aside the question of these deliberate editorial additions and improvements, we should consider that Abraham's biographers (the authors of Genesis) were very much of a different time and place, whether Abraham lived in Ebla in 2500

B.C., in Ur in 2000 B.C., or in Mitanni in 1500 B.C. Inevitably, then, a great many of the details of Abraham's story are anachronistic—that is, they describe a social background that is quite different from the way things actually were in Abraham's own times (and here the plural seems strangely appropriate).

In Genesis 12:16, for example, Pharaoh rewards Abraham with, among other things, "he asses," "she asses," and "camels." But we know that camels were not domesticated until the thirteenth century B.C., at least two hundred years too late for Abraham to have owned one. Before that, as this passage correctly implies, pack mules were the customary beasts of burden; a mule could carry a load of up to about 150 pounds. But these mules, though they were a much hardier breed than their modern descendants, still had to be watered at least once a day. This meant that the caravan routes had to be laid out fairly circuitously, planning for a water hole every fifteen miles or so— a reasonable day's journey for a train of pack mules. It wasn't until the sturdy dromedary replaced the pack mule that caravans could travel for several days without making a detour toward a water hole, which greatly decreased travel time across the desert between one market and another.

To be sure, this is a minor discrepancy, especially when we consider the enormous problems that Abraham has created for historians and archaeologists—to say nothing of the difficulties that theologians and moralists have had to deal with when they try to turn this lusty old patriarch into a spotless saint on a pedestal. Clearly, Abraham was no saint; and it is his various flaws and weaknesses that make him such an appealing character. He certainly seems much more human and accessible to us than most other Old Testament personalities. For one thing, he had a sense of humor:

Then Abraham fell upon his face, and laughed . . .

—GENESIS 17:17

This is the first time that the Bible mentions anyone's laughing, and we can see what Abraham thinks is so funny: the Lord has assured him that he will father a son, at the age of ninety-nine. A few verses later, the Lord (in the guise of an angel) repeats these tidings to his wife, Sarah, who is also "well stricken in age." She, at least, tries to stifle her laughter, but the Lord speaks rather reprovingly to her afterward. (Sarah, by the way, is the only woman in the Old Testament to whom God speaks directly.)

Abraham's own conversations with his God have an informal, almost raffish quality that seems particularly compelling to the modern reader. The most famous of these occurs at the end of Genesis 18, where Abraham haggles and chops logic with the Lord and generally carries on—apart from a few conventionally self-deprecating formulas ("I . . . which am but dust and ashes" and the like)—as if he were talking to an equal, as one experienced man of the world to another. To be sure, Abraham has a personal stake in the outcome of this discussion. The Lord is determined to find out whether the citizens of Sodom and Gomorrah are really such a pack of degenerates as they are reported to be. If so, the cities will be destroyed. Because Abraham's nephew Lot lives in Sodom, Abraham suggests a more discriminating approach to the problem:

> *Wilt thou also destroy the righteous with the wicked?*
> *Peradventure there be fifty righteous within the city: wilt thou also destroy and not spare the place for the fifty righteous that are therein?*

> —GENESIS 18:23–24

He goes on to remind God that there are certain standards to uphold, after all:

> *That be far from thee to do after this manner, to slay the*

80

righteous with the wicked. . . . Shall not the Judge of all the earth do right?

—GENESIS 18:25

The Lord accepts Abraham's initial bid, and so Abraham presses his advantage:

Peradventure there shall lack five of the fifty righteous: wilt thou destroy all the city for lack of five?

—GENESIS 18:28

The Lord still seems amenable, so Abraham decides to press on—"to sop up the gravy," as they say in business-administration circles:

Peradventure there shall be forty found there.

—GENESIS 18:29

Once again, the Lord agrees to come down a few points, but Abraham has built up too much momentum to be content with that. What if there were only thirty, for example, or twenty? Or ten? The bargain is struck at ten, and "the Lord went his way, as soon as he had left communing with Abraham." But, as we know, even ten proved to be too high a quota of righteousness for the Cities of the Plain—though the Lord indulgently waives his right of foreclosure until Lot and his family are safely outside the city limits.

The Middle Eastern passion for driving the hardest possible bargain is very neatly captured in this brief vignette. The contrast between Abraham's properly deferential manner and his relentless exploitation of the psychological moment seems so realistic, so real in fact, that it may be hard for even the most reverent modern reader to read this passage all the way through and keep a straight face. It is even harder to understand how sobersided biblical scholars of the previous century could have read this same passage and still be convinced that Abraham was a purely imaginary figure—a legal fiction, as they say, who was created solely in order to give the Israelites a clear title to the Land of Canaan. If this were really true, surely the authors of Genesis would have given him a much more conventional, much more venerable personality, and not quite so many ordinary human frailties. After all, legendary ancestors are a lot easier to invent than real human beings.

The modern reader may not be terribly concerned with Abraham's mysterious origins or his moral peccadilloes, but the problem of the language remains. A certain amount of Abraham's story will still be lost in translation, unfortunately, until these strange words and stranger customs can be properly explained. And even though scholars and archaeologists have been very successful in solving the lesser mysteries of the Book of Genesis, the average reader, who must be content with King James or Luther, is still left in the dark. For example, take this simple sentence:

> And the LORD appeared unto him in the plains of Mamre. . . .

> —GENESIS 18:1

This is straightforward enough, but only because the King James panel decided to gloss over a small textual problem here, one that Luther and his German successors preferred to meet head-on. The German version reads: ". . . by the terebinth of Mamre." A terebinth is a small tree, a kind of pistachio in fact, which was considered sacred in ancient times. Earlier in the Book of Genesis we are told that Mamre was a sanctuary near the city of Hebron where Abraham built his "altar to God." But wouldn't it be simpler just to say "by the sacred grove of Mamre"? In the German Bible this phrase is intelligible only to the reader who happens to know already about terebinths and their properties; in the English Bible this engaging bit of background lore has dropped out altogether.

Similarly, in Genesis 21:33, the King James says that "Abraham planted a grove in Beersheba," which is less explicit but probably more informative than Luther's ". . . a tamarisk in Beersheba." Perhaps both clarity and accuracy could be served by adopting a compromise version: "a grove of tamarisks."

It should be a relief, after all this, to skip ahead to the romantic story of Abraham's grandson Jacob, who becomes involved in a curious triangle with the lovely Rachel and her "tender-eyed" older sister, Leah. Jacob agrees to work for Laban, their father, for several years in return for Rachel's hand. The authors of Genesis have compressed the whole story of Jacob's seven years' ordeal into a single sentence that for its beauty and simplicity can hardly be matched in all of world literature:

> *And Jacob served seven years for Rachel; and they seemed unto him but a few days, for the love he had to her.*

> —GENESIS 29:20

This verse is made all the more poignant by what follows. On their wedding night, after the seven years are up, it is not Rachel but Leah, her older sister, who joins Jacob in the nuptial chamber. It is not until the next morning that he discovers the substitution, though, and he naturally protests to Laban. Laban's answer is disarmingly simple:

> *It must not be so done in our country, to give the younger before the firstborn.*

> —GENESIS 29:26

(This is one of those self-evident axioms of rural life that would still be understood in many parts of the world today.) Jacob seems to be persuaded by this, and he agrees to serve another seven years for Rachel's sake. By now all three sides of the triangle are firmly locked in place: Jacob loves Rachel, Rachel loves Jacob, Leah loves Jacob, and before long the older sister bears him a son. The atmosphere in Laban's household is crackling with tension, the suspense is mounting—and then the story seems to trail off into another botanical digression, though this time the subject is not terebinths or tamarisks, but mandrakes.

> And Reuben [Jacob and Leah's son] went in the days of wheat harvest, and found mandrakes in the field, and brought them unto his mother Leah. . . .

—GENESIS 30:14

Glancing down the page, we see that these mandrakes actually play a crucial role in the story:

> And Rachel said, Therefore he [Jacob] shall lie with thee to night for thy son's mandrakes.

—GENESIS 30:15

What is this all about exactly? The German reader is left with no more of a clue than his English counterpart; Luther just says cryptically that Reuben found "dudaim berries" in the fields, which other German versions of the Bible translate as "love apples" (an old name for a kind of eggplant) or simply "mandrake." "Love apples" should give us a hint at least. As all of King James's subjects knew perfectly well, the mandrake root was a powerful aphrodisiac. This explains how Leah managed to lure Jacob back into her bed, even after he had finally married her younger sister.

Back to our story. Jacob, having fathered many children and accumulated "much cattle, and maidservants, and menservants, and camels [!], and asses," incurs his father-in-law's displeasure and decides to abscond with his wives and their children and as much as they can carry. In addition, Rachel stole "the images that were her father's." When Laban catches up with them, he reproachfully asks Jacob, "Wherefore hast thou stolen my gods?" Jacob flatly denies having done so ("for Jacob knew not that Rachel had stolen them") and suggests that Laban search their tents. He fails to discover the stolen images, however, because Rachel "had taken the images, and put them in the camel's furniture [saddle, saddle blanket, and so on], and sat upon them." She explains regretfully to her father that she can't get up, "for the custom of women is upon me," and the images remain safely hidden.

The images that Laban is so anxious to recover are his household gods *(theraphim)*. (Little sandstone figurines of this type, no more than six or eight inches tall, have been dug up by the hundreds; every self-respecting museum has whole cabinets and storage closets full of them.) This makes sense. Laban, a pious, god-fearing pagan, is naturally intent on getting them back (though as far as his daughters, his flocks, and his other chattels are concerned, he is willing to arrive at a reasonable settlement with Jacob). But why has Rachel hidden them, instead of just handing them over? This is a question that scholars have been able to answer only since 1937, when the legal tablets of Mitanni were discovered. Whichever member of the family had possession of the household gods automatically became the heir to the family estate. Rachel was not being a disobedient daughter so much as a prudent mother—trying to secure her children's inheritance against the claims of her brother's families. Actually, Jacob had promised Laban that whoever had made off with the *theraphim* would be put to death, so Rachel was in fact endangering her own life for her children's sake. It is comforting to know that this problematical tale has a moral after all, even if it took twenty-five hundred years for scholars to puzzle it out.

In the next chapter of the Book of Genesis we come upon the

story of Jacob's meeting with the angel, which for Christians is one of the most important parables of the Old Testament:

> And Jacob was left alone; and there wrestled a man with him until the breaking of the day.
>
> And when he saw that he prevailed not against him, he touched the hollow of his thigh; and the hollow of Jacob's thigh was out of joint, as he wrestled with him.
>
> And he said, Let me go, for the day breaketh. And he said, I will not let thee go, except thou bless me.
>
> —GENESIS 32:24–26

For Christians, the operative phrase here is "I will not let thee go, except thou bless me," which seems to say in a very short space almost everything that can be said about the unrelenting struggle between the Holy Spirit and the human spirit. For Orthodox Jews this passage has a much more literal application, and even today the ultra-pious Jew still refrains from eating the hip tendon of any animal, in commemoration of Jacob's all-night bout with the angel, from which he emerged not only with a dislocated hip but also with a new name: Israel, "he who struggled with God."

Before we move on to the first generation of the children of Israel, though, a final note on grandfather Abraham. In late biblical times, when the great compilation of Jewish laws called the Talmud was being written, the honored dead were said to rest "in Abraham's bosom." The most famous instance of this phrase occurs in the Gospel According to Saint Luke, in the parable of the rich man and the beggar Lazarus. (The Gospel does not tell us the name of the rich man, though later tradition refers to him as Dives, which is Latin for "rich man.")

> And it came to pass that the beggar died, and was carried by the angels into Abraham's bosom; the rich man also died, and was buried.

86

The Old Testament

> *And in hell he lift up his eyes, being in torments, and seeth Abraham afar off, and Lazarus in his bosom.*

—LUKE 16:22–23

To the authors of the Book of Genesis, Abraham was the first of the patriarchs, the living embodiment of the most ancient tradition of the Jews, the first to dwell in the Land of Canaan. Here, in the words of Jesus, he appears as the symbol of the continuity of the law of the prophets: Father Abraham, the spiritual father of his people.

> *And Israel dwelt in the land of Egypt . . .*

—GENESIS 47:27

Joseph; or, Up from Slavery

The career of Joseph, one of the twelve sons of Jacob, introduces an unexpected international complication into the pastoral tale of the house of Abraham. The Book of Genesis suddenly shifts its focus from family history to world history and the destinies of great nations. This all comes about because of the jealousy of Joseph's brothers, who are so resentful of their father's favorite son that they arrange to have him kidnapped by a passing caravan and sold into slavery in Egypt, sold to Potiphar, "an officer of Pharaoh's, and captain of the guard."

Dreams and dream interpretation, as well as family rivalry, play an essential part in the biblical story of Joseph, which is perhaps what inspired Thomas Mann to attempt a modern psychological treatment of this subject in his three-part novel, *Joseph and His Brothers*. Mann's protagonist, like the biblical Joseph, is an egocentric dreamer who rises to become a trusted minister of state. *Joseph and His Brothers* is far from being the usual biblical potboiler, on the order of *Quo Vadis?* or *Ben Hur*, though the original plot is lurid enough. The biblical Joseph's rise to power begins with a botched seduction—Potiphar's wife "caught him by his garment, saying, Lie with me." Joseph prudently takes to his heels, leaving the garment in the hands of his temptress. Potiphar's wife nevertheless denounces Joseph to Potiphar and produces the garment to corroborate her story. Joseph is thrown into "the prison, a place where the king's prisoners were bound." One of the latter is Pharaoh's butler, who is impressed by Joseph's skill at interpreting prophetic dreams. Two years later, when Pharaoh has an especially troubling dream that leaves his regular staff of soothsayers baffled, he sends for Joseph. The upshot is that Joseph is appointed Pharaoh's viceroy, to rule over all of Egypt.

This is, at least, a rough outline of the biblical account of Joseph's early career (which can be found in Genesis 37–41). None of these picaresque details has been confirmed by any of the surviving Egyptian records from the period, which do not even mention Joseph by name. This means that, as far as historians and archaeologists are concerned, Joseph is an even more shadowy figure than Abraham. It does not mean, though, that the biblical story of Joseph is necessarily a fable or an out-and-out fabrication. The next question, then, as usual, is how much of the "deep background" of the biblical story can be verified by referring to other sources—namely, the wealth of reliable information about this period that Egyptologists have collected. To anticipate slightly, it does seem fairly safe to conclude that the original author of the story of Joseph was well acquainted with the patterns of everyday life in ancient Egypt and what we might call the Egyptian national character. To begin with, an example that has been alluded to already:

And it came to pass after these things, that his master's wife cast her eyes upon Joseph; and she said, Lie with me.

—GENESIS 39:7

Did all Egyptian women have such roving eyes, and were they accustomed to play such an aggressive sexual role? Herodotus remarked on the unusual freedom that Egyptian women enjoyed in his day (about a thousand years later); unlike their Athenian sisters, they were definitely not slaves of their husbands or prisoners of the family hearth. They went to market by themselves, for example (Herodotus found this worthy of note, because in Greece it was the men who took care of such things), and generally managed to get around a great deal in public. Egyptian women liked to be seen, and to be admired, which is probably why the Egyptians made such great advances in the applied arts of cosmetology, hairdressing, and *haute couture*; they had already discovered the principle that lies at the heart of all civilization and technology: there is no work of nature that cannot be improved on.

This applied to the human body especially, beginning with manicures and pedicures; Egyptian women painted the soles of their feet with henna, a versatile product that has been around for five thousand years or so. The other raw materials that went into the Egyptian cosmetics chest were fairly exotic by our standards, but the basic techniques have not changed very much since the time of Potiphar's wife. Egyptian women adorned and accentuated their eyelids with powdered lapis lazuli (a bright blue semiprecious stone), their eyelashes with antimony (a lustrous gray metallic powder), and their eyebrows with galena (lead sulfide, a glossy black mineral pigment). A brilliant shade of crimson lipstick could be manufactured from cochineal, an organic dyestuff made from pulverized scale insects (an idea that is almost as unappealing as the ingredients of many of our modern perfumes and cosmetics).

Women who were not quite satisfied with their natural hair color might try a henna rinse, or they might prefer to put themselves in the hands of a reliable wig maker (though the methods of these ingenious craftsmen were so painstaking that a fitting generally took several hours). An elongated skull was considered especially attractive, and so Egyptian babies often had their heads bound to a flat cradleboard. The prospects of a good night's sleep were not much better in later life; both men and women slept with their heads propped up by a forked neck rest—something like a miniature crutch—to protect their elaborate hairdos. Today, when we come upon one of these grotesque devices in a museum display case, we can only wonder why the ancient Egyptians—always made out to be such a practical people, with a genuine flair for engineering and design—never came up with a more elegant, or at least more comfortable, solution to this problem.

When she awoke, with every hair in place presumably, the lady of fashion was assisted in her toilette by a whole platoon of maids and servants, including a lady's maid to attend to the combs, hairpins, and curlers; an apothecary to mix the perfumes and fragrances; another to grind the cosmetics on a palette; plus a flower arranger and a page with a fan, to provide the proper boudoir atmosphere. After two or three hours, the mistress of the house was ready to face the world; if she was planning a more intimate encounter—"to make a beautiful day of it," as the Egyptians said—she might also wear an amulet filled with aromatic herbs between her breasts. (The fashions of the period tended toward extreme décolletage.) I can only refer you to the Song of Solomon (1:13) if you are wondering what all this has to do with the Bible:

> A bundle of myrrh is my well-beloved unto me; he shall lie all night betwixt my breasts.

It seems clear, then, that women in ancient Egypt were considerably more independent than their contemporary sisters in Mitanni or the Land of Canaan. This did not, however, prevent the typical Egyptian husband from claiming the more usual privileges of Near Eastern domesticity: to keep a harem if he could afford it, or if not, simply to take one or more attractive serving maids as his mistress. This, in turn, seems to have made it easier for his wife to deceive him—as attested by this fragment by an Egyptian poet, who was apparently less steadfast than Joseph in resisting the entreaties of the mistress of the house: "I was like a dog that slept in the house, like a pet greyhound in my lady's bed, beloved of his mistress." My lady's bed, by the way, was not the sinuous gilded couch so beloved of Hollywood set designers, but rather a kind of monumental hammock, a wicker frame set on four carved legs of ebony or ivory, so high off the ground that my lady and her captive poet needed a mounting block with three steps just to climb into it (though the back of a crouching slave was equally convenient and a good deal cheaper). The bed itself was furnished with bolsters and cushions and, needless to say, was wide enough to accommodate two quite comfortably.

For those who required further encouragement or instruction in the art of love, there were illustrated papyrus sex manuals, some of which are extant, though usually locked away in the "special collections" of modern libraries and museums. The most famous of these, Papyrus 5501, now reposes in the "Poison Cabinet" of the Museo di Antichità in Turin, Italy; it depicts the antics of a shaven-headed priest and a Theban harlot in a style that is no less drastically explicit than later Oriental productions of this kind. This does suggest, then, that the sexual propensities of Potiphar's wife were not all that unusual.

> *And Joseph's master took him, and put him into the prison, a place where the king's prisoners were bound: and he was there in the prison.*

> —Genesis 39:20

Potiphar was the captain of the guards (literally, "slaughterers," or executioners), and the royal prison served both as a death row for condemned prisoners and as a common lockup—preventive detention—for prisoners awaiting trial. (Those who had already been convicted of noncapital crimes were sent off to work in the mines or the papyrus swamps.) With no individual cells, all the inmates who were being held at Pharaoh's pleasure lived in a single room. Loopholes picked in the walls allowed a certain amount of contact with the outside world; friends and relatives were expected to keep the prisoners supplied with food and other necessities as long as they remained in custody. Sentence could be passed only after a formal hearing was held; the Egyptians were great sticklers for precedent and procedure, and the papyrus texts of their civil and criminal codes represent one of the oldest of the many zealously preserved traditions that collectively defined the culture of the land of the pharaohs.

> *And they dreamed a dream both of them, each man his dream in one night, each man according to the interpretation of his dream [Luther translates "each of them a dream of special significance"], the butler and the baker of the king of Egypt, which were bound in the prison.*
>
> —GENESIS 40:5

Two of Joseph's cellmates had "offended their lord the king of Egypt" and were convinced that the "special significance" of their dreams would give them a timely warning of what Pharaoh proposed to do with them. Dream interpretation was a serious art, more of a science in fact, in ancient Egypt. "God created dreams to point out the way for men, since they are incapable of seeing into the future"—or so we are informed by the author of an Egyptian dream book, a compilation of the more common dream patterns and symbols along with their "correct" interpretations.

Sometime later, Pharaoh himself has two very unsettling

dreams. As Joseph explains, both have the same meaning—
"recurring dreams," to use our modern psychoanalytic terminology. The real content is identical, although the dramatic form is
different in each case. Joseph's interpretation of the dream of
"the seven fat years and the seven lean years" is so compelling
that Pharaoh immediately appoints him chief economic adviser
and, when the time comes, administrator of the Egyptian famine
relief program. Previously, as related in Genesis 37 and 38,
Joseph's attempts at amateur soothsaying, though no less accurate, are a great deal less successful. When he tells his father,
Jacob, about his dream that the sun, moon, and eleven stars
bowed down to him, he is dismissed with a stern patriarchal
rebuke. Then, when he correctly prophesies that the butler will
be restored to favor and that the baker will be hanged, the butler
promptly forgets about him and the baker is obviously in no
position to do him any good.

> But he [Pharaoh] hanged the chief baker: as Joseph had
> interpreted to them.
>
> —GENESIS 40:22

Here, admittedly, the author slipped up. Though Pharaoh
had the power of life and death over his subjects, he could not
possibly have had his chief baker hanged, simply because that
particular form of capital punishment was unknown in ancient
Egypt. Very few crimes were actually punishable by death;
adultery was, but only for the male offender. Rebels and
incorrigible enemies of the state might be put to the sword or
burned alive, whereas high officials and other dignitaries were
given the opportunity to poison themselves as a special dispensation. Lesser felons were punished by a term at hard labor as
described previously, by flogging, or by the sort of exemplary
mutilation that was practiced in medieval Europe and is still

known in parts of the Near East today—nose-slitting, ear-cropping, loss of one or both hands, and the like.

And Pharaoh took off his ring from his hand, and put it upon Joseph's hand, and arrayed him in vestures of fine linen [literally, "garments from Byssus"], and put a gold chain about his neck.

—GENESIS 41:42

This corresponds in every detail to the actual Egyptian ceremony for the investiture of a high official. Pharaoh's ring bears the royal seal and is thus the emblem of Joseph's authority as Pharaoh's viceroy. The gold chain is equivalent to an order of merit or a decoration, and "garments from Byssus"—made from an especially costly fabric, linen interwoven with threads of cotton—were the traditional court dress. The Egyptians, after all, invented high fashion; even their everyday clothes were made of a linen that was literally almost as smooth as silk. Men wore a kind of kilt or apron that left the upper body free; and, as in more recent times, hemlines rose and fell with the vagaries of fashion.

Egyptian women, as we have already seen, had long since discovered that fashion could be both an end in itself and a means of furthering their own interests. This trend began innocently enough with separate wardrobes—hampers, actually; the wardrobe hadn't been invented yet—for summer and winter, for indoor and for outdoor wear. The basic prototype, subject to endless modish variations, was a long, pleated linen skirt with shoulder straps. When all possible variations on this theme had been exhausted, an additional outer garment, a cloak or mantle, was introduced, and the process began all over again. Highborn women of fashion had to exercise a great deal of ingenuity to outclass their most dangerous rivals, the professional dancing girls, who customarily danced naked except for a narrow girdle around their hips. The only other Egyptians who were totally unaffected by the fashion craze were the gods themselves, who were always pictured wearing the traditional loincloth of pre-historic times, and children, who rarely wore anything at all.

And Pharaoh called Joseph's name Zaphnath-paaneah; and he gave him to wife Asenath the daughter of Poti-pherah priest of On. . . .

—Genesis 41:45

The real meaning of Joseph's new name is likely to remain a mystery, but On (the name of a city, not a god) is better known by its Greek name, Heliopolis. A mound of rubble at the edge of the desert northeast of Cairo is about all that is left to mark the site, apart from an obelisk and a few graves. This was the city that Amenhotep IV, who called himself Akhenaten, first used as a base and principal sanctuary from which he spread his mono-theistic cult of the sun god. Shortly after his death, the priests of the older gods put an end to his precocious experiment.

If we accept the Mitanni theory concerning Abraham, Jacob must have lived about 1400 B.C., which would mean that Joseph might conceivably have been a contemporary of Akhenaten. It also seems easy to imagine that Joseph, a foreigner, could have advanced politically so far under Akhenaten's relatively liberal (by Egyptian standards, ultra-radical) regime. Unfortunately, almost all the records and monuments of Akhenaten's brief reign were obliterated in the priestly counterrevolution that followed; so we are left with still another hypothesis that will probably never be proved.

And their father Israel said unto them, If it must be so now, do this; take of the best fruits in the land in your vessels, and carry

down the man a present, a little balm, and a little honey, spices,
and myrrh, nuts, and almonds.

—GENESIS 43:11

When the famine predicted by Joseph finally arrives, his father, Jacob (who is still home on the faraway banks of the Jordan), advises his sons to take a handsome present to Pharaoh's viceroy in the hope of obtaining enough "corn" (wheat) to last them through the famine. Balm, spices, and myrrh were always in great demand in Egypt, because they were used in embalming, as the word itself implies. (*Balm* in this context is probably a collective name for the dried sap or gum of various plants which became viscous when soaked in water but would not dissolve in the mixture of alcohol and resin that the Egyptians used as embalming fluid.) Luxury items of this kind were imported into Egypt in great quantities. Even at this early date a vast trade network extended far beyond the shores of the Mediterranean. Egyptian glass beads and African ivory carvings have been found as far inland as Hallstatt in the Austrian Alps; the Egyptians (or enterprising middlemen from other countries) often exchanged these trade goods for salt in Europe during the Bronze Age. Even silk from China eventually reached Egypt, though by a more circuitous route, probably overland by way of India.

The almonds and the "nuts" (pistachios, to be precise) of the Jordan valley, a more humble and less impressive gift (or bribe), were also not ordinarily available in Egypt. (Almonds, as well as tomatoes, oranges, lemons, and many other fruits and vegetables, were not cultivated in Egypt until Hellenistic and Roman times, over a thousand years later.) Honey, on the other hand, had always been a staple of the Egyptian diet, because sugarcane was still unknown in that part of the world. In fact, the earliest hieroglyph symbol for "the pharaoh of Upper Egypt" was a stylized picture of a bee; Egyptian beekeepers had been tending their beehives since prehistoric times. What was the point, then, of offering "a little honey" to the prime minister of a country that was already pretty well saturated with the stuff? Actually, what Jacob had in mind was wild honey, which has a sharp, smoky taste. A great delicacy among the Egyptians, wild honey usually was imported from as far away as Syria, and later even from Greece.

And they set on for him by himself, and for them by themselves, and for the Egyptians, which did eat with him, by themselves: because the Egyptians might not eat bread with the Hebrews; for that is an abomination unto the Egyptians.

—GENESIS 43:32

The word *abomination* implies that some sort of religious taboo was involved, a fear that these uncouth strangers might contaminate their food in some way. But it is more likely that this was mere fastidiousness on the Egyptians' part ("loathing" in Luther's translation), inspired by prejudice. Presumably the prohibition applied to all foreigners, though the Egyptians seem to have had a particularly low opinion of their immediate neighbors to the east:

Behold the miserable Asiatic, wretched is the place in which he dwells, poorly watered and inaccessible in the thick of the forest. He has no settled home, but his feet are always wandering . . . He has been fighting since the time of Horus, but he never wins the honors of victory; he can pilfer a lonely farmstead, but he can never conquer a populous city.

What sort of meal was it that Joseph's brothers were so pointedly excluded from? First of all, the Egyptians ate while crouching around small, short-legged tables; there were no utensils to speak of, but finger bowls were provided at each place. Roast goose was the universal favorite, followed by ox cooked in batter (beef Wellington, more or less), mutton, and goat; pork was strictly taboo. Quail and pigeon were so plentiful that they were considered to be poor man's food exclusively. Chicken was still unknown, and many of the fish from the Nile—catfish in particular, because of their indiscriminate feeding habits—were thought to be unclean. Because fresh meat spoils so quickly in a hot climate, animals were always slaughtered very shortly before the meal was about to be prepared—"slay, and make ready," as Joseph instructs his steward, "for these men shall dine with me at noon." The Egyptians, as the original wine snobs, kept cellar lists with notations of vintage years and vineyards; they also distinguished five different kinds of beer, the choicest of which, "beer of the harbor," was imported. For less refined palates there were several varieties of unfermented grape juice, cider, and a wine made from fermented dates.

> And put my cup, the silver cup, in the sack's mouth of the youngest, and his corn money. . . .
> Is not this it in which my lord drinketh, and whereby indeed he divineth?
>
> —GENESIS 44:2, 5

Indeed! A drinking cup that foretells the future sounds like a fairly remarkable device, but several of these wide, bowl-shaped drinking vessels have been recovered from Egyptian gravesites. In fact, the technique—the Egyptian equivalent of tea-leaf reading—was very simple. The diviner poured a drop of wine into the cup and studied the pattern the wine made on the bottom. Alternatively, the cup was filled with wine, a drop of oil was passed into it, and the divination was based on the shifting patterns made by the oil on the surface. To the Hebrews this sort of behavior must have seemed both scandalous and incomprehensible, because any form of "soothsaying" or divination was expressly forbidden.

Now thou art commanded, this do ye; take you wagons out of the land of Egypt for your little ones, and for your wives, and bring your father, and come.

—GENESIS 45:19

The mention of "wagons" here is a little difficult to account for; the Egyptians took to the idea of using wheeled vehicles for transporting heavy cargo much later than other Near Eastern peoples, even though they were already familiar with the spoked wheel in the guise of the waterwheel, an Egyptian invention. Two very good reasons explain this, both of which involve the proximity of the River Nile. First, river transport was considerably cheaper and more convenient, whether by raft, oared galley, or lateen-rigged sailboats (which looked very much like the feluccas that can still be seen in the Nile today). Second, a heavily loaded wagon would almost certainly sink up to its hubs in the heavy clay along the riverbank. Sledge runners were much more practical for this sort of job, and the Museum of Antiquities in Cairo contains an impressive collection of sledges and stoneboats of many different designs.

Getting back to the wagons again—Joseph also sends his father "ten asses laden with the good things of Egypt," the normal method of transporting bulky cargo overland. This seems to imply that Pharaoh's "wagons" sent to collect Joseph's family were strictly passenger vehicles, probably two-wheeled hunting chariots. Such chariots were used as jaunting cars, as well as by royal couriers and by the cavalry (more about this later). If so, this was a handsome gesture on Pharaoh's part, and it seems more in keeping with this passage's tone of pageantry and magnificence to imagine a fleet of chariots skimming across the desert than a procession of lumbering oxcarts.

And God spake unto Israel in the visions of the night, and said, Jacob, Jacob. And he said, Here am I.

—Genesis 46:2

This was the proper response to a summons from the Almighty, a phrase that occurs many times in the Old Testament, though it seems also to have been used to indicate respectful obedience to the voice of authority in general (as when Jacob instructs the young Joseph to join his brothers in Shechem and help them tend the flocks, to which he replies, "Here am I"). This formula was borrowed directly from the Egyptians, who, of course, were almost obsessively preoccupied with thoughts of the life to come. They buried with their dead little figurines, called *ushabti*, which were expected to answer on behalf of the deceased when his or her soul was summoned before Osiris, the divine judge. Also, living Egyptians were obliged to donate their labor to the state for a fixed period of time; the souls of the dead had a similar responsibility, to replace the sand that was carried off from the right bank of the Nile with fresh sand from the left bank. The *ushabti* was supposed to stand in for the dead man's soul by performing his labor service for him in the afterworld. One of these figurines, which was recovered from an Egyptian tomb, bears this inscription: "O thou Ushabti, when I am called by name, and my name is read from the roll that I might perform all manner of tasks that are ordained in the underworld, say thou then, Here am I."

Incidentally, several other features of the Osiris cult were later incorporated into the rituals of the Christian church. For example, the bishop's crozier was originally the shepherd's crook, used by Osiris in his alternate role as the good shepherd;

100

and Osiris's high-crowned, pointed headdress served as the prototype of the triple crown of Saint Peter, the papal tiara.

*That ye shall say, Thy servants' trade hath been about cattle
. . . for every shepherd is an abomination unto the Egyptians.*

—GENESIS 46:34

Joseph is coaching his father and brothers for their audience with Pharaoh, but the crucial distinction he draws between cowherds (honest sons of the soil) and shepherds (pariahs and riffraff) seems more than usually obscure. We might think, for example, that a streetcar conductor who was determined to pass himself off as a railway conductor was engaging in a particularly irrational form of social snobbery; but in this case Joseph is being perfectly reasonable. This is simply another instance of the settled Egyptian's deep-seated disdain for his nomadic neighbors. Shepherds, who followed their flocks to greener pastures as the seasons changed, were nomads by definition; cowherds and stock breeders rarely strayed far from home and therefore were respectable. The Egyptians found the nomads' migratory habits particularly irksome in times of famine, when they arrived in great numbers to pasture their flocks on the banks of the Nile.

*And Joseph gathered up all the money that was found in the
land of Egypt. . . . And Joseph said, Give your cattle; and I will
give you for your cattle, if money fail.*

—GENESIS 47:14, 16

This makes the Egyptian economic system sound more sophisticated than it actually was. As in Mitanni and everywhere else, there was no standardized coinage, though copper ingots and gold rings were a common medium of exchange in barter transactions. Silver ("white gold," the Egyptians called it) had an even greater purchasing power than gold. A few verses later, when the farmers' money runs out, they are forced to turn their lands over to Pharaoh. This was not a case of simple extortion—as it must have seemed to the nomadic Hebrews, who were unfamiliar with such civilized refinements as land surveys and tax assessments—but of foreclosure for nonpayment of taxes. Taxes were paid in kind (that is, a certain percentage of the year's harvest), and as the Bible correctly reports in verse 22, "only the land of the priests bought he not." In other words, temple property was tax-exempt, because in theory it belonged to the gods and in practice to the priests, and Pharaoh was well advised to cultivate the goodwill of both if he wanted everything to go smoothly for him in this world and the next.

> *. . . and the physicians embalmed Israel.*
> *And forty days were fulfilled for him; for so are fulfilled the days of those which are embalmed: and the Egyptians mourned for him threescore and ten days.*

> —GENESIS 50:2–3

Herodotus, who was fascinated with mummies and the whole process of mummification, reported that it took seventy days, not forty, for a corpse to be prepared for burial. Who is right?

The significance of the seventy-day period of mourning probably had more to do with the Egyptians' otherworldly preoccupation with astrology than with the requirements of mummification. Sirius, and the other bright stars by which the Egyptians measured the passing of the hours at night, disappeared below the horizon for about seventy days every year. This (presumably) came to be thought of as the naturally ordained interval between death and rebirth—and thus the duration of the soul's journey to the afterworld—and so the prescribed period of mourning and preparation for burial was fixed accordingly.

Two other possibilities could explain the discrepancy between forty and seventy days. The embalming process could be more or less elaborate, depending on how much the survivors were willing to pay to ensure their loved one's immortality, and perhaps Jacob was given only a second-class send-off. This seems unlikely. That the procedure had become much more complicated and time-consuming by Herodotus's time seems far more probable.

So Joseph died, being an hundred and ten years old: and they embalmed him, and he was put in a coffin in Egypt.

—Genesis 50:26

So ends the story of Joseph, and the Book of Genesis, the first of the five books of Moses. The possibility that Joseph's grave might someday be discovered is perhaps remote, but not to be discounted entirely. Professor Moussa, an Egyptian archaeologist who has been systematically excavating the "royal cemetery" at Sakkara since 1962, announced in 1978 that the locations of about 75 percent of the graves in the area were still unknown, and Sakkara is only one of many of the Egyptian "cities of the dead."

So far, over the past century or so, archaeologists have confined the search largely to royal tombs, though it was not just the pharaohs (at least in later Egyptian history) who were buried in great state and with ample provisions made for the soul's material comfort in the life to come. The hastily embalmed bodies of ordinary Egyptians were laid out in plain wooden coffins and placed in sepulchers hollowed out of the face of a cliff. Rich men and high officials—and Joseph appears to have been both—were buried in spacious underground vaults, called *mastabas*, which were divided into two chambers. The outer chamber, which mourners, priestly caretakers, or curious passersby could enter freely, was decorated with murals and hieroglyphic inscriptions illustrating the deceased's exploits. The actual burial chamber, which contained the mummy in its sarcophagus and the grave goods, could be entered only through a narrow vertical shaft, which was sealed off after the burial to make it inaccessible.

Even if Joseph's grave is ever found—and this is one of the fondest dreams of archaeologists and biblical scholars alike—he will probably remain a fairly ambiguous character. He was undoubtedly a great man, but the final reward of his greatness was that his people gave up their freedom to become the semicivilized dependents, the slaves eventually, of a powerful empire. It was left to Joseph's successor, Moses, to lead them out of bondage in Egypt and to fulfill God's promise to Jacob, that he would make of his people a great nation.

And the LORD spake unto Moses face to face, as a man speaketh unto his friend.

—EXODUS 33:11

Moses

My mother bore me in secret and set me in a little ark of rushes and entrusted me to the river.

Here is a passage that we should have no trouble interpreting, for this is easily the most memorable episode in a very familiar story. The Hebrews have been living in Egypt for over a generation by now, and their numbers have increased so alarmingly that the Egyptians have begun to regard them as a very serious threat—which they decide to neutralize first by drafting them into slave-labor gangs and finally by outright extermination. Pharaoh decrees that all male Hebrew children shall be killed; Moses' mother tries to save him by setting him adrift in a basket made of bulrushes, "entrusting him to the river."

So far so good. The trouble is that this was clearly too good a story to be used only once. The lines quoted above are not from the Bible. They were inscribed on tablets over a thousand years before the Book of Exodus was written; the river is the Euphrates, not the Nile; and the child, who is eventually rescued of course, grows up to be Sargon of Akkad, one of the greatest of the Mesopotamian kings.

Easily half a dozen such stories tell of infant heroes of history and legend and their hair's-breadth escapes from destruction—Hercules, Perseus, Alexander the Great, Romulus and Remus, even the infant Jesus, who was saved from the murderous King Herod by a timely flight into Egypt. All these stories were probably composed to illustrate a particular point: the hero has been deliberately spared from destruction—chosen, in other words—by a higher power, which has preserved his life in order to allow him to fulfill his special destiny. The hero goes on to lead his people to greatness, or to perform some remarkable exploit.

But why was it, in the case of Moses and Sargon, at least, that their mothers decided to save them by casting them adrift on the river? To us this may seem a fairly desperate remedy, but for them the river was not only a sacred place but also the body of the river goddess herself (spitting in the river, for example, was considered a particularly disgusting and sacrilegious practice). In other words, Moses' and Sargon's mothers were entrusting them to the goddess's care, just as we still hear stories of abandoned babies turning up on the steps or on the altars of churches.

Moses' mother clearly did the right thing, because the Nile goddess promptly hands him over to Pharaoh's daughter, who decides to adopt him on the spot. She gives him the name Moses, because, as the Bible has her explain, "I drew him out of the water." *Mose* means "to draw forth" in Hebrew, and the authors of the Book of Exodus apparently thought that it was perfectly natural for an Egyptian princess to speak fluent Hebrew. But Mose was also a common Egyptian name, written like this: mʃʒ . The *m* and the *s* are perfectly recognizable—Egyptian script has no vowels—and the last character is not really a letter but what is called a determinant, in this case a kind of shorthand symbol for a pair of (male) buttocks, which makes it absolutely clear that Mose was a man's name. The syllables *mo-se* can also be found in a great many other Egyptian names, notably those of the pharaohs Thutmose, Ahmose, and even Ram(o)ses.

A Coptic church eventually was built on the supposed site where the princess found Moses among the bulrushes, to the south of Cairo. But because neither the site nor the story is authentic and the church is not especially interesting in itself, the tourist who is on the trail of Moses would do better to head north to Tanis, in the eastern delta of the Nile. The ruins there are probably those of "Raamses" in Exodus 1:11, one of the "treasure cities" of Pharaoh Ramses II. Today Raamses lies well clear of the usual tourist routes, a vast field of rubble and broken brick, fallen obelisks and "trunkless legs of stones," the remnants of colossal statues. Ramses II moved his court there from the old capital of Memphis because the Memphite priesthood had grown too powerful and had taken to meddling in affairs of state.

The walls of Raamses, according to the Book of Exodus, were mortared with the blood and sweat of the tribes of Israel. Overseers—"taskmasters"—urged them on with whips and cudgels, and "all their service, wherein they made them serve, was with rigour."

Sometime later, after the Hebrews had managed to deliver

their quota of sun-dried bricks for the houses and buildings of Raamses, Pharaoh decided to make their "service" even more oppressive. They would not be given any more straw (which was used as a binding material to keep the dried bricks from crumbling), but they were still expected to produce just as many bricks as before: "So the people were scattered abroad throughout all the land of Egypt to gather stubble instead of straw." This was not quite so hopeless a task as it sounds. In ancient Egypt only the kernels of the grain were harvested; the rest of the stalk was left standing in the fields.

(Before the Hebrews were commandeered as slave laborers for the royal treasure cities of Pithom and Raamses, they had settled as farmers in the fertile land of Goshen on the eastern edge of the delta, not far away. The modern name for Goshen is Wadi Tumilat; it is still a fertile region, though the wheat fields of antiquity have long since been replaced by fields of cotton.)

The next that we hear of Moses he has grown to manhood. Though to all intents and purposes he is still a member of the Egyptian royal family, he has evidently become curious about the plight of his fellow countrymen. While visiting one of Pharaoh's grandiose construction sites, he sees an Egyptian overseer beating a Hebrew laborer. He kills the Egyptian and thus is forced to flee from Egypt, to the land of Midian, in the south of modern Jordan. He takes a Midianite woman, Zipporah, as his wife and is introduced to the Midianite religion, the worship of a deity called "Jahweh." The Bible describes the events leading up to Moses and Zipporah's marriage in some detail, but though we are told that she was the daughter of Jethro, the high priest of Midian, the Bible says nothing at all about this god of the Midianites, Jahweh, the future God of Israel, the God who spoke to Moses face to face.

The biblical account of Moses' life, as usual, supplies only enough details for a very sketchy biography: a young courtier impulsively kills a man, flees the country, and is befriended by a foreign patriarch, who gives him his daughter in marriage. On the other hand, if we stick to the authentic "historical"—that is, nonbiblical—evidence, we are left once again with precisely nothing. We have become quite familiar by now with the first law of biblical criticism—speculation flourishes when facts are in short supply—and one of the most durable speculations is, quite predictably, that Moses never existed at all, that he was purely a product of the imagination of later scribes and storytellers.

But before we allow Moses to be swept away, along with Noah and Abraham, in this wholesale purge of Old Testament heroes, we should consider the counterargument that any great historical event on the scale of the Exodus from Egypt strongly suggests the presence of a great political leader. This has certainly been the case in later, better-documented historical periods; why should the Exodus be an exception?

Even with the absence of convincing nonbiblical evidence, historians are still inclined to believe that such a man, who may actually have been called Moses, did live during the reign of Ramses II, about 1250 B.C. Ramses himself, as we have already seen, was quite an impressive figure in his own right; apart from the treasure cities of Pithom and Raamses, he was also responsible for the great temple complex at Abu Simbel and the first shipping canal between the Nile and the Red Sea. Thus, the confrontation between Moses and Pharaoh that is described in the Book of Exodus was, to put it mildly, a clash between two extremely forceful personalities.

After he has spent some time in exile among the Midianites, Moses returns to Egypt with explicit instructions from the Lord: "bring forth my people the children of Israel out of Egypt." This instruction is prefaced by the spectacular apparition of an "angel of the Lord . . . out of the midst of a bush: and he looked, and, behold, the bush burned with fire, and the bush was not consumed."

Whether we take this episode of the burning bush to be a

metaphor or a literal account of a miracle, it clearly requires some explanation. German theologians, struck by the fact that the bush is called a "thornbush" in Luther's version of the Bible, interpreted this as a symbol of Moses' inner struggle with the pricks and burning pangs of conscience. The flames could also be seen as flowers that burst into bloom in the sunlight of the divine presence.

The Rosicrucians and other mystical writers who saw almost everything as a clue to ancient occult secrets helpfully pointed out that the hawthorn was also called a "rosebush" until about the ninth or tenth century A.D. This suggests a connection between, among other things, the Crown of Thorns, the Ark of the Covenant (which they believed was made from hawthorn wood), and the Christian hymn (inspired by the Song of Solomon) "I am the Rose of Sharon, like a lily among the thorns." Later, more advanced thinkers also cited the story of Sleeping Beauty (hidden behind her impenetrable thorny hedge), as well as the alchemical device of "a rose surrounded by thorns" as further parallels to their own interpretation of the occult significance of the burning bush: namely, that anyone who wishes to penetrate the innermost secrets must first pass through the thorny thicket that protects and conceals them from the uninitiated.

At any rate, botanists eventually put an end to this luxuriant growth of symbolism with one simple, reasonable question: Could there actually be a plant that burns but is not consumed? In fact, there is one, a shrub called fraxinella ("the little ash tree"), more popularly known as "the gas plant" or just "the burning bush." It can be found in any well-stocked botanical garden, probably under its Latin name of *Dictamnus albus*. The several subspecies of fraxinella are sparsely distributed all across the Eurasian landmass, from China and the Near East to the Balkans and as far west as the Rhineland. *Dictamnus* prefers chalky soil and a warm, dry climate. Its sturdy white (hence, *albus)* rootstock sends up numerous stiff, vertical stalks bearing tough, dark green leaves that are shaped something like the leaves of an ash tree. The rose-colored blossoms—which look, appropriately enough, like miniature candles—appear in early summer. The entire plant is honeycombed with tiny oil sacs that secrete large quantities of volatile oils in hot weather. Direct rays of the sun may ignite the oil, which then burns off so quickly that the plant itself does not catch fire; in other words, it is not consumed. Visitors to Israel may have the opportunity to see any number of burning bushes in the desert if the sun is hot enough.

The Lord also arranged that Moses' younger brother, Aaron, assist him in his appeal to Pharaoh, because Aaron had the gift of eloquence, and Moses was, by his own admission, "slow of speech, and of a slow tongue." It would have been fairly simple to obtain an audience with Pharaoh. The living god of Egypt was expected to be accessible to even the least of his subjects; the modern Parkinsonian plagues of executive secretaries and appointment calendars seem to have been unknown in the days of the pharaohs.

The Book of Exodus gives a detailed account of the brothers' remarkable meeting with Pharaoh:

> And Moses and Aaron went in unto Pharaoh, and they did so as the LORD had commanded: and Aaron cast down his rod before Pharaoh, and before his servants, and it became a serpent.
>
> Then Pharaoh also called the wise men and the sorcerers: now the magicians of Egypt, they also did in like manner with their enchantments.
>
> For they cast down every man his rod, and they became serpents: but Aaron's rod swallowed up their rods.
>
> —EXODUS 7:10–12

It may seem here that Aaron is just trying to dazzle Pharaoh and his magicians with flashy magic tricks, but there is a bit more to it than that. The serpent was one of many creatures that the Egyptians held sacred; they believed that certain species were endowed with supernatural powers and with wisdom that was denied to mortal men. Consequently, when Aaron's serpent devours the others, it is taken as a sign that Aaron himself is wiser and more powerful than the magicians. Nevertheless, Pharaoh is unconvinced. Jahweh, anticipating this of course, is prepared to unleash seven plagues on the Egyptians in order to bring Pharaoh around. Each plague was a natural catastrophe that was depressingly familiar in ancient Egypt, as other contemporary evidence makes very clear, though the biblical interpretation of these events—that they were sent by the Lord to deliver his people from bondage—is entirely new.

In the biblical account of the Egyptians' final ordeal—the extermination of "all the firstborn in the land . . . even unto the firstborn of the maidservant that is behind the mill"—the authors of the Book of Exodus have assigned a new ritual meaning to the old nomadic custom of preparing a sacrificial banquet to celebrate the tribe's arrival at a new encampment and fresh pastureland. This is the origin of the Jewish festival of Pesach, or Passover, the ritual commemoration of the Exodus from Egypt. The Lord had instructed the Israelites to smear the doorposts of their homes with blood from a freshly slaughtered lamb or kid, so that "the LORD will pass over [*pesa* in Hebrew] the door, and will not suffer the destroyer [the Angel of Death] to come in unto your houses to smite you." This is also the source of the Christian image of Jesus as the sacrificial lamb—"Are you washed in the blood of the Lamb?"—and, indirectly, of the Last Supper, which was simply the last Passover seder that Jesus shared with his disciples before his crucifixion. For Christians the Jewish feast of liberation, the symbol of a new beginning, has become the commemoration of Jesus' farewell to his disciples and of his final days on earth.

And the children of Israel journeyed from Rameses to Succoth, about six hundred thousand on foot that were men, beside children.

—EXODUS 12:37

Taking this passage at face value, we can readily assume that there were over a million people altogether, counting women and children—a single marching column some sixty miles long, in other words. There were simply not enough fields and pastures, even in the fruitful Land of Goshen, to support such a multitude (let alone in the quarries and clay pits of Pithom and Raamses).

But here, as usual, things (large numbers especially) are not necessarily what they seem. The word *elef* ordinarily means "thousand," but it also has the secondary meaning of "clan," or as we would say today, "extended family." This is perhaps what the authors of Exodus had in mind—that six hundred families followed Moses out of Egypt, which also might explain why the Egyptian chroniclers didn't bother to waste even a single hieroglyph on the disappearance from their midst of a few hundred miserable nomads.

And as many millions of our contemporaries know from bitter experience, a band of refugees in hostile country does not take to the road all at once, in formation, like a triumphant army on the march, as the Hollywood cast-of-thousands spectaculars would have us believe. Instead, single families and small groups share the same road for a while, then go their separate ways. This is probably how we should imagine the Exodus—individual clans, perhaps entire tribes, setting out, though not all at once, toward the east. We can understand how the children of Israel might well have spent forty years in the wilderness (assuming that this figure is accurate): the difficulty of the terrain and the scarcity of food and forage along the way would have made any kind of continuous mass migration just about impossible.

When we think of the Exodus as a much stealthier, smaller-scale operation, even the biblical account of the parting of the Red Sea and the annihilation of Pharaoh's armies begins to seem much more plausible. Instead of all Pharaoh's chariots and spear carriers following in pursuit of the tribes of Israel, we might imagine that one of those scattered refugee bands was harried by a squadron of three or four chariots from an isolated frontier post—a routine border incident, hardly worth reporting, let alone carving in immortal stone. (And in any case, the Egyptian military annals, especially in the days of Ramses II, consisted of nothing but victory communiqués. Anything short of that, as they saw it, was best forgotten.) On the other hand, in retrospect, the sum total of these small evasions, especially after many retellings around a desert campfire, might easily add up to a miraculous great escape, as reported in Exodus 14:21–22, 28:

> *. . . and the* LORD *caused the sea to go back by a strong east wind all that night, and made the sea dry land, and the waters were divided.*
>
> *And the children of Israel went into the midst of the sea upon the dry ground . . .*
>
> *And the waters returned, and covered the chariots, and the horsemen, and all the host of Pharaoh that came into the sea after them; there remained not so much as one of them.*

In more recent translations of the Bible, the locale has been changed from the Red Sea to the "Sea of Reeds," a literal translation of the Hebrew words *yam suf* which appear in the earliest manuscript texts. Whatever this Sea of Reeds might have been, it is clearly not the same as the Red Sea, which has never had reeds growing along its shores; its eastern shore, the Sinai Peninsula, is completely barren. Even so, not everyone has accepted this editorial annotation. There are those who would argue that the Bible does not specify precisely where this miraculous parting of the waves actually occurred; not far from "the wilderness of the Red [or Reed] sea" is all we are told in Exodus 13:18. Thus, even if we could think of a plausible, "rational" explanation for such a phenomenon, we would not have any way of verifying it.

Whether the Israelites carefully picked their way through a tidal marsh (a sea of reeds) in which Pharaoh's chariots foundered, or whether an undersea earthquake temporarily exposed the seabed, or whether a rapid incoming tide simply caught the Egyptians (the landlocked Israelites were presumably unacquainted with tides)—all these are merely speculations, more or less ingenious attempts to provide a biblical miracle with respectable scientific credentials.

Other wonders that the Israelites encountered in the course of their forty-year trek through the wilderness can be explained more readily, because they appear to have been local natural phenomena with which the Israelites were simply unfamiliar. For example:

> And the Lord went before them by day in a pillar of a cloud, to lead them the way; and by night in a pillar of fire, to give them light: to go by day and night.

> —EXODUS 13:21

The "pillar of a cloud" may well have been an enormous dust devil, a shimmering funnel of sand that a whirlwind can raise to a height of sixty feet or more, the desert equivalent of a waterspout. And the "pillar of fire" may just as easily have been a flare-up of a natural petroleum spring, which would be visible from a considerable distance at night. The Israelites interpreted both as signs that the Lord was blazing a trail for them, and anyone who has ever spent the night in a sleeping bag out on the open desert knows how grateful one can be, despite maps and compasses and everything else, to find such natural beacons in the desert emptiness.

The modern reader can interpret the miracles performed by Moses during the trek through the wilderness in either of two ways: as straightforward miracles, physical manifestations of the Lord's concern for the preservation of his people, or as examples of what we might call the practical "survival skills" of the desert tracker and pathfinder. Readers who prefer the first approach do not require any further explanation than that (and may as well skip over the next few pages). Those who are still not satisfied with the biblical account of these occurrences—that manna fell from the skies or that water flowed from the rock that Moses struck simply because the Lord was watching over his people and was always there to provide them with food and water when they were hungry and thirsty—are invited to consider the following hypothetical (and nonsupernatural) solutions to the logistical problems of the Israelites in the wilderness.

Biblical miracles always seem a little harder to believe than accounts of equally implausible events in other sources. Thus, we are quite willing to accept that Hannibal could have marched a troop of war elephants through the snowcapped peaks of the Alps, but when we read that Moses turned the brackish lake at the oasis of Marah into a reservoir of fresh drinking water, we begin to shake our heads in disbelief.

> . . . *and the* LORD *shewed him a tree, which when he had cast into the waters, the waters were made sweet . . .*

> —EXODUS 15:25

There is nothing especially miraculous about this, though; today, Bedouin shepherds of this region still use the branches of the barberry bush to make alkaline water sweet, or at least drinkable. A little later on, the children of Israel began to grow mutinous because they had no idea where their next meal was coming from:

And it came to pass, that at even the quails came up, and covered the camp . . .

—Exodus 16:13

You may recall from the previous chapter that quail were almost as common as sparrows in ancient Egypt. In the spring, flocks of thousands of quail, exhausted by the rigors of their migratory flight to the north, can be found roosting on the desert floor. Catching them is child's play, and the month of April is closed season on quail in modern Egypt.

The timely arrival of the quail is followed the next morning by a more mysterious incident, the fall of manna, the bread of heaven:

And when the dew that lay was gone up, behold, upon the face of the wilderness there lay a small round thing, as small as the hoar frost on the ground.

And when the children of Israel saw it, they said one to another, It is manna: for they wist not what it was. [In biblical Hebrew, man-hu? *means "what is this?"] And Moses said unto them, This is the bread which the LORD hath given you to eat.*

—Exodus 16:14–15

Until about twenty years ago, botanists believed that manna was actually a sweet-smelling, viscous secretion produced by certain species of tamarisk tree when they are infested with aphidlike scale insects. Then Professor Avinoam Denin of the University of Jerusalem discovered that manna was produced not by the tamarisk but by another shrub with the mellifluous name of *Hammada salicornica.* Professor Denin identified seven different plants, all of them native to the Sinai, which secrete small, sticky-sweet droplets when their bark is punctured by insects. In other words, despite the Sinai's many other disadvantages, there seems to be no shortage of manna.

116

Another relic of the Exodus that tour guides are always eager to show off to visitors to the Sinai is the "rock in Horeb" that Moses struck with his staff to bring forth water for the children of Israel. Today at least half a dozen such rocks make an attractive backdrop for group photographs (though of course there is no particular reason to believe that Moses ever struck any of them). Modern desert trackers and herdsmen are familiar with several reliable dowsing techniques by which certain rocks can be made to yield at least enough fresh water for a small group of travelers and their animals. Moses, who had spent many years in the land of Midian grazing his father-in-law's flocks, might simply have found a promising spot on a limestone outcrop where a crumbling chunk of limestone could be dislodged to reveal a hidden spring. Or perhaps he used his staff as a divining rod— instead of striking the rock, letting his staff drop on the spot where his dowser's instincts led him to suspect that groundwater could be found directly below the surface.

But the greatest miracle of the Exodus did not take place in the desert but on a mountaintop, where God spoke to Moses and presented him with the tablets of the Law. This mountain goes by several different names in the Bible—Mount Sinai, Mount Horeb, or simply "the mountain of God"—and we are still not certain of its precise location. This kind of indecisiveness is not very good for the tourist trade, however, and pilgrims and tourists with a biblical bent have always had the foremost of the three granite peaks of the Sinai massif pointed out to them as Jebel Musa, "Mount Moses." Although it has a monastery at its base and a chapel near the summit, it is more the feeling of the landscape, with the mountains rising up like a great clenched fist of stone, that makes this seem like the authentic "mountain of God," even though the biblical Mount Sinai may well have been somewhere else altogether.

When Moses "brought forth the people out of the camp to meet with God," the Book of Exodus reports:

And mount Sinai was altogether on a smoke, because the
LORD descended upon it in fire: and the smoke thereof ascended
as the smoke of a furnace, and the whole mount quaked greatly.

—EXODUS 19:18

This, as Bible-reading nineteenth-century geologists were
quick to point out, is an excellent description of a volcanic
eruption. No volcanoes exist in the Sinai Peninsula, however,
though there are traces of volcanic activity some distance to the
east, in the land of Midian, where Moses watched over Jethro's
flocks before his return to Egypt. But this explanation was too
simplistic for those subtler scientific critics who were determined
to find a "rational" explanation for these phenomena—an
explanation that was just as esoteric and implausible as the
original, biblical one.

The Book of Exodus speaks of "thunders and lightnings, and a
thick cloud upon the mount, and the voice of the trumpet
exceeding loud." Moses, therefore, must have invented gunpowder and set off a charge to put the credulous Israelites in the
proper frame of mind to receive the Ten Commandments! In
fact, thunder and lightning, storms and fire from heaven, were
all attributes of the pagan nature gods, and it is perfectly
understandable that the children of Israel would have continued
to associate these awesome manifestations with their new god,
Jahweh.

The Bible tells us that Moses was called up to Sinai a second
time to receive the commandments that the Lord himself had
written on tablets of stone, but the idea of a divine lawgiver is not
original with the Book of Exodus either. The most famous of the
ancient Near Eastern legal codes, the Code of Hammurabi, was
inscribed on a great standing stone—a stela, as archaeologists
call it. The upper panel shows Hammurabi with a long beard
and a turban, dressed as if for a long journey, sitting opposite the
sun god, Shamash, who is placing the tablets of the law in the

118

hero's outstretched hands. Hammurabi, a Babylonian king, lived around 1728–1686 B.C., at least four hundred years before the time of Moses.

No other important artifact of Hammurabi's reign has survived, but this alone is enough to secure him an important place in history. The bulky diorite slab, which stands over seven feet tall, is probably the most precious of all the treasures of the Louvre, next to the *Mona Lisa*. Its phallic shape is no accident; this symbolized the divine origins of the law, which in the ancient Near East was enforceable only after it had been written down and prominently displayed for all to see. Hammurabi, then, was the creator of the world's first uniform code of laws, which included such provisions as:

> *If a man shall put out the eye of another, then let his own eye be put out.*
>
> *If a man shall knock out the teeth of another who is higher in rank, then let his own teeth be knocked out.*

Moses reduced this to a simpler formulation:

> *And if any mischief follow, then thou shalt give life for life,*
> *Eye for eye, tooth for tooth, hand for hand, foot for foot.*
>
> —EXODUS 21:23–24

Either way, this seems cruel enough, if not all that unusual, to us, but in Hammurabi's (and Moses') time, the introduction of statutory penalties for violent crimes must have caused a sensation comparable to the one that preceded the abolition of the death penalty in our own century. Hammurabi's Code was remarkable in that it was the first real attempt to make the punishment fit the crime. The customary law of the vendetta which it replaced emphasized massive retaliation rather than justice, and the customary punishments, inflicted by the kinsmen of the injured party, were a great deal more ferocious: "Kill seven of them [to avenge] your brother that they have struck down."

The parallels between Hammurabi's Code and the laws of Moses are so striking that some biblical scholars have surmised that Abraham must have been familiar with Hammurabi's Code and was so impressed with the evenhandedness of its precepts that he passed it on to his sons and grandchildren as the unwritten law of his clan. It was thus available to Moses as a paradigm when he assumed the role of lawgiver for the children of Israel.

Hammurabi's Code begins with a surprisingly modern-sounding preamble, which states that its purpose is to "bring forth the victory of righteousness, and thereby prevent the strong from unjustly prevailing over the weak . . . and to instruct the nation and to further the well-being of the people." Here the principle of equality before the law is affirmed in theory, perhaps, but not in practice—all of the 282 separate subdivisions of Hammurabi's Code describe different penalties and criminal procedures, depending on whether the wrongdoer or the victim is a priest or an official, a freedman or a slave. (Still, one remarkably progressive section of the code provides for a kind of crime-victim's insurance scheme: "If a robber is not taken, the city and the elders where the robbery took place shall restore everything to the householder of which he was despoiled as soon as he demands before a court that this be done.")

Other parallels with the laws of Moses can be found in another contemporary source, the so-called Egyptian Book of the Dead, which coached its readers to give the right sort of testimony when their souls were summoned before the forty-two judges of the underworld as a preliminary to their entrance into the kingdom of the dead. This does not imply by any means that the Ten Commandments were completely unoriginal. First of all, a certain similarity is bound to exist between any two sets of laws that are established to regulate the affairs of a complex society, especially when both originated in the same broad cultural context. In addition, two crucial concepts, found nowhere else in the ancient world, were definitely set forth for the first time in the laws of Moses:

> *I am the* LORD *thy God . . .*
> *Thou shalt have no other gods before me.*
>
> —EXODUS 20:2–3

The idea of a transcendent, immaterial God is totally without precedent, even in the radical theology of the pharaoh Akhenaten, whose state religion of Aten, the solar disk, was only an old-style nature cult raised to a slightly higher power.

The second of these ideas is, if possible, even more fundamental:

> *Thou shalt love thy neighbor as thyself.*
>
> —LEVITICUS 19:18

This has been called the most important of all the commandments of Judaism, one that Jesus later invoked to illustrate the essential difference between his teachings and the laws of the prophets:

> *Ye have heard that it hath been said, Thou shalt love thy neighbor, and hate thine enemy.*
> *But I say unto you, Love your enemies, bless them that curse you . . .*
>
> —MATTHEW 5:43–44

The single phrase "Thou shalt love thy neighbor as thyself" would have been reason enough for incorporating the entire Old Testament into the Christian Bible, even if thousands of other reasons did not already exist. The words "as thyself"—no more and certainly no less—are clearly what make this commandment

both meaningful and practicable. No great act of self-renuncia-
tion is required; only balance, fairness, and empathy.

Passing from the sublime to the mildly ridiculous, we come
now to the problem of Moses' horns. Both Saint Jerome's Latin
Vulgate and the German Bible (until earlier in this century)
described Moses' descent from Mount Sinai in more or less these
words:

> *When Moses came down from the mountain, he knew not, that
> there were horns upon his countenance.*

Both Michelangelo and Rembrandt, following a well-established artistic convention, depicted Moses with a magnificent set
of horns, though the King James version of this passage seems
disappointingly tame by comparison:

> *And it came to pass . . . when he came down from the mount,
> that Moses wist not that the skin of his face shone . . .*

> —EXODUS 34:29

There seems to be a substantial difference of opinion here
between the King James scholars and Saint Jerome—perhaps the
result of an editorial conspiracy or a cover-up to spare His
Majesty's godfearing Anglican subjects from the awful truth. But
in fact more recent scholarship has confirmed that the original
Hebrew word that is in dispute here is *qaran*, "to be radiant, to
shine," which when written without the vowel points is indis-
tinguishable from *qeren*, "to bear horns." Saint Jerome saw
nothing strange in this, apparently; he translated *qrn* as *cornuta*
(Luther, who was not much of a Hebrew scholar, followed suit
with *gehornt*). Later Church Fathers came up with an ingenious
gloss for this text: Moses was given a pair of horns, along with the
Ten Commandments, to protect him against evildoers when he

rejoined sinful human society after his forty days on Mount Sinai.

Now the archaeologists have decided to reopen this controversy by asserting that Saint Jerome may very well have been right in the first place. The figure of a horned god was very common in the ancient Near East and in pre-Christian Europe; and images of Baal, the great god of the Canaanites and the Phoenicians, are horned. Perhaps Moses' horns were actually a vestige of this pagan symbol of strength and potency. The question is still unresolved, and Moses has not yet necessarily shed his horns.

It is interesting that some of the coins and medals struck by Alexander the Great show him wearing horns—in his case, an attribute of the Egyptian sun god Ammon, who took the form of a ram. Horns were the classical equivalent of the power look, long before Wagner's Valkyries brought them back into fashion.

Another of Saint Jerome's less defensible lapses made Moses not only the lawgiver of the Jews but the patron of medieval Christians who were afflicted with bad teeth. The Vulgate describes the death of Moses in these words:

> Moses centum et viginti annorum erat quanto mortuus est;
> non caligavit oculus eius, nec dentes illius moto sunt.
>
> *(Moses was one hundred and twenty years old when he died; his*
> *eye was not clouded, nor were his teeth loosened.)*

This error has long since been corrected in the Latin Bible, but readers of the King James may feel that something has been lost in the translation when they turn to Deuteronomy 34:7:

> *And Moses was an hundred and twenty years old when he died;*
> *his eye was not dim, nor his natural force abated.*

It seems that Moses was responsible for only a small part, if that, of the text of the five books of the Bible that are traditionally ascribed to him. Biblical scholars still cannot say with certainty which passages were actually composed by Moses and which by other authors. At least it is certain that the so-called lost or apocryphal books of Moses that are sometimes displayed in occult bookstores are forgeries concocted during the Middle Ages.

A great deal of the text of the five genuine books of Moses is devoted to matters of ritual which have not been practiced since the second destruction of the Temple, in A.D. 70. These contain a strange combination of the esoteric and the mundane that has made passages such as the following one, in which the Lord supplies detailed specifications for the construction of the Ark of the Covenant, a fertile ground for all sorts of curious speculations:

> And they shall make an ark of shittim [acacia] wood: two cubits and a half shall be the length thereof, and a cubit and a half the breadth thereof, and a cubit and a half the height thereof.
>
> And thou shalt overlay it with pure gold, within and without shalt thou overlay it, and shalt make upon it a crown of gold round about.
>
> And thou shalt cast four rings of gold for it, and put them in the four corners thereof; and two rings shall be in the one side of it, and two in the other side of it.
>
> And thou shalt make staves of shittim wood, and overlay them with gold.
>
> And thou shalt put the staves into the rings by the sides of the ark, that the ark may be borne with them. . . .
>
> And thou shalt put into the ark the testimony which I shall give thee.
>
> And thou shalt make a mercy seat of pure gold. . . .
>
> And thou shalt put the mercy seat above upon the ark. . . .
>
> —Exodus 10–14, 16–17, 21

The instructions in their entirety take up almost three printed columns—three times as long as the Ten Commandments. The Ark would have been almost four feet long and about two feet tall, about the size of an old-fashioned steamer trunk (the Hebrew word that is translated as "ark" simply means "trunk" or "coffer" in ordinary contexts). "Mercy seat" is a free rendering of the Hebrew *kapporeth*, which in this case means something like "a covering to keep out sin." The *kapporeth* was intended to protect the purity of the Ark's contents: the book in which "Moses wrote all the words of the LORD" (Exodus 24:4), the tablets of the Law, an omer (about five pints) of manna, and Aaron's "rod [that] was budded, and brought forth buds, and bloomed blossoms" (Numbers 17:8), as a token of the supremacy of Aaron's tribe, the Levites, the hereditary priesthood.

Later commentators subsequently amended this list to suit the tastes of later centuries. During the Middle Ages the alchemists believed that the philosopher's stone, the elusive substance that would enable them to transmute the baser metals into gold, was also hidden in the Ark.

At the beginning of our technical age the Ark was thought (by some) to be a kind of electrical storage battery which endowed its possessor with superhuman powers, though unauthorized persons could approach it only at their peril (see II Samuel 4:3–11, II Samuel 6:6). More recently, Erich von Däniken has theorized that the Ark actually served as an electronic relay station that monitored transmissions from extraterrestrial space-craft, broadcasting messages of spiritual uplift and encouragement to our backward planet. Needless to say, there is nothing in the Bible to suggest that the Ark was ever used for any purpose except to house the sacred relics of the Exodus. The Ark itself, like so many other treasures, disappeared during the sack of Solomon's Temple; according to one early legend it was spirited off by the prophet Jeremiah to await the coming of the

Messiah—or perhaps (if later theories are correct) the electrician.

Probably the most striking feature of the Ark is that it was equipped with rings and staves so that it could be carried along with the Israelites whenever they took to the roads in search of fresh pastures. We know that other nomadic peoples carried similar portable sanctuaries on their migrations, though these sanctuaries were more like sedan chairs in which their gods could be borne along in state, invisibly, until whenever they chose to visit their devotees. The Israelites, whose God was both immaterial and omnipresent, had all the more reason to remind themselves—as the incident of the golden calf had shown—that the Lord was always with them. The Ark of the Covenant and the relics concealed inside it were the physical symbols of Jahweh's promise to dwell among the tents of Israel wherever their wanderings took them and for all eternity.

So far we have paid attention only to the first two books of Moses—Genesis and Exodus—and neglected the other three—Leviticus, Numbers, and Deuteronomy. All five are collectively called the Torah ("the law") in Hebrew and the Pentateuch ("divided into five parts") in Greek, a term that is still used by Christian scholars. Only Genesis, the first half of Exodus, and short sections of Deuteronomy make very interesting reading, unfortunately. The rest are concerned largely with sacrifices, statistics, and long lists of place names.

The third book of the Bible is called Leviticus because it was intended primarily as a handbook for the priests of Jahweh, the Levites. The Levites were not strictly priests in the usual sense but more like deacons, laymen who assisted the priests in performing certain rites. Thus, they were not an elite minority but an entire social class in themselves, the tribe of Levi. By King Solomon's time they numbered some twenty-four thousand, and so a kind of quota system had to be imposed to screen the candidates more selectively.

The contents of the Book of Leviticus are so dry and technical that the ability to read a passage from it served as the standard test of literacy in the Middle Ages. This was particularly important because priests, or persons claiming to be priests, who were accused of serious crimes were allowed to go free if they could successfully invoke the "benefit of clergy"—that is, if they could read through a line or two of difficult liturgical Latin without stumbling over too many of the words.

The fourth book of Moses, Numbers, also does not have much to offer the modern reader. As its name implies, it is a detailed census report of the twelve tribes of Israel, along with a checklist of the dates prescribed for certain sacrifices and festivals, a survey of the boundaries between the grazing grounds allotted to the various tribes, and a complete itinerary of their early migrations.

The title of the fifth book, Deuteronomy, means "the second law" in Greek (the other titles come from Latin, by the way). This is essentially a restatement of the laws of Moses as set forth in the Book of Exodus—moral precepts suited to most ordinary (and extraordinary) occasions, the proper punishments for disobedience of the same, and a brief account of the last days of Moses:

> *And Moses went up from the plains of Moab unto the mountain of Nebo, to the top of Pisgah, that is over against Jericho. And the LORD shewed him all the land of Gilead, unto Dan,*
>
> *And all Naphtali, and the land of Ephraim, and Manasseh, and all the land of Judah, unto the utmost sea,*
>
> *And the south, and the plain of the valley of Jericho, the city of palm trees, unto Zoar.*
>
> *And the LORD said unto him, This is the land which I sware unto Abraham, unto Isaac, and unto Jacob, saying, I will give it*

*unto thy seed: I have caused thee to see it with thine eyes, but
thou shalt not go over thither.*

*So Moses the servant of the LORD died there in the land of
Moab, according to the word of the LORD.*

—DEUTERONOMY 34:1–5

Why is the Lord tantalizing Moses like this? The Bible gives
no explanation, but there is one nevertheless: if we were actually
to follow in Moses' footsteps and climb to the summit of Mount
Nebo on the clearest, sunniest day of the year, we would still not
be able to see nearly all the territory that is described in this
passage. And Moses, for all that his eye was not dimmed, could
not have done much better three thousand years ago. This is not
just a geographical oversight on the part of the authors; they
knew perfectly well what they were up to.

From earliest times down to the settling of the American West
and the South African Great Trek of the nineteenth century, the
unwritten law of the conquering settler has been that the
homesteader or the patriarch of an invading tribe can claim for
his descendants all the land that extends "as far as the eye can
reach." Moses' first and last glimpse of the Promised Land was
enough to establish a valid title on behalf of the children of Israel
in perpetuity.

The last verses of Deuteronomy (34:10–12) sum up the
awesome, enigmatic career of this "servant of God" in a few
incisive phrases, which would serve very well as both his eulogy
and his epitaph:

*And there arose not a prophet since in Israel like unto Moses,
whom the LORD knew face to face,*

*In all the signs and the wonders, which the LORD sent him to
do in the land of Egypt to Pharaoh, and to all his servants, and to
all his land,*

128

And in all that mighty hand, and in all the great terror which Moses shewed in the sight of all Israel.

There is very little else that historians can add to this passage, which is just as well. Two of our greatest artists have already shown us the living man Moses. Rembrandt's white-bearded prophet and Michelangelo's horned demigod, together, have given us the monument to match this epitaph. And all Moses' biblical successors, however gifted as prophets, judges, and men of war, would always be measured by the absolute standard of his achievements. The first of these was Moses' lieutenant Joshua, whom he chose to lead the Israelites into Canaan.

Truly the LORD hath delivered into our hands all the land . . .

—JOSHUA 2:24

The Conquest of Canaan

The Book of Joshua: Mythology or Military History?

Moses was 120 years old when he died, Abraham was all of 130, and Joshua 110—or so we are told in the Bible. These figures, of course, were not intended to represent their actual chronological ages but to serve as a relative index of their accomplishments. Certainly a man like Moses, with so many remarkable exploits to his credit, must have lived a very long time indeed—almost two normal life spans—to have achieved so much.

The Book of Joshua, short and compact, reads like military history, which is more or less what it purports to be: a pithy

129

account of the Israelites' invasion and conquest of the Land of Canaan. Using the traditional reckoning, this must have taken place around the twelfth or thirteenth century B.C.; however, scarcely anything in the archaeological record confirms this. What has been found tends to support a much later date for the conquest—it may not have been concluded until two or three hundred years later. Each of the two possible explanations for this discrepancy is endorsed by several eminent biblical scholars: either the Book of Joshua is correct, and the archaeologists simply haven't been looking in the right places; or the conquest of Canaan was not an ordinary military campaign, which began with an armed invasion of enemy territory and continued until all resistance had been crushed.

There is much to be said for the second point of view, and it does begin to seem that this conquest, like the Exodus, was a fairly lengthy enterprise that may have taken decades, perhaps centuries. Rather than a concerted invasion, a series of armed incursions by the Israelites penetrated various points along the frontier. Finally they found themselves the masters of all the territory that Moses had seen (and had not seen) spread out at his feet on Mount Nebo.

The Book of Joshua itself was not written for the benefit of scholars and historians in the remote future but for the more immediate descendants of the combatants themselves, to preserve the memory of the great feats of arms which their ancestors had achieved. In other words, it is a heroic saga, like *Beowulf* or the Arthurian legend, in which dates and place names are not as important as personalities. Joshua is a heroic rather than a historical figure, a composite of many different men who lived in several different centuries. The authors of the Book of Joshua wanted to recapture the excitement and the emotional impact of these events, not to re-create the exact circumstances in which they took place.

And the conquest of Canaan was, from a strictly military

standpoint, a formidable objective. The cities of Canaan were fortified, and the nomadic Israelites had no siege engines or battering rams to reduce these Canaanite strongpoints. Unless the garrison could be lured out into the open by a ruse of some sort, the Canaanites could be taken only by storm. In either case, both courage and tactical acumen were clearly required, because the odds were always with the defenders.

The most famous of these sieges—the most famous in history, in fact—was the battle of Jericho:

> *And ye shall compass the city [the* LORD *instructs Joshua], all ye men of war, and go round about the city once. Thus shalt thou do six days.*
>
> *And seven priests shall bear before the ark seven trumpets of rams' horns: and the seventh day ye shall compass the city seven times, and the priests shall blow with the trumpets.*
>
> *And it shall come to pass, that when they make a long blast with the ram's horn, and when ye hear the sound of the trumpet, all the people shall shout with a great shout; and the wall of the city shall fall down flat, and the people shall ascend up every man straight before him.*
>
> —JOSHUA 6:3–5

Although the walls came tumbling down, this had nothing to do with trumpet blasts, or with Joshua. The walls of Jericho were destroyed long before his time by an earthquake. And the city of Ai, southeast of Bethel (which Joshua takes with the help of another strategem suggested by the Lord), was already a heap of ruins by the time Joshua's troops arrived there. Ai is simply the Hebrew word for "ruins." The biblical account of the bloody "conquest" of those ghost cities lends credence to the theory that Joshua's Old Testament biographers gave him a great deal more credit than he was really entitled to.

A few chapters before the fall of Jericho is another interesting episode that is often overlooked by readers who are eager to get on to the trumpets and the tumbling walls. Joshua sends out two "men to spy secretly" in the Land of Canaan, instructing them to "Go view the land, even Jericho"—a covert operation, as we would say today. Joshua's spies make their way to Jericho, where they take refuge in the house of a "harlot" called Rahab. The Bible mentions that "her house was upon the town wall, and she dwelt upon the wall," which was quite usual, because prostitutes were expected to entertain their clients outside the residential section of the city.

Rahab has not merely taken a fancy to these dashing agents; she has heard stories of the Israelites' miraculous victories over the Egyptians and the Amorites, and she has decided to embrace the Israelite cause wholeheartedly. This turns out to be a very sensible decision:

> And the city shall be accursed [Joshua later tells the people] . . . and all that are therein, to the LORD; only Rahab the harlot shall live, she and all that are with her in the house, because she hid the messengers that we sent.
>
> —JOSHUA 6:17

"All that are with her in the house," by the way, does not refer to her ordinary peacetime clientele but to her family and possibly other inhabitants of Jericho—fifth columnists, so to speak—who as partisans of the Israelites were working to undermine their fellow citizens' determination to resist, now that the conquering army was actually at the gates. The original purpose of Joshua's unorthodox tactics—the rams' horns and the war cries—was probably to demoralize the defenders even further and intimidate them into surrendering without giving battle.

Rahab the harlot is mentioned once again in the Bible—in the New Testament, surprisingly enough. The long list of "begats" at the beginning of the Gospel According to Saint Matthew includes the sentence "And Salmon begat Booz of Rachab," which is to say that Jesus was considered a direct descendant of the harlot Rahab. As you may recall from our earlier discussion of the genealogy of Jesus, this was meant only metaphorically, as a symbol of the fact that Jesus was of the true line of Abraham and of the House of David. Still, it is interesting that three of the four women who are mentioned by name in this passage were what the authors of the New Testament would call "sinners."

The Church Fathers were somewhat at a loss to explain what two harlots (Tamar and Rahab) and a notorious adulteress (Bathsheba) were doing in this illustrious company. They finally chose to interpret this as a sign that anyone who had sufficient goodwill was ready to receive the true faith.

We might also take this to mean that the authors of the Old Testament did not regard the practice of the oldest profession as anything unusual or even disreputable. Among the worshipers of Baal, as with the Babylonians of Herodotus's time, temple prostitution was an honorable, even an obligatory, form of service to their god, and ritual intercourse was a perfectly legitimate means of achieving communion with the godhead. Jahweh, after all, was the first ancient divinity who was thought of as incorporeal, and therefore sexless.

After Jericho and Ai were duly conquered, the walled town of Gibeon mysteriously surrendered without a fight. After its capitulation, however, Gibeon was besieged by a confederation of hostile Amorite tribes and called on Joshua for help. Joshua set off on a forced march at night to relieve Gibeon. The Amorites were routed, and:

> It came to pass, as they fled from before Israel . . . that the LORD cast down great stones from heaven upon them . . . and they died: they were more which died with hailstones than they whom the children of Israel slew with the sword.

—JOSHUA 10:11

Even so, there were still quite a few Amorites left, and the Lord was persuaded to intervene even more decisively—to suspend the most elementary laws of physics—on behalf of the children of Israel:

> Then spake Joshua to the LORD . . . and he said in the sight of Israel, Sun, stand thou still upon Gibeon; and thou, Moon, in the valley of Ajalon.
> And the sun stood still, and the moon stayed, until the people had avenged themselves upon their enemies. . . .

> —JOSHUA 10:12–13

But we know that the earth revolves around the sun and not the other way around, so it must have been the earth that stood still. The sun and the moon transfixed in their courses across the sky, not to mention the stones falling from heaven—at one time this was a favorite passage of reactionary theologians who cited it as proof that the earth really was the center of the solar system.

More recently this cosmic extravaganza has challenged the boldest of our modern armchair theoreticians, and it goes without saying that they have risen to the challenge admirably: evidently, the earth was broadsided by an enormous comet (hence the stones, intergalactic debris from the melting head of the comet). This collision caused such terrible perturbations in the earth's orbit that the earth not only stood still but actually reversed its direction. (Thus, the battle of Gibeon was an important milestone for our entire planet, not just for the Israelites and the Amorites. Before that day the sun must have risen in the west!)

But these audacious theorists could have spared themselves, to say nothing of the stars and the planets, a great deal of trouble if they had only read the next line of the text: "Is not this written in the book of Jasher [or "in the Book of the Righteous"]?" In other words, the short poem (or incantation) that Joshua declaims to his troops before they go off in pursuit of the fleeing Amorites is a quotation, a literary allusion. It appears that not only Joshua and the Israelites but also the authors of the Book of Joshua and their prospective readers (or listeners) were very familiar with the ancient heroic epic, the book of Jasher. And the whole point of such an allusion is that the audience can be expected to fill in the rest of the story for themselves. It is as if today we heard someone talking about Birnam Wood coming to Dunsinane and a man who was not of woman born, we would know immediately that he was referring to the last act of *Macbeth*, not to teleportation and cloning.

This still leaves the hailstorm unaccounted for, and once again we have many theories to choose from. The most plausible-sounding theory was advanced by a retired army officer, a major with considerable combat experience. Joshua's troops, he has suggested, would have been exhausted after their all-night march (Joshua 10:9). Ordinarily it would have been highly inadvisable to send them directly into combat, except under certain circumstances. A sudden rainstorm, for example, would have refreshed Joshua's worn-out foot soldiers and afforded them a brief respite before battle. More important, the heavy war chariots of the Amorites would have been bogged down, unable to take to the field. The ensuing hailstorm would have been enough to cause the dismounted Amorite warriors to break ranks and beat a disorderly retreat, with the Israelites in full pursuit and no quarter given.

If we have to invoke some sort of superhuman agency to explain Joshua's victory, it seems much more satisfactory to rely on General Mud, a familiar hazard of the battlefield, rather than hurtling comets and worlds in collision. This is still only a hypothesis, though, and those who are interested in working out their own reconstruction of the battle can examine the original terrain at el Jib in Israel, which is thought to be the site of the ancient city of Gilboa.

Even after so many victories, the Israelite conquest of Canaan would not be complete until they had conquered the city of Hazor, strategically the most important of the Canaanite strongholds. Joshua took Hazor, "burnt it with fire," and destroyed it utterly, according to the Bible.

In fact, many different references to the destruction of Hazor are scattered through the Old Testament; biblical scholars had taken this as an instance of editorial carelessness on the part of the authors. But Hazor has now been more thoroughly excavated than almost any other ancient site, by a team of Israeli archaeologists led by Yigael Yadin, former chief of staff of the Israeli army. When General Yadin published the results of their findings, it became clear that these apparently contradictory or redundant accounts of Hazor's destruction were not simply the result of faulty proofreading; they discovered twenty-one different levels of occupation between the nineteenth and the second centuries B.C. Hazor had already been "destroyed utterly" and subsequently rebuilt perhaps half a dozen times before the Israelites arrived in the Land of Canaan.

The Bible also mentions that after his victory over the king of Hazor and his allies,

> . . . Joshua did unto them as the LORD bade him: he houghed [hamstrung] their horses, and burnt their chariots with fire.
>
> —JOSHUA 11:9

Joshua had not thought of appropriating the horses and chariots for his own use in future campaigns because the Israelites at that time fought exclusively on foot, and horse breeding was not practiced seriously in Judah until the time of King Solomon.

After Hazor fell, the conquered territories were parceled out to the tribes of Israel, which makes for very dull reading indeed— reminiscent of the Book of Numbers—and the action does not really pick up again until the last two chapters.

A bloodthirsty tale, this Book of Joshua. Yet it contains a core of valid historical information, even if the chronology is hopelessly confused. For many years, though, German biblical scholars were convinced that the biblical account of the conquest of Canaan was no more than a puffed-up propaganda tract, and that the Israelite settlement of Canaan was actually a peaceful migration into a sparsely settled region whose nomadic inhabitants were occupied elsewhere with the more serious threat posed by "Nordic" invaders on the coast (such as the Philistines).

Over the last few decades French archaeologists have provided us with an entirely different picture, in light of their discoveries at Ras Shamra, the site of the Canaanite city of Ugarit. First of all, the Canaanites were already a settled agricultural people by the fourteenth century B.C. Jewelry found in their gravesites is of a very high standard of workmanship. And their religion, the cult of the nature god Baal and his extended family of lesser gods and goddesses, was firmly rooted in the folk culture and everyday life of the Canaanite people. Most important of all—and this came as quite a surprise—the people of Ugarit used a kind of cuneiform script which reduced the unwieldy Sumerian array of hundreds of characters to a mere thirty. Thus, the Canaanites were already well on their way toward inventing the alphabet.

But all this does not really explain why this saga of chauvinistic blood and thunder belongs in the Christian Bible. Read the Book of Joshua and you will understand at once. Every verse proclaims the new religion of Jahweh—a God who does not simply manifest himself in the remote forces of nature but who intervenes directly in human affairs, to serve and guide his people. The phrases "and the LORD commanded" and "Joshua spake unto the LORD" occur repeatedly; God has become a decisive force in human history for the first time.

And this is not just a new idea, but in fact was to be the

dominant idea of our Judeo-Christian culture for almost two thousand years.

> *In those days there was no king in Israel: every*
> *man did that which was right in his own eyes.*
>
> —JUDGES 21:25

The Book of Judges: History Written in Blood

The title alone—the Book of Judges—has a faintly ominous ring to it, as if we might be in for a reprise of Leviticus or Deuteronomy. In fact, the judges were the elected leaders of the twelve tribes. When the people "came up to them for judgment," judges were expected to provide bold council and decisive leadership, not closely reasoned opinions; they were the executive branch, in other words, not the judiciary. Judges were all completely autonomous; none of them was set above the rest except by virtue of his or her personal prowess and achievements.

The Book of Judges takes up immediately where Joshua leaves us and provides us at the outset with a clear picture of the progress of the Israelite conquest of Canaan. The land, occupied for some time, was still not subdued. Pockets of resistance were everywhere, and the Israelites were constantly called upon to take up arms to preserve what they had already won.

"What makes this book so lively and exciting is the diversity and the contrasts exhibited by the personalities who appear in it"—or so we are assured by Joseph Dheilly in the Glossary to the five-volume Andreas edition of the Bible, which appeared in 1975. Two years earlier, the definitive *Handbuch zur Bibel* (Handbook of the Bible) commented that "The human actors in the Book of Judges are a depressing lot, and the destiny of the

138

Jewish people is played out in a series of monotonous cycles." Even the Bible sometimes plays to mixed reviews.

After Joshua's death the Israelite conquest had begun to lose momentum. As might be expected, the Israelites found themselves living in uneasy proximity to the various other tribes they had not succeeded in exterminating or driving off. Although these people are called Hittites in many editions of the Bible, they were not the Indo-European empire builders of that name, but a miscellaneous collection of peoples who had settled in Canaan long before the arrival of the Israelites.

There was extensive contact between the Israelites and their neighbors, both on the battlefield and in bed. The authors of the Old Testament approved of indiscriminate slaughter as an expression of the will of God. They frowned on indiscriminate procreation, however, and the phrase "The people did evil in the sight of the LORD" recurs constantly in the Book of Judges, whenever the Israelites took foreign women as wives and adopted their gods as their own.

The reasons for this backsliding are easy enough to understand. It was not that Baal was thought to be greater, better, or more powerful than Jahweh, but simply that he was more comprehensible, more of an immediate, palpable presence than the sexless, invisible God of Moses and Joshua. Baal was a fertility god, a farmers' god. The Greeks later identified him with the sun god, Helios, and his principal sanctuary, Baalbek, was later renamed Heliopolis. Barren women had only to sleep with one of Baal's priests to become fruitful and bear children. The Israelites, who were now tilling their own fields for the first time in their history, naturally felt closer to this potent god of the harvest than to the mysterious Jahweh.

Needless to say, the worship of Baal is repeatedly forbidden in the laws of Moses, beginning with the first commandment, explicitly and implicitly:

There shall be no whore of the daughters of Israel, nor a sodomite of the sons of Israel.

Thou shalt not bring the hire of a whore, or the price of a dog, into the house of the LORD thy God for any vow: for even both these are abomination unto the LORD thy God.

—DEUTERONOMY 23:17–18

This refers to the Canaanite practice of ritual prostitution, which wayward young Israelites of both sexes apparently engaged in. The "price of a dog" was the bounty paid to male prostitutes who allowed themselves to be sodomized, dog-fashion, by patrons of the temple, and who even wore dog masks of various kinds in the interest of anonymity and symbolic realism.

As noted earlier, Baal was not an only child. He had seven brothers and sisters, all offspring of El ("The lord"), the first and greatest of the Canaanite gods. This idea of a pantheon or a host of heaven seems to have made a strong impression on the Israelites; presumably this is why the angels, the messengers of God, figure so much more prominently in the Book of Judges than elsewhere in the Bible. Jahweh evidently needed to call up this squadron of visible auxiliaries to keep from being outnumbered and outshone by his Canaanite rival.

If we want to imagine the angels of the Lord as the authors of the Old Testament saw them, first we will have to forget the dimpled cherubs and the languid, hermaphroditic creatures that decorate our greeting cards. The angels of the Old Testament are fiercely masculine; they carry swords or staves; their voices are like thunder. All in all, they are quite terrifying, which is why so many of the messages that they deliver on earth begin with the words "Fear not. . . ." Their wings are not the delicate, almost vestigial appendages of our familiar cherubs, but a visible emblem of superhuman power; they are not subject to the ordinary limits of space and time.

140

The idea of these winged demigods originated in Persia, and they are represented on Sumerian cylinder seals, Assyrian bas-reliefs, and Babylonian vase paintings. Mercury, the winged messenger of the Olympian gods, was one of their direct descendants. Only much later did angels take to plucking harps, waving palm fronds, singing psalms (several of which were originally composed as hymns to Baal, by the way), and the rest of the insipid behavior that was attributed to them in the Middle Ages and the Renaissance.

The Book of Judges takes much the same attitude toward the ordinary calamities of a settler's life in a hostile countryside that is already apparent in the Book of Joshua. Enemy raids, and the ensuing theft or destruction of the harvest, are regarded as punishments sent down by God because the Israelites have strayed from the path of righteousness.

The task of the judges was to cope with these external and internal threats to the security of the Israelite settlements in Canaan. So for the most part the judges were not white-robed prophets but battle-scarred tribal chieftains who often worked in strange ways to discomfit the enemies of Israel. The authors of the Book of Judges make no attempt to conceal their sympathy for these raffish characters, and their more distinguished dirty tricks and feats of rascality are recounted in loving detail. Here, the children of Israel are crying out to be delivered from Eglon, king of Moab, who has forced them to pay tribute:

> But when the children of Israel cried unto the LORD, the LORD raised them up a deliverer, Ehud the son of Gera, a Benjamite, a man lefthanded: and by him the children of Israel sent a present unto Eglon the king of Moab.
>
> But Ehud made him a dagger which had two edges, of a cubit length; and he did gird it under his raiment upon his right thigh.

141

And he brought the present unto Eglon king of Moab: and Eglon was a very fat man.

And when he had made an end to offer the present, he sent away the people that bare the present.

But he himself turned again from the quarries [graven images] that were by Gilgal, and said, I have a secret errand unto thee, O king: who said, Keep silence. And all that stood by him went out from him.

And Ehud came unto him; and he was sitting in a summer parlour, which he had for himself alone. And Ehud said, I have a message from God unto thee. And he arose out of his seat.

And Ehud put forth his left hand, and took the dagger from his right thigh, and thrust it into his belly:

And the haft also went in after the blade; and the fat closed upon the blade, so that he could not draw the dagger out of his belly; and the dirt came out.

Then Ehud went forth through the porch, and shut the doors of the parlour upon him, and locked them.

When he was gone out, his servants came; and when they saw that, behold, the doors of the parlour were locked, they said, Surely he covereth his feet [doeth his easement] in his summer chamber.

And they tarried till they were ashamed: and, behold, he opened not the doors of the parlour; therefore they took a key, and opened them: and, behold, their lord was fallen down dead on the earth.

—JUDGES 3:15–25 (The words in brackets are variant readings supplied by the King James translators.)

Very few national epics would be so forthright—first to pin the murder of an unsuspecting fat man on one of their national heroes, and then to re-create the crime with almost sadistic relish. (Archaeologists have confirmed the background details of the story. The palace of the king of Moab may very well have had a veranda with a door that locked and indoor plumbing, consisting of a series of conical clay tubes that could be linked together to make a wastepipe for Eglon's "chair of easement.")

> *And the children of Israel again did evil in the sight of the LORD, when Ehud was dead.*
>
> *And the LORD sold them into the hand of Jabin king of Canaan, that reigned in Hazor; the captain of whose host was Sisera . . .*

> —JUDGES 4:1–2

So begins another biblical tale of intrigue and political murder, which occurred some twenty years later, when the prophetess Deborah was the judge of one of the tribes of Israel. This crime was even more heinous than Ehud's, because it involved a breach of the law of hospitality, which above all else was sacrosanct in the ancient world: Sisera, the Canaanite general, is defeated by the Israelites. He abandons his chariots and escapes on foot to seek asylum at the tent of Jael, the wife of Heber, who was an ally of his master, the king of Canaan. Jael goes out to meet him and welcomes him:

> *And Jael went out to meet Sisera, and said unto him, Turn in, my lord, turn in to me; fear not. And when he had turned in unto her into the tent, she covered him with a mantle.*
>
> *And he said unto her, Give me, I pray thee, a little water to drink; for I am thirsty. And she opened a bottle of milk, and gave him drink, and covered him.*
>
> *Again he said unto her, Stand in the door of the tent, and it shall be, when any man doth come and enquire of thee, and say, Is there any man here? that thou shalt say, No.*
>
> *Then Jael Heber's wife took a nail of the tent [tent peg] and took an hammer in her hand, and went softly unto him, and*

143

smote the nail into his temples, and fastened it into the ground:
for he was fast asleep and weary. So he died.

—JUDGES 4:18–21

The entire story is later retold in metrical verse, a victory hymn that the Bible attributes to Deborah and Barak, the Israelite commander:

Blessed above women shall Jael the wife of Heber the Kenite be,
blessed shall she be above women in the tent.
He asked water, and she gave him milk;
she brought forth butter in a lordly dish.
She put her hand to the nail, and her right hand to the
workmen's hammer;
and with the hammer she smote Sisera,
she smote off his head,
when she had pierced and stricken through his temples.
At her feet he bowed, he fell, he lay down:
at her feet he bowed, he fell:
where he bowed there he fell down dead.

—JUDGES 5:24–27

The vigor of the language and the hypnotic rhythmic structure of the verses is perfectly suited to the violence of the deed itself, which is re-created, almost gloatingly, in every detail. The song concludes with a purely imaginary scene in which Sisera's mother looks out her window and anxiously asks her "wise ladies" why her son's chariot has not yet returned from the battle. She answers her own question in a beautiful little aria that has the unexpected poignancy of a lullaby after the operatic violence of Deborah's victory hymn:

Have they not sped?
have they not divided the prey [booty];
to every man a damsel or two;

to Sisera a prey of divers colours,
a prey of divers colours of needlework,
of divers colours of needlework on both sides,
meet for the necks of them that take the spoil?

—JUDGES 5:30

But once again "the children of Israel did evil in the sight of the LORD," and the Lord retaliates by allowing the Midianites and other desert marauders to pillage their settlements. Finally, though, he relents and chooses a young man called Gideon to lead an army against the Midianites.

Gideon, skeptical at first, asks for a sign that the Lord intends to follow through on this unpromising scheme. Being a farmer's son, he proposes that he should leave a fleece out in a field (not "in the floor," as the King James has it); in the morning he expects to find the fleece soaked with dew, but the ground all around it completely dry. "And it was so: for he rose up early on the morrow . . . and wringed the dew out of the fleece, a bowl full of water." Then, hesitantly, Gideon asks the Lord to repeat the miracle, only this time "let it now be dry only upon the fleece, and upon all the ground let there be dew." The Lord has great hopes for Gideon, and he obligingly "did so that night: for it was dry upon the fleece only, and there was dew on all the ground."

Gideon is convinced; he gathers an army and prepares to attack. His stratagem would make the perfect climax to any Hollywood Western; each of his men carries a torch concealed in a clay pot while the army advances stealthily toward the enemy camp. At Gideon's signal, the troops smash the pots to the ground, brandish their torches, sound their trumpets, and the enemy flees in confusion.

After several more victories over the Midianites, the Ammonites, the Ephraimites, and others, Gideon has accumulated enough battle trophies to melt down and make "an ephod

145

thereof, and put it in his city, even in Ophrah: and all Israel went thither a whoring after it . . ."

Biblical scholars have expended a great deal of effort in trying to figure out exactly what an *ephod* might be. The word is used many times in the Old Testament, with a different meaning almost every time. Sometimes it is a priestly vestment, sometimes merely a loincloth, and sometimes—as here—a "graven image," or a pagan cult object of one kind or another. The Israelites were still apparently eager to cultivate the gods of their enemies, even if they prayed to them only to make doubly sure that someone up there was listening.

After Gideon's death the land was plunged into anarchy and idolatry once more. Gideon's son Abimelech was a thoroughgoing scoundrel who intrigued to have himself made king, having first killed all his seventy brothers ("Gideon had many wives") to clear the title. The less said about this Abimelech the better, except for a single arresting detail. When Abimelech destroyed the rebellious city of Shechem, the Bible reports that he "beat down the city, and sowed it with salt."

Salt was primarily an agent of ritual purification; every sacrifice was sprinkled with salt before it was laid upon the altar. In this case, though, Abimelech is practicing a different kind of sympathetic magic. Just as nothing will grow on a salted field, so—the conqueror hoped—a city "sowed with salt" would never rise again from the ruins. (Perhaps Abimelech didn't use quite enough salt, because Shechem was rebuilt about 150 years later.)

Interestingly, both practices have survived as common superstitions in our own culture. Spilling the salt portends disaster for the entire household. Fortunately, disaster can be averted by throwing a pinch of salt over one's shoulder in a gesture of ritual purification.

Of the many tribes and peoples mentioned in the Book of

Judges who have since vanished from the face of the earth, the Ammonites, whose kingdom lay beyond the River Jordan, at least have a permanent memorial in the city of Amman, the capital of the modern kingdom of Jordan. The Ammonites succeeded the Midianites, their neighbors to the south, as the archenemies of Israel, and the Bible reports that one of the later judges, Jephthah,

> . . . *vowed a vow unto the* LORD, *and said, If thou shalt without fail deliver the children of Ammon into mine hands,*
>
> *Then it shall be, that whatsoever cometh forth of the doors of my house to meet me, when I return in peace [that is, victorious] from the children of Ammon, shall surely be the* LORD'S, *and I will offer it up for a burnt offering.*

> —JUDGES 11:30–31

Jephthah quickly comes to regret this impetuous offer. The first living creature that he meets on his victorious return home is his daughter, his only child. She agrees that Jephthah's vow to the Lord must be fulfilled at all costs. And though we have come a long way since the barbarous days of Abraham and Isaac, no angel of the Lord appears to stay Jephthah's upraised hand, and no fire comes down from heaven to smite him. No one says a word, in fact, until quite a bit later, when Jephthah rates a very favorable mention in the New Testament as one of the great pillars of righteousness in the days of the prophets (Hebrews 11:32).

Still, whatever we might think of Jephthah, he at least deserves some credit for a very clever stratagem he devised in a later campaign, to prevent the defeated Ephraimites from slipping through the Israelite lines. The sentries were instructed to order everyone to repeat the word *shibboleth*, which the Ephraimites had trouble pronouncing; the best they could do was "sibboleth." Anyone who returned the sentries' challenge with a sibilant "sibboleth" was sure to be an Ephraimite, which is to say, done for.

Most famous of the heroes of the Book of Judges is Samson, immortalized in great poetry and grand opera, masterly painting and mediocre films.

Certainly there is a wealth of dramatic material here to work with—the champion of the Israelites who slew a thousand warriors with the jawbone of an ass; the vulnerable superman whose strength was miraculously preserved by the "seven locks of his hair" and treacherously stolen by a beautiful woman; the fallen colossus, blinded and shorn, who won his greatest victory at the moment of his death . . .

Quite a story, in short, and no wonder—the biblical "biography" of the last of the judges is actually a kind of anthology of the highlights of many different heroic sagas. These were carefully selected, according to modern biblical scholars, to point a very specific moral: that even a man chosen by God to be set above all other men can be brought low if he fails to live up to his vocation.

Fortunately, the authors of the Book of Judges were shrewd enough to disguise this morality tale as a first-rate melodrama. The sex and violence speak for themselves, of course, but a few other matters deserve a word of explanation. First, this business about Samson's hair. As he himself confesses to Delilah, after considerable nagging on her part:

> *There hath not come a razor upon mine head; for I have been a Nazarite unto God from my mother's womb: if I be shaven, then my strength will go from me, and I shall become weak, and be like any other man.*

> —JUDGES 16:17

The Nazarites were a kind of elite corps of ascetics who had dedicated their lives to the service of the Lord. Among the various special prohibitions and restrictions the Nazarite was bound to observe:

> *All the days of the vow of his separation there shall no razor come upon his head . . . he shall be holy, and shall let the locks of the hair of his head grow.*

> —NUMBERS 6:5

Samson has not *chosen* to become a Nazarite; he was consecrated to the Lord's service by his parents, as he explains to Delilah, before he was born. Nor is he much of an ascetic. But his Nazarite vow is the key to his superhuman strength. Thus, nothing is especially magical or mysterious about his "seven locks," except that they symbolize his "separation" as a chosen servant of the Lord. But when he confides his secret to his Philistine mistress—who immediately lulls him to sleep with his head in her lap and signals to an accomplice with a razor—his vow is broken, his strength deserts him, and "he wist not that the LORD was departed from him."

Delilah is only one of many villainous Philistines in the Old Testament. The Philistines remained a constant source of anxiety for the Israelites from the days of the judges until the reign of King David. The Israelites hated and feared them, not so much because they were warlike and aggressive, which they were, but because they had already learned the secret of forging iron weapons from their distant cousins the Hittites. The Israelites, with their obsolete bronze swords and shields, were hopelessly outmatched in combat.

The Bible has a great deal to say about the Philistines, most of it derogatory. Yet we have little reliable information about them. Most serious scholars believe that they originally came from

Crete; others have identified them with the Pelasgians, the semilegendary inhabitants of the Greek mainland in pre-Hellenic times. (German scholars of the old school, as mentioned earlier, were very attached to the theory that the Philistines were actually a race of biblical Vikings, a North Germanic people who somehow found their way from the Baltic to the Aegean and points east.)

All that we can say for certain is that the Philistines were an Indo-European people who suddenly appeared on the coast of Canaan at about the same time the Israelites were moving in from the interior. Probably, as mercenaries in the service of Pharaoh Ramses III, they were first settled in garrison towns along the northern border of the Egyptian Empire. Then, sometime around 1200 B.C., they founded their own city-states and set about the conquest of their Semitic neighbors.

Given the attitude of the authors of the Old Testament toward the Philistines, it is hardly surprising that in more recent times the word *Philistine* has been used as an all-purpose term of abuse. Today, however, it generally means something like "lowborn," "money-grubbing illiterate," or "ignoramus"— qualities that we can't necessarily pin on the Philistines of the Old Testament. In fact, the origin of this modern usage of the word is only indirectly connected with the Bible.

In seventeenth-century German universities, the students (who naturally thought of themselves as the chosen people) called all nonstudents *Philister*. The arch-*Philister* were the landladies and boardinghouse keepers in university towns, who were regarded as being morbidly suspicious, prudish, tight-fisted, and generally "petty bourgeois."

In the nineteenth century, British writers like Thomas Carlyle and Matthew Arnold anglicized this term and applied it to a different target: the prosperous Victorian middle class and everyone else whom they believed to be the enemies of culture and enlightenment. As Matthew Arnold explained it: "The people who believe that most of our greatness and welfare are proved by our being very rich, and who must give their lives and thoughts to becoming rich, are just the very people we call Philistines."

Another etymological spin-off of the Philistines is the word *Palestine*, which was originally *Philistia*, the land of the Philistines. This term, unknown in Old Testament times, was first used by the Romans in the year A.D. 135. The Jewish Bar Kokhba revolt had just been suppressed, with great difficulty, by a Roman punitive expedition. After the Romans had finished plundering and crucifying their rebellious subjects, they decided to take a more lasting revenge by obliterating the very name of the Jewish homeland. The province of Judea was accordingly named Philistia, after the ancient enemies of the Jews, as a particularly humiliating reminder of their subjugation by the Romans.

The dates of events described in the Book of Judges cannot be fixed exactly (assuming that they actually took place and were not—like the exploits of Samson—simply borrowed from earlier literary sources). The basic time period is approximately 1200–1000 B.C., about the same time as the Trojan War. Contemporary events in Canaan did not have much in the way of epic grandeur, though, and no Israelite Homer celebrated the cattle raids, blood feuds, and all-around moral depravity of the days of the Judges. As a kind of isolated postscript, however, we finally come upon the strangely familiar story of an old man of Gibeah—his name is not mentioned—who invites two stranded travelers, a Levite and his concubine, to stay in his house for the night. While they are feasting and making merry, a pack of unruly neighbors surrounds the house and starts pounding on the door—the Bible calls them "sons of Belial," which simply means that they were worthless characters, up to no good, which is indeed the case:

> *. . . Bring forth the man that came into thine house, that we may know him.*
>
> *. . . Nay, my brethren, nay [the old man answers], I pray you, do not so wickedly; seeing that this man is come into mine house, do not this folly.*
>
> *Behold, here is my daughter a maiden, and his concubine; them I will bring out now, and humble ye them, and do with them what seemeth good unto you . . .*
>
> —JUDGES 19:22–24

This, of course, is the story of Lot, the angels of the Lord, and the men of Sodom all over again, almost word for word from Genesis 19:5. Was there a very good reason for telling it a second time? Biblical scholars say no. This was simply a widely circulated anecdote that two different authors appropriated to serve their own particular dramatic purposes. Just as with the story of Jephthah's daughter, the Book of Judges stops short of the dramatic climax of the Genesis version and supplies a more predictably gruesome and pessimistic conclusion: the sons of Belial spurn the offer of the old man's daughter, the Levite brings out his concubine instead, and "they knew her, and abused her all the night until the morning."

The Levite finds his mistress dead on the old man's doorstep the next morning. He speaks to her—"Up, and let us be going." When she doesn't answer, he simply slings her body onto his mule and returns home.

> *And when he was come into his house, he took a knife, and laid hold on his concubine, and divided her, together with her bones, into twelve pieces, and sent her into all the coasts [that is, to the twelve tribes] of Israel.*
>
> —JUDGES 19:29

An intertribal council is convened to decide on the proper

retaliation for this appalling crime. The Levite gives them a rather self-serving account of what actually took place:

> And the men of Gibeah rose against me, and beset the house
> . . . and thought to have slain me: and my concubine have they
> forced, that she is dead.

> —JUDGES 20:5

Of course this is inaccurate on two vital points: the men of Gibeah wanted to "know" him, not to kill him, and he himself handed his mistress over to them, knowing full well what the consequences would be. At this point, though, the Levite is interested only in whipping up war hysteria, and the tribes of Israel accommodate him by marching against the men of Gibeah. (Students of English history may remember a similar bizarre episode, the so-called War of Jenkins's Ear, which broke out after the English smuggler Robert Jenkins displayed a severed human ear in the House of Commons—his own, allegedly cut off by Spanish customs officers. Jenkins, like the Levite, had his revenge: the war lasted for nine years and raged over half of Europe.)

After the men of Gibeah have been dealt with, the Book of Judges suddenly switches from sordid melodrama to a rowdy sexual farce, a kind of biblical version of the satyr play that followed every performance of a classical Greek tragedy. What has happened is that although the men of the tribe of Benjamin have lost most of their womenfolk—who have been killed or carried off in various wars—the other eleven tribes have sworn not to give their daughters in marriage to the Benjamites (because they refused to join the expedition against Gibeah, as a matter of fact). The Benjamites, like all the other tribes of Israel, forbidden to marry foreigners, are threatened with extinction. The other tribes manage to scrape up "four hundred young virgins," survivors of a community massacred for some infraction (see Judges 27:8–12 for details). Not enough, the Benjamites reply. Things seem to have reached an impasse.

The solution, simple and ingenious, is not very elegant. The elders of Israel finally announce that the tribes have sworn not to *give* their daughters to the men of Benjamin, but they haven't sworn to prevent the Benjamites from carrying them off by force. The festival of the new wine is about to begin at Shiloh; the elders advise the men of Benjamin to lie in wait in the vineyards:

> . . . *and, behold, if the daughters of Shiloh come out to dance in dances, then come ye out of the vineyards, and catch you every man his wife of the daughters of Shiloh . . .*

—JUDGES 21:21

And to pacify their future in-laws if they should happen to take it amiss:

> *And it shall be, when their fathers or their brethren come unto us to complain, that we will say unto them . . . ye did not give [your daughters] unto them at this time, that ye should be guilty.*

—JUDGES 21:22

Thus the elders of Israel, and the men of Shiloh, are left with a clear conscience, and the tribe of Benjamin is happily saved from extinction. Although the authors make no attempt to provide a moral for this story, a hint of an apology in the very last verse incisively sums up all that has gone before:

> *In those days there was no king in Israel: every man did that which was right in his own eyes.*

—JUDGES 21:25

> . . . *Intreat me not to leave thee, or to return*
> *from following after thee . . . whither thou*
> *goest, I will go . . .*
>
> —RUTH 1:16

The Book of Ruth: A Good Man Is Hard to Find

Now it came to pass in the days when the judges ruled, that there
was a famine in the land. . . .

> —RUTH 1:1

At first it may seem as if we are in for more of the same, but
the Book of Ruth is a story of the domestic side of life in the days
of the Judges. Simply and briefly told, it is one of the finest love
stories in all of world literature. It also contains one of the most
beautiful lines in the Bible, which has since found its way into
some Christian marriage services: "for whither thou goest, I will
go . . . thy people shall be my people, and thy God my
God . . ."

In the Book of Ruth, however, these words are spoken by a
daughter-in-law, Ruth, to her mother-in-law, Naomi. Ruth is a
widow, and the two of them set out for the village of Bethlehem,
five miles south of Jerusalem, from Ruth's native land of Moab.

They arrive in Bethlehem just as the barley—the Israelite
staple crop—is being harvested (which means, incidentally, that
it was the month of May). Ruth goes out into the fields to glean
the stalks of barley that have been overlooked by the harvesters or
have fallen out of the sheaves. (This was—and is—the special
prerogative of the poor, a right that was guaranteed in the Book
of Leviticus. Today you can still see old women and small
children gleaning in the dry, stony fields of the Middle East,
stooped over in the broiling sun, picking up a few handfuls of
grain that can be ground into meal or parched in a copper pot.)

155

The "reapers" who are cutting the barley are not farmers bringing in their own harvest but farm laborers, supervised by a foreman, all employees of a wealthy landowner called Boaz. As it happens, Boaz is a relative of Naomi's. An eligible bachelor, he has already been fully briefed (presumably by Naomi) about Ruth's loyalty, devotion, and other excellent qualities.

Naomi, of course, is delighted by Boaz's attentions to Ruth; he even encourages his laborers to cut the barley sloppily and to let Ruth "glean even among the sheaves"—to gather stalks that the harvesters have already cut and tied, which would be strictly out of bounds for ordinary gleaners. Naomi explains to Ruth that there is another very good reason this relationship should be cultivated:

The man is near to kin unto us, one of our next kinsmen.

—RUTH 2:20

Glancing over at the margin, we see that the King James translators have supplied a variant reading (a literal translation in this case) which is less redundant but not really very enlightening: a "near kinsman" is also "one that hath the right to redeem." What this actually means is that Boaz is one of the heads of the family, the "godfather" as it were, who is obliged by Israelite law to bail out any of his relatives who find themselves in financial difficulties.

The "redeemer" was so called because he was expected to redeem the pledges of any of his relatives who got into debt. If a relative's house or land was attached by creditors, the redeemer would discharge the lien on the property. Most important as far as the story of Ruth is concerned, if any of his brothers died childless, the redeemer was also expected to marry his brother's widow and have children by her to carry on the line—"to preserve their inheritance," as the Bible says.

At this point we begin to suspect that Ruth may not have

wandered into Boaz's field by chance, and that Naomi has arranged the whole thing. For one thing, although Boaz is not necessarily the only member of Naomi's clan who has the right to "redeem" her son's widow, Naomi is determined that Boaz will be the first to press his claim.

Thanks to Ruth's special privileges as a gleaner, she comes home after her first day's work with an ephah of barley—about three-quarters of a bushel, or close to fifty pounds! Ruth stays on as one of Boaz's "handmaids," gleaning profitably in his fields through the end of the wheat harvest, which means that the spring harvest is almost over. Naomi decides that further delay would be fatal, and that it is time for the coup de grâce:

> . . . *Behold [she tells Ruth], he winnoweth barley to night in the threshing floor.*
>
> *Wash thyself therefore, and anoint thee, and put thy raiment upon thee, and get thee down to the floor . . .*
>
> *And it shall be, when he lieth down, that thou shalt mark the place where he shall lie, and thou shalt go in, and uncover his feet, and lay thee down; and he will tell thee what thou shalt do.*
>
> —RUTH 3:2–4

(We may wonder why Ruth needs to be told all this, because she herself was married for ten years or so.)

Ruth makes her way down to the threshing floor and lies down at Boaz's feet. When he awakes, he fails to recognize her in the dark, and Ruth explains:

> . . . *I am Ruth thine handmaid: spread therefore thy skirt [the hem of his robe, that is] over thine handmaid; for thou art a near kinsman ["redeemer"].*
>
> —RUTH 3:9

This sounds to us as if Ruth is asking Boaz, in an indirect, poetic way, to take her under his protection, which she is. But more specifically, she is asking him point-blank to propose to her, because this gesture of spreading his robe hem over her would be tantamount to an offer of marriage. Though willing, Boaz has one small problem. He has to consult with one of his kinsmen—who apparently has priority as the family redeemer—and persuade him to waive his claim to Ruth's hand and her inheritance. Boaz handles the matter very skillfully; he manages to persuade his kinsman that he is taking a burdensome family responsibility off his hands. The kinsman signals his assent by taking off his shoe and handing it to Boaz, which, as the Bible carefully explains,

> . . . was the manner in former time in Israel concerning redeeming . . . for to confirm all things; a man plucked off his shoe, and gave it to his neighbour [partner]: and this was a testimony in Israel.

—RUTH 4:7

(Evidently this curious custom was already obsolete by the time the Book of Ruth was written, and contemporary readers would have been just as baffled as we would without a word or two of commentary.)

Naomi's matchmaking has paid off at last. Boaz and Ruth are married. Their son Obed—who is nursed by his doting grandmother, of course—turns out to be the grandfather of King David. Thus, the story of Ruth and Boaz, which so far has seemed to be no more than a pleasant digression, actually has a fine political point to it. Ruth was born in Moab, and the Moabites were distant relatives of the children of Israel, which did not prevent them from going for each other's throats from time to time. It was King David who finally subdued the Moabites and forced them to pay tribute. In other words, the incorporation of Moab into the Israelite empire is romantically prefigured by the marriage of Ruth and Boaz, a portent that the two nations were destined to be ruled by the House of David.

*. . . for the sword devoureth one as well as
another.*

—II S<small>AMUEL</small> 11:25

First and Second Samuel; or, the
Kingmaker of Canaan

Squeezing tribute out of the Moabites, however, hardly compares with one of David's earlier exploits: his victory over Goliath. The encounter between the shepherd boy with his slingshot and the Philistine giant in armor is certainly the most famous of literary duels—or have we already left the realm of fiction entirely, for the First Book of Samuel, which includes the story of David's early career, is considered to be one of the "historical" books of the Bible?

Archaeologists are inclined to think that much of the information in the two books of Samuel is highly reliable, "good history," or as Professor Anton Jirku puts it, "historical source material of unparalleled quality." Perhaps we should see how reliable the historians are by taking a closer look at the First Book of Samuel's account of the battle between David and Goliath:

> And he [David] took his staff in his hand, and chose him five smooth stones out of the brook, and put them in a shepherd's bag which he had, even in a scrip; and his sling was in his hand: and he drew near to the Philistine.
>
> And the Philistine came on and drew near unto David; and the man that bare the shield went before him.
>
> And when the Philistine looked about, and saw David, he disdained him: for he was but a youth, and ruddy, and of a fair countenance.
>
> And the Philistine said unto David, Am I a dog, that thou comest to me with staves? And the Philistine cursed David by his gods.

*And the Philistine said to David, Come to me, and I will give
thy flesh unto the fowls of the air, and to the beasts of the field.*

—I SAMUEL 17:40–44

David amiably replies that he intends to leave the entire
Philistine host as crowbait and carrion. After a few more verses
of righteous intimidation, the ritual exchange of insults is over,
and the real battle can begin in earnest:

*And David put his hand in his bag, and took thence a stone,
and slang it, and smote the Philistine in his forehead, that the
stone sunk into his forehead; and he fell upon his face to the earth.*

—I SAMUEL 17:49

These slings were deadly weapons, not children's toys, nor
were they used exclusively by simple shepherds. Assyrian,
Greek, and Roman armies all included special units of sharp-
shooters equipped with slings, and the Bible mentions elsewhere
that some of those expert marksmen were so accomplished that
they also "slang" left-handed.

*So David prevailed over the Philistine with a sling and with a
stone, and smote the Philistine, and slew him; but there was no
sword in the hand of David.*
*Therefore David ran, and stood upon the Philistine, and took
his sword, and drew it out of the sheath thereof, and slew him,
and cut off his head therewith. . . .*

—I SAMUEL 17:50–51

The Philistines flee, leaving David in possession of the field.
An exciting story, with a wealth of circumstantial detail—could
it actually have happened that way? If so, what are we to make of
this sentence from the *Second* Book of Samuel:

And there was again a battle in Gob with the Philistines, where

Elhanan and the son Jaare-oregim, a Beth-lehemite, slew the
brother of *Goliath the Gittite [of Gath, the Philistine capital),
the staff of whose spear was like a weaver's beam.*

—II SAMUEL 21:19

The translators have added the words *the brother of* because
they believed that David, not Elhanan, killed Goliath, and
because a passage in the Book of Chronicles (20:5) confirms that
Elhanan killed a Philistine giant called Lachmi, the brother of
Goliath of Gath, "whose spear was like a weaver's beam."

Modern biblical scholars, however, are convinced that it was
not David who killed Goliath at all—and it may quite possibly
have been someone called Elhanan. Only much later, after
David had won his reputation as a mighty warrior on other
battlefields, did biblical chroniclers retroactively decide to make
him the hero of the Goliath story as well. (Note that the authors
tried to cover their tracks by introducing Goliath's brother into
the Elhanan story in First Chronicles; apparently they forgot to
take the same precaution in Second Samuel.) This kind of
retouching of the historical record, common enough in our own
century, is all the more predictable in this case, because the
original reports of Elhanan's victory over Goliath were probably
written about 950 B.C. and the story of David and Goliath about
580 B.C.—more than 350 years later.

Scholars are quite confident about this latter date, which was
arrived at not by the usual laborious and inconclusive techniques
of the historical linguist, but as the result of a single logical
deduction. Luckily, the retouchers gave the game away by
making an elementary historical blunder. The David and
Goliath story goes on to describe how David "took the head of
the Philistine, and brought it to Jerusalem," where he was taken
immediately before King Saul. But Saul's capital was Gibeah, in
Judah, and Jerusalem was not even part of his kingdom; it was
annexed much later, by David himself, seven years after Saul's

161

death. (David financed this expedition out of his own pocket; he recruited an army of mercenaries and took the city, which became his private fief, by right of conquest, and thus quite literally "the city of David.")

So, then, it seems clear that the story of David and Goliath must have been composed much later, after Jerusalem had become the capital of Israel and Judah—perhaps one of the rare instances in which we have actually learned something from the mistakes of the past.

David's reputation seemed to have received another rude shock when the twenty-five thousand cuneiform tablets of the city archives of Mari were deciphered. The word *davidum* crops up repeatedly—so often, in fact, that scholars finally decided that *davidum* was not a personal name at all but a military title, something like "generalissimo" or "commander in chief." As Werner Keller observed in the first edition of *The Bible As History:* "The name Caesar was later adopted as a title . . . in David's case it seems to have been the other way around." This in turn suggested several intriguing possibilities: David, like the Emperor Augustus, simply exchanged his name for his title; or perhaps there were many other Davids—many great commanders—whose exploits were later attributed to David by the same myth-making process we have already observed in the case of Joshua.

Then, in 1978, the scholars announced that there had been a regrettable error. *Davidum*, it turns out, does not mean "commander" at all, but "a rout, a disastrous defeat"—quite a different thing after all, even if the two ideas are often linked in practice. So, after a century of scholarly pursuit, the historical David remains as elusive as ever. And even such unparalleled source material as the First Book of Samuel still presents serious problems for historians and archaeologists. This leaves us free to read the story of David in the spirit in which it was written, as our grandparents did—as an example of how the weak can easily defeat the strong when they are inspired by their faith, "armed in righteousness," as the Bible says. In other words, the poet Schiller's "God favors the brave" wins out over the general's cynical *bon mot* (attributed both to Napoleon and to Frederick the Great): "God is always on the side of the big battalions."

Looking at the story of David from this perspective, we can be more tolerant of occasional redundancies and contradictions. These mean only that the story was composed by many different authors, drawing on a remarkable variety of historical and nonhistorical sources. For example, in one place we are told that David began his career as a harpist at the court of King Saul; in another, that he was a shepherd—bringing his brothers ten loaves of bread and "an ephah of this parched corn" from home, plus ten cheeses for "the captain of their thousand"—who joined the Israelite host by accident. But these are minor points in comparison with the surprises that David has to offer. These begin with Saul.

Saul, the first king of the Israelites, was chosen and anointed by the prophet Samuel about 1000 B.C., at a time when the Land of Canaan was still being devastated by Philistine raids, more so than ever, in fact. Samuel was a reluctant kingmaker, because his prophetic gifts had shown him all too clearly what this sort of thing could lead to:

> And he said, This will be the manner of the king that shall reign over you: He will take your sons, and appoint them for himself, for his chariots, and to be his horsemen; and some shall run before his chariots.
>
> And he will appoint him captains over thousands, and captains over fifties; and will set them to ear his ground, and to reap his harvest, and to make his instruments of war, and instruments of his chariots.
>
> And he will take your daughters to be confectionaries, and to be cooks, and to be bakers.

And he will take your fields, and your vineyards, and your oliveyards, even the best of them, and give them to his servants.

And he will take the tenth of your seed, and of your vineyards, and give to his officers, and to his servants.

And he will take your menservants, and your maidservants, and your goodliest young men, and your asses, and put them to his work.

He will take the tenth of your sheep: and ye shall be his servants.

And ye shall cry out in that day because of your king which ye shall have chosen you; and the LORD will not hear you in that day.

—I SAMUEL 8:11–18

Evidently Samuel is what we would call a rabid democrat, yet the Israelites remain unconvinced:

. . . Nay; but we will have a king over us; That we also may be like all the nations [goyim, or Gentiles] . . .

—I SAMUEL 8:19–20

Apparently these nomads, having finally settled down into a sedentary routine of tending crops and fending off the Philistines, want a king—to prove to themselves, and the "nations," that they are just as civilized as anyone else. Samuel shrewdly tries to make the best of this bad business by choosing a king from the tribe of Benjamin, the smallest of the tribes of Israel (even after the abduction of the daughters of Shiloh, the Benjamites are still just barely scraping along).

Saul is thirty years old when he is chosen king. When he first meets Samuel, he is looking for a "seer"—a prophet or clairvoyant—to help him find a herd of his father's mules that have gone astray. Instead, as the Bible trenchantly puts it, "he found a kingdom." This kingdom, unfortunately, is still little more than a vassal state of the Philistines, who had forced on the Israelites a policy of unilateral total disarmament to preserve the secret of their own military supremacy:

> *Now there was no smith found throughout all the land of Israel: for the Philistines said, Lest the Hebrews make them swords or spears:*
>
> *But all the Israelites went down to the Philistines, to sharpen every man his share, and his coulter, and his axe, and his mattock.*

—I SAMUEL 13:19–20

Although Saul successfully defies the Philistine arms embargo and holds his own against his enemies well enough, he is not made out to be a very attractive character in the First Book of Samuel. Saul is hot-tempered, repressive, and deceitful. We need not take this too seriously, however, for it is entirely possible that Saul was painted so black only to make David shine all the more brightly. Saul was the man the times required, and we would do better to remember him at the head of his armies in battle rather than sulking in his place. Saul dies heroically in battle, with an antique Roman flourish: encircled by the Philistines, mortally wounded by their arrows, he instructs his armorbearer:

> . . . *Draw thy sword, and thrust me through therewith; lest these uncircumcised come and thrust me through, and abuse me. But his armourbearer would not; for he was sore afraid. Therefore Saul took a sword, and fell upon it.*

—I SAMUEL 31:4

The ruins of Saul's palace at Gibeah have been uncovered at a place called Tel el-Ful, a few miles north of Jerusalem on the road to Samaria. Although the site is a popular tourist attraction, visitors are likely to be disappointed. Not a trace of Oriental splendor enhances this squat rectangular structure, whose interior courtyard measures only about forty-two yards by twenty-five. The flat roof of the palace, as of any ordinary house, served as a kind of promenade deck as well as a sleeping porch on hot summer nights; these are the "high places" where Samuel communes with Saul in I Samuel 9:25 and from where David first catches sight of Bathsheba while he is restlessly pacing "the roof of the king's house" at night.

King David was richly endowed—by the chroniclers who compiled the Books of Samuel—with all those human qualities in which Saul was deficient. He was not only a "mighty valiant man," but "cunning in playing"—a gifted poet and musician—"prudent in matters, and a comely person," beloved of his people, and a great lover of women. He is said to have had four hundred children; allowing for the usual tenfold exaggeration, fathering even forty children is still a respectable lifetime record.

We may wonder why so many of those who antagonized, or merely inconvenienced, this glittering paragon happened to die at the opportune moment—usually of unnatural causes. David's defenders might point out that he always showed remarkable restraint as far as King Saul was concerned, despite the many occasions on which Saul tried to have him killed. And there is the friendship—"passing the love of women"—between David and Saul's son, Jonathan, whose own story is a perfect illustration of the conflict between love and duty, the favorite theme of French classical dramatists. Like a couple of characters from Racine or Corneille who have unaccountably wandered into Macbeth's castle, David and Jonathan display a high-minded affection that contrasts strikingly with Saul's baseness and treachery. David has more than one opportunity to kill the king; the closest he comes is snipping off a corner of Saul's mantle as

166

he sleeps. Even then he suffers agonizing pangs of conscience for this symbolic outrage against "the Lord's anointed."

After several lucky escapes from Saul's more serious attempts on his life, David finally wearies of his hand-to-mouth existence as an outlaw and flees the country to offer his services to one of the kings of the Philistines. By this time David is a true soldier of fortune; he would rather fight in the service of Israel's enemies than not fight at all. This also gives him an opportunity to study the tactics of the most formidable army in Canaan. He manages to persuade the king of Gath that he has been raiding Saul's territory, though actually he has led his troops against the Amalekites, far to the south.

But why is Saul so relentlessly determined to kill David in the first place? On the surface his motive seems to be simple jealousy of David's military prowess and his popularity with the people. "Saul hath slain his thousands, and David his ten thousands" (I Samuel 29:5), the Israelite women cry out, rather tactlessly, as David returns from battle. From what we have already learned of Saul's character, he seems broody and obsessive enough to plot the murder of anyone who has outshone him like this. But in fact, Saul has a more practical motive: he is not simply envious of David's ruddy countenance and his war record; he fears and mistrusts him as a potential rival.

Saul has fallen out of favor with Samuel, the kingmaker. Samuel, according to the Bible, had already anointed David as Saul's successor while David was still an untried boy tending his father's flocks:

> Then Samuel took the horn of oil, and anointed him in the midst of his brethren: and the Spirit of the LORD came upon David from that day forward. . . .
>
> —I SAMUEL 16:13

Saul has lost the mandate of heaven, in other words, and

David is the popular pretender to the throne. Saul wavers between trying to fix David "to the wall" with his javelin and sending him off on various high-risk combat missions—notably when he orders David to bring back the foreskins of a hundred Philistines as the bride-price for his daughter Michal. (Biblical scholars cite this strange scavenger hunt as indirect proof that the Philistines, because they did not practice circumcision, were not Semites.)

To imagine David as he really must have been, we have to look beyond Michelangelo's colossal statue—the idealized but slightly awkward adolescent with the distinctive creases around his nostrils—and the extravagant praise lavished on the future king of Israel in the Books of Samuel. What we are really looking for is the sort of information that is mentioned only in passing or carefully tucked away between the lines.

For example, it is hard to imagine Michelangelo's noble youth, or the author of the Psalms, running a protection racket. But that was apparently the case. While David is still a fugitive in Israel, he becomes the "captain" of a ragtag army of drifters, absconding debtors, and other social misfits:

> And every one that was in distress, and every one that was in debt, and every one that was discontented, gathered themselves unto him. . . .

> —I SAMUEL 22:2

A few chapters later we are given a highly sanitized but still unmistakable account of David's extortion methods. He sends an unarmed advance party to the house of a wealthy landowner called Nabal—or he sends "messengers" to "salute" him, as the Bible puts it. They explain to Nabal, in true Mafioso style, that though David's band of desperadoes has been camping out on Nabal's grazing land for some time now,

> . . . thy shepherds which were with us, we hurt them not, neither

was there ought missing unto them, all the while they were in Carmel.

—I Samuel 25:7

But Nabal "churlishly" refuses to pay off—to hand over "whatsoever cometh to thine hand unto thy servants, and to thy son David"—and David sets out with four hundred armed men for Nabal's farmstead.

Nabal's shepherds, naturally mindful of the prospect of having their kneecaps smashed by David's "messengers," warn Nabal's wife, Abigail, pointing out that David's demands are perfectly reasonable and that Nabal is just being perversely stubborn: "for he is such a son of Belial, that a man cannot speak to him." Abigail, "a woman of good understanding," goes out to meet David with a pack train laden with "two hundred loaves, and two bottles of wine, and five sheep ready dressed, and five measures of parched corn, and an hundred clusters of raisins, and two hundred cakes of figs" to buy him off. Ten days later, "the Lord smote Nabal, that he died," and David takes the lovely widow as his second wife.

David's passion for another beautiful woman, Bathsheba, later involves him in a more famous, and even more discreditable, episode. By this time we are already well into the Second Book of Samuel, and David, now king, is more inclined than ever to waive the rules. Bathsheba, unfortunately, is already married to Uriah the Hittite, one of David's officers. David sends Uriah off to the front with a sealed dispatch for his commander, which reads as follows:

. . . Set ye Uriah in the forefront of the hottest battle, and retire ye from him, that he may be smitten, and die.

—II Samuel 11:15

Joab, David's general in the fields, is clearly disturbed by all this when he sends back a messenger with a report of Uriah's death. David replies with world-weary cynicism, telling Joab, in effect, to forget about the whole thing and get on with it:

> . . . *Thus shalt thou say unto Joab, Let not this thing displease thee, for the sword devoureth one as well as another: make thy battle more strong against the city, and overthrow it. . . .*
>
> —II SAMUEL 11:25

This episode has predictably mixed results. On the one hand, the second son of David and Bathsheba—they are married as soon as the obligatory period of mourning is over—grows up to be King Solomon, the greatest of the kings of Israel and Judah. On the other hand, as the author drily remarks,

> . . . *the thing that David had done displeased the LORD*
>
> —II SAMUEL 11:27

David's military record, at least, is excellent; he defeats the Philistines in almost every encounter. (The Egyptian Empire was in full decline by David's time, which meant that small expansionist states like Israel and Judah could move with impunity into what had once been Egyptian territory.) David seems to have profited a great deal from his four years in the service of the Philistines, and he clearly had a high regard for their military prowess. His royal bodyguard was composed exclusively of Cretans and Philistines, though the Bible, loath to admit this, calls them "Cherithites and Pelethites."

David's musical gifts are equally in evidence throughout both Books of Samuel—though whether the Psalms of David were actually composed by David, or merely written at his behest or dedicated to him, is still disputed. In one version of the story, David's skill as a harpist is what first brings him to the attention of King Saul:

And it came to pass, when the evil spirit from God was upon Saul, that David took an harp, and played with his hand: so Saul was refreshed, and was well, and the evil spirit departed from him.

—I SAMUEL 16:23

(This therapy was very effective when Saul was depressed, though when he was in a manic phase he was just as likely to reach for his javelin.)

Still, despite one thing and another, David manages to reign for many years without bringing himself into serious disfavor with the Lord. And even then he is given the special dispensation of choosing his punishment—seven years of famine, three months of flight "before thine enemies," or three days of pestilence. David chose the plague, because, as he explains to the prophet Gad, the Lord's confidential agent in this matter:

I am in a great strait: let us fall now into the hand of the LORD; for his mercies are great: and let me not fall into the hand of man.

—II SAMUEL 24:14

We can easily think of three or four capital (or pestilential) crimes that David has already committed: extortion and robbery with violence, conspiracy with intent to murder, high treason, and consorting with the enemy. Yet curiously enough, David is now being chastised by the Lord for *obeying* one of his commandments:

And again the anger of the LORD was kindled against Israel, and he moved David against them to say, Go, number Israel and Judah.

—II SAMUEL 24:1

It was perfectly all right for Moses to take a census of the

171

twelve tribes after the Exodus from Egypt, but when David does the same thing—no doubt to find out how many men of military age he could mobilize in an emergency—he immediately finds himself in a great strait.

No one—neither theologian, historian, nor archaeologist—has yet been able to reconcile the punishment with the crime in this case. And contemporary readers were apparently just as baffled as we are. In First and Second Chronicles, which were composed sometime during the fourth century B.C., about two centuries after Samuel, this story has been substantially revised. Here it is not God but Satan who "provoked David to number Israel" (I Chronicles 21:1). (This, by the way, is Satan's first appearance in the Old Testament, and merely a walk-on compared with the starring role he plays later, in the Book of Job.) The authors of Chronicles, with the advantage of two centuries' hindsight, thought it best to reinterpret this incomprehensible act of God as the work of the Devil, which is why members of certain Fundamentalist sects steadfastly refuse to send in their census forms.

Certainly the most decisive event of David's reign was selecting Jerusalem as the capital of the dual monarchy of Israel and Judah. Urusalima—"the city of peace"—was an ancient stronghold of the Canaanite tribe called the Jebusites. David's decision did not make much sense from a strictly geographical standpoint. Jerusalem was not on the banks of a great river or at the confluence of any important caravan routes; it had no outlet to the sea. Why, then, was David's choice of this inaccessible eyrie as his capital such a political masterstroke?

First of all, the territory of the tribe of Judah—the only one of the twelve to acclaim David as king after the death of Saul—lay directly to the south. The territory of the other tribes—who continued to recognize the authority of Saul's son until his death—lay to the north. Jerusalem was a kind of free city in the neutral corridor between them. David hoped to reunite these two entities into a single nation, with Jerusalem as the keystone of the new political structure.

Jerusalem was also the site of a pagan temple dedicated to the supreme god of the Jebusites. David was simply reaffirming an ancient tradition when he brought the Ark of the Covenant there. As so often in the past, the Israelites rededicated a pagan sanctuary to the worship of Jahweh. The Ark had come to rest at last; it would no longer accompany the tribes of Israel in their migrations and campaigns. Instead, the Israelites would have to come to it, making Jerusalem a great pilgrimage center.

The Jebusite settlement that David and his mercenaries conquered occupied only the southeastern corner of the later city, a hill on the western slopes of the Vale of Kidron that the Jebusites had named Mount Zion. Looking out over this site today from the Mount of Olives, the modern visitor to Jerusalem is likely to be disappointed in the celebrated Mount Zion. It seems hardly large enough to accommodate a modest village. The Zion of the Psalms, however, does not refer just to the mountain but to the entire city of Jerusalem, as it later came to be, the sanctuary of Jahweh, the dwelling place of the Lord.

The choice of Jerusalem as the capital of David's dual monarchy was the first step toward unifying all the neighboring kingdoms—not only Israel and Judah, but Ammon, Moab, Edom, and Zobah—into a single Judaic state; the Israelite conquest of of Canaan had entered the imperial phase. And the task of uniting and administering those territories was left to Solomon, David's son and successor, who began his long and glorious reign most inauspiciously by almost letting the kingship slip through his fingers.

> *Give therefore thy servant an understanding*
> *heart to judge thy people, that I may discern*

between good and bad: for who is able to judge
this thy so great a people?

—I KINGS 3:9

Splendor and Majesty: The Legacy of Solomon

The First Book of Kings: Concerning David and Abishag, Bathsheba and Adonijah, Solomon, and Many Others

As the First Book of Kings begins, David is nearing the end of his forty-year reign. He is an old man now, very frail, and very cold: ". . . they covered him in clothes [blankets], but he gat no heat." Fortunately, his servants have a perfect home remedy for the king's persistent chill:

Let there be sought for my lord the king a young virgin; and let
her stand before the king, and let her cherish him, and let her lie
in [his] bosom, that my lord the king may get heat.

—I KINGS 1:2

A "fair damsel" called Abishag the Shunammite was recruited to cherish and minister to the king in this particularly intimate capacity, "but"—we are told quite explicitly—"the king knew her not." That David later takes Abishag as his wife is not really the point of this gossipy tale of Jerusalem behind closed doors.

Politics, not sex, is the key to it all, though the background is a little complicated: David has still not chosen a successor, and it was not yet customary for the eldest son to inherit the throne. This is likely to cause a serious dynastic crisis, as David knows perfectly well, but he is still reluctant to make the choice (his favorite son, Absalom, is long dead by now).

Solomon's half brother, Adonijah, puts an end to the suspense with a forthright, though premature, public announcement: "I will be king."

And perhaps he would have been, had Bathsheba not been so determined to see her own son, Solomon, on the throne. Accompanied by the prophet Nathan, she goes before King David and informs him that Adonijah has already proclaimed himself king. This is not strictly true. All that Adonijah has actually said is that he wants and expects to become king, not that he already has. But this is enough to persuade David that the moment of decision has come. He confirms Solomon as his successor, Solomon is anointed by the high priest, and David dies shortly afterward.

Cold-blooded pragmatism, rather than Solomonic wisdom and an understanding heart, is the keynote of Solomon's first few months on the throne.

He begins with a bloodbath of his major political rivals in which Abishag plays an important role. Adonijah has already been pardoned by David for his impetuousness; now he asks Bathsheba to intercede with the new king to grant him a special favor. He wants to marry Abishag, who is not only, ex officio, the hottest-blooded woman "in all the coasts of Israel," but also the late king's widow. Bathsheba (who has presumably already foreseen the outcome of all this) speaks to Solomon; Solomon refuses and orders Adonijah put to death.

This is not because he covets Abishag for himself, but because—as we have already learned from the story of Ruth—under Israelite law a man who marries a widow automatically has a strong legal claim to her husband's estate, in this case, the kingdom of Israel and Judah. Solomon understands this perfectly well, of course: "Ask for him the kingdom also; for he is mine elder brother," he says to Bathsheba. In other words, Adonijah, as the elder brother, still has certain rights to his father's inheritance: if he marries one of the old king's wives, this, according to ancient customary law, would give him a plausible claim to Solomon's throne as well.

The solution as far as Solomon is concerned is to get rid of

Adonijah, which he does, along with his entire shadow cabinet (including old General Joab, to whom Solomon has every reason to be grateful). The authors of the Old Testament were just as eager as he was to clear up any flaw in Solomon's title to the throne. This is why they make a special point of mentioning that though David and Abishag slept together and were later married, "he knew her not." The marriage was thus legally invalid, and Adonijah's claim to the throne was null and void. So, then, the charming story of David and Abishag was included in the First Book of Kings not to gratify our prurient curiosity but to settle an important question of high dynastic politics.

After a few months all of Solomon's rivals were safely underground, and "the kingdom was established in the hand of Solomon." Solomon was now undisputed ruler of the most powerful state between Egypt and Assyria. The greatest mistake of his reign, however, was to concentrate on outward show and external recognition at the expense of the unity and stability of his own disparate territories. This mistake has since been made by rulers of greater and lesser realms than his. In many ways Solomon was unquestionably one of the greatest statesmen in the history of the world. His record of accomplishment in both foreign and domestic affairs is quite impressive. That he released the Israelites from their self-imposed cultural isolation, after so many centuries, is in itself a highly important achievement. In a related sphere, his understanding of the principles of political economy—notably the benefits to be derived from foreign trade—showed a remarkable sophistication for a prince of the tenth century B.C. (972–932, to be precise).

He created a centralized administration for Israel and Judah, which were divided into twelve provinces, along tribal lines, with a "prince" (governor) for each province. The kingdom of Ammon was ruled directly from Jerusalem, Moab by a puppet ruler (a "duke," the Bible calls him) whom Solomon himself had put on his throne. Solomon's viceroys administered the client

176

states of Edom and Aram, which, like the Philistine city-states, were obliged to pay tribute. So far, so good.

But the revenues from the Israelite homeland and the tributary states were not enough to support all the grandiose projects that Solomon had in mind. So he introduced the Egyptian practice of compulsory labor service; his subjects were required to donate their labor to the state for one month out of every three—which was not so good.

Worst of all, in terms of the long-term political stability of this pluralistic empire, was the favoritism he showed the Israelites, who were apparently exempt from forced labor:

> *But of the children of Israel [as opposed to the "Hittites," the Amorites, the Jebusites, and other subject peoples] did Solomon make no servants for his work; but they were men of war, and chief of his captains, and captains of his chariots and horsemen.*

—II CHRONICLES 8:9

Here the phrase "chief of his captains" probably refers to high-ranking civil servants rather than to military men, but it was also during Solomon's reign that the first Israelite standing army was organized. That this included a cavalry arm of "forty thousand" or "one thousand and four hundred" chariots (depending on whether you look in Second Kings or Second Chronicles) was a striking development—just a few years before, David, like Joshua, could think of nothing better to do with captured enemy war-horses than to hamstring them.

Solomon established garrisons—"chariot cities"—for these mobile troops at various strategic points along the frontier. Archaeologists have used a great deal of printer's ink on Solomon's chariot cities over the past few decades, praising Solomon's strategic wisdom in deploying these prototypes of the Cossacks and the Bengal Lancers along his borders so skillfully and so carefully. Yigael Yadin has proved conclusively, however, that the garrison system was actually organized some-time after Solomon's death. This came as a great blow not only to Yadin's fellow archaeologists but to the Israeli tourist ministry as well. Solomon's chariot cities were a popular feature on the itinerary of the ministry's excursion buses, and what country would voluntarily deprive itself of a lucrative tourist attraction? The buses still make the circuit of the chariot cities of Hazor, Megiddo, and Gedser, though now the phrase "Solomon's stables" has been carefully enclosed in quotation marks in all the ministry's brochures.

A certain amount of confusion seems to have surrounded the subject of "Solomon's stables" from the beginning. The end of chapter 10 of the First Book of Kings describes how the chariot cities were established and how Solomon's merchants carried out a brisk trade in war-horses and chariots with "all the kings of the Hittites, and for the kings of Syria." We are also told that the breeding stock of the royal stud farm was "brought out of Egypt and linen yarn: the king's merchants received the linen yarn at a price" (I Kings 10:28). If linen yarn seems a bit of a digression here, it is. In fact, it represents a valiant attempt by the King James translators to make something out of the phrase "the horses were brought out of *mitzrain* [Egypt] and *koa.*" *Koa*, it turns out, was not "linen yarn" but a small city-state in Asia Minor mentioned later in the Bible as a hotbed of idolatry, so the next sentence should accordingly be revised to read: "The king's merchants brought them out of Koa for a price." "Egypt" is a mistake, too, though a much more venerable one, because it was made by a Hebrew scribe who misinterpreted the place name *Muzri*, a neighboring city in Asia Minor, as *mitzrain*.

After you have seen "King Solomon's stables," you might also want to visit "King Solomon's mines" at Wadi Timnah. There the entrances of ancient mineshafts can still be seen in the sheer cliffs of a massive rock formation. The smoke and the loud rumblings emanating from the modern copper mine nearby furnish convincing background effects, but archaeologists assure us that these ancient shafts were worked at various times before and after—but not during—the reign of King Solomon. "King Solomon's Copper Mines" were definitely not King Solomon's, and they too have to be discreetly framed in quotation marks.

Fascination with King Solomon's mines was not inspired by the Bible, which never mentions them, or by overzealous archaeologists, but by H. Rider Haggard's famous adventure story, which first appeared in 1892. The Bible does mention that Solomon went through enormous amounts of copper. What with all the bronze and "brasen" fixtures that he included in his Temple, the copper must have come from somewhere—and *King Solomon's Mines* makes a wonderful title for a novel. *King Solomon's Mines* takes place in a mythical country in Central Africa, of course, but the tourist who arrives in Israel hoping to see "King Solomon's mines" is not about to be disappointed.

The flaw in Rider Haggard's otherwise impeccable reasoning is that King David had evidently been stockpiling not only brass and iron but gold, silver, and other precious metals during his long career of conquest. The First Book of Chronicles mentions three specific instances of this:

> *And David took the shields of gold that were on the servants of Hadarezer [the king of Zobah], and brought them to Jerusalem.*
>
> *Likewise from Tibhath, and from Chun, cities of Hadarezer, brought David, very much brass, wherewith Solomon made the brasen sea, and the pillars, and the vessels of brass.*
>
> —I CHRONICLES 18:7–8

> *And David prepared iron in abundance for the nails for the doors of the gates, and for the joinings; and brass in abundance without weight [that is, more than could be weighed]; . . .*
>
> —I CHRONICLES 22:3

. . . gold and silver . . . that I have prepared for the holy house,
Even three thousand talents of gold, of the gold of Ophir, and
seven thousand talents of refined silver, to overlay the walls of the
houses withal: . . .

—I Chronicles 29:3–4

David had donated most of the spoils of his own campaigns in Zobah, Moab, Edom, Ammon, Amalek, and Philistia; he also required the tribes of Israel to contribute to this building fund, because it had long since been decided to build a temple to the Lord in Jerusalem. David had already drawn up the plans, down to the last detail, and entrusted them, along with his well-stocked treasury, to Solomon, so that he could bring the work to completion. Because David had already cornered the market in strategic metals, there was no reason for Solomon to go out prospecting.

The land of Ophir, mentioned in the last of these quotations, is the biblical El Dorado. We are told that both King Hiram's (or Hurum's) Phoenicians and Solomon's own treasure fleet made several voyages to Ophir and brought back cargoes of "gold . . . great plenty of almug trees [actually *algum* trees, probably a kind of sandalwood], and precious stones" (I Kings 10:11). Ophir is mentioned only this once in connection with David, and because the Israelites were still hopeless landlubbers in David's time and Ophir was accessible only by sea, it seems likely that this was an interpolation by a later scribe, intended to add greater luster to David's reputation as a treasure finder (or perhaps, by his time, "gold from Ophir" had simply become a stock phrase like "Siberian sable" or "Nova Scotia salmon").

Solomon was the father of the Israelite merchant navy, and the mysterious land of Ophir seems to have become a regular port of call (I Kings 9:28, 10:11; I Chronicles 8:18, 9:10) as long as the Temple was under construction. It was usually the Phoenicians, however, who supplied the vessels, crews, and nautical expertise. On one occasion they came back laden with "four hundred and fifty talents of gold," which is equivalent to something on the order of a million troy ounces, or about a ton of gold! But whether this cargo was acquired by barter or by piracy, and more important, where this golden land of Ophir was actually located, the Bible doesn't say. Adventurers and treasure hunters have looked in all the likely spots—India, the western coast of Arabia, the east coast of Africa, even the Ural Mountains in Russia, far from the shores where the almug tree grows. For a century or so it was thought that the ruined "lost city" of Zimbabwe in Central Africa must have had some connection with the biblical land of Ophir. This impressive fortress complex of round towers and unmortared stone walls inspired some romantic scholarly theories (in addition to H. Rider Haggard's *King Solomon's Mines*). The fortress itself was unmistakably Phoenician in design; gold dust and gold artifacts were found on the site, even a Roman coin in one of the collapsed underground galleries. Finally, in 1950, a fragment of wood from Zimbabwe was tested by the carbon-14 dating method. The results were disappointing; Zimbabwe could not have been built before A.D. 500, at the very earliest, fifteen hundred years too late for Hiram and Solomon.

Zimbabwe was too recent, India too far away, the Urals too cold—but in 1978 American geologists discovered an ancient gold mine in the mountains between Mecca and Medina in Saudi Arabia, and this will have to remain our best guess, at least until another candidate arises. It does seem likely that Ophir was somewhere on the shores of the Red Sea. About fifty years before Solomon's time, the energetic Egyptian queen Hatshepsut, who had recently dispensed with her husband and had herself acclaimed as pharaoh (false beard and all), sent out five thirty-oared galleys to the "land of Punt" to bring back myrrh for her father's tomb at Deir el Bahri.

The garrulous Egyptians decorated the burial chambers of

Deir el Bahri with a very detailed account of this and ten later voyages to the land of Punt, including a list of the ship's captains and a complete cargo manifest: "ivory and ebony, silver, gold, and sandalwood, myrrh and cinnamon, apes and panthers." This sounds remarkably like the land of Ophir, but unfortunately the one detail that Hatshepsut neglected to mention was how to get there. Trade routes were closely guarded secrets in those days, and because Solomon later "made an affinity with Pharaoh" and married an Egyptian princess, it is tempting to speculate that her dowry might have included precise sailing directions for the land of Punt.

At any rate, Solomon was clearly eager to exploit the possibilities of foreign commerce. So far, though, the Israelite maritime experience had been limited to crossing the Red Sea some four hundred years earlier. Rather than trying to turn his shepherd and farmer subjects into sailors overnight, Solomon enlisted the aid of his ally, King Hiram of Tyre. This turned out to be a profitable joint venture. Besides these expeditions to the land of Ophir, the Bible also mentions that Hiram and Solomon outfitted a merchant fleet that made regular voyages across the Mediterranean:

> For the King [Solomon] had at sea a navy of Tharshish with the navy of Hiram: once in three years came the navy of Tharshish, bringing gold, and silver, ivory, and apes, and peacocks.

> —I KINGS 10:22

Unfortunately, it is not clear whether the phrase "navy of Tharshish" refers to the fleet's destination or its cargo: Tharshish (or Tarshish) may have been the Phoenician port of Tarlessus on the Spanish coast (the apes, ivory, and peacocks do suggest a proximity to North Africa). *Tarshish* was also the Phoenician word for "smelter" or "furnace," so the Tarshish ships may have been a fleet of oreboats returning from the copper mines of

Sardinia or Cyprus. The authors of the Bible seem to have used this term with the landsman's typical disdain for the finer points of nautical terminology; sometimes the phrase "ships of Tarshish" seems to mean any coastal trading vessel of the type built by the Phoenicians, as:

> *Jehoshaphat [a later king of Judah] made ships of Tharshish to go to Ophir for gold: but they went not; for the ships were broken at Ezion-geber.*

—I Kings 22:48

Later on, in II Chronicles 20:36, we are told that these same ships were intended "to go to Tarshish," but Ezion-geber was a port built by Solomon on the Gulf of Aqaba, an arm of the Red Sea. This is a moot point, though, because Jehoshaphat's ships were apparently broken up at their moorings by a storm or were simply too unseaworthy to leave port. Solomon at least was sensible enough to rely on Phoenician shipwrights to build his treasure ships and Phoenician convoys to get them safely to Ophir and back. Even the journey to Tarshish (in Spain) was a fairly routine voyage, for the Phoenician galleys, with their square sails and ten banks of oars, had been known to sail as far as Britain. They may even have circumnavigated Africa a few centuries later and (just possibly) have reached Brazil.

The Bible also mentions that Hiram of Tyre sent Solomon a corps of architects and engineers to assist in the building of the Temple. The Tyrian architects already had some experience with the construction of high-rise buildings; Tyre was built on an island that was connected to the mainland by a narrow causeway, and residential space was at a premium—buildings of as many as six stories were not uncommon.

The building of the Temple was a seven-year project, for which Hiram supplied not only the expert manpower but some of the raw materials as well:

*And Hiram sent to Solomon, saying, I have considered the
things which thou sentest to me for: and I will do all thy desire
concerning timber of cedar, and concerning timber of fir [cypress].*

*My servants shall bring them down from Lebanon unto the sea:
and I will convey them by sea in floats unto the place that thou
shalt appoint me. . . .*

—I KINGS 5:8–9

(Today the famous cedars of Lebanon are an endangered species,
but they may still be seen, as the tide of battle permits, in a
national park at the foot of Mount Lebanon [Jebel Machmal],
about a dozen miles from Beirut.)

To use cedar beams for the roof of his Temple was not just
another one of Solomon's extravagances. The pharaohs had
already been importing cedar logs from Lebanon for a good two
thousand years—the Lebanese cedar trade was probably the
oldest systematically organized export business in the history of
the world. The cedar of Lebanon was the only tree growing
between the Nile and the Euphrates that was sturdy enough for
structural beams and timbers.

But in building the Temple other, less practical factors had to
be considered:

*And the [LORD's] house . . . was built of stone made ready
before it was brought thither: so that there was neither hammer
nor axe nor any tool of iron heard in the house. . . .*

—I KINGS 6:7

In other words, the block had to be dressed in the quarries.
This was not in the interests of efficiency or to avoid profaning
the Temple site with an ungodly racket of hammering and
sawing; Solomon is simply following one of the Lord's commandments—the letter at least, if not the spirit—as set forth in
Deuteronomy 27:5–6:

*And there shalt thou build an altar unto the LORD thy God,
an altar of stones: thou shalt not lift up any iron tool upon them.*
   *Thou shalt build the altar of the LORD thy God of whole
[uncut] stones. . . .*

Here, as so often happens, is a fundamental disagreement
between the architect and his client. The Lord has made it clear
that a cairn of rough stones piled together will do perfectly well;
Solomon has something far more elaborate in mind. Certainly a
few conservative members of the priesthood with old-fashioned,
simple tastes were inclined to make an issue of this. In any case
Solomon tactfully agreed to keep all "tools of iron" off the
building site. The scratches and grooves made by Solomon's
quarry men can still be seen on the cliffs below the Old City of
Jerusalem. The Temple itself, however, was completely destroyed, so that not one stone lies upon another, in the biblical
phrase—unless we choose to count, as pious Israelis do, a few of
the hewn stone blocks in the Wailing Wall which are said to
have originally belonged to the Temple.

   We also do not have a very clear idea of what Solomon's
Temple actually looked like. We have no contemporary descriptions of it, except those found in the Bible, and there the text is
very corrupt and the meanings of many of the technical terms
that are used can only be inferred from the context. It is clear,
though, that the Temple was designed and built by Hiram's
Phoenician architects:

*And Solomon's builders and Hiram's builders did hew them
[the foundation stones of the Temple], and the stonesquarers: so
they prepared timber and stones to build the house.*

—I KINGS 5:18

   The "stonesquarers"—master masons, in other words—are
also called "Giblites," and Gebal was another Phoenician city,
better known to us by its Greek name, Byblos. Art historians

have thus felt fairly safe in concluding that Solomon's Temple must have looked something like the temples of El, the supreme god of the Phoenicians and the Canaanites. The trouble is that so far all the temples of El that have been uncovered were built either sometime before or sometime after the tenth century B.C. The ground plan of these temples nevertheless seems to correspond pretty well to the specifications for Solomon's Temple that are given in the Bible, as nearly as we can interpret them.

The Temple dimensions suggested by modern scholars vary between 170 feet by 80 feet and 90 feet by 35 feet; the Bible is not precise on the point. Its walls may have been over 60 feet high, or perhaps less than 40 feet. Archaeologists at least agree that the Temple was surrounded by a walled courtyard, and that it consisted of a porch or vestibule, an outer sanctuary, and an inner sanctuary—the Holy of Holies—which only the high priest was permitted to enter. The "molten sea," which Solomon cast from the "great quantity of brass" that David brought back with the spoils of Zobah, stood in the outer courtyard of the Temple. This was an enormous brass basin, "ten cubits from the one brim to the other: it was round all about, and his [its] height was five cubits: and a line of thirty cubits did compass it round about" (I Kings 7:23). This basin—a "laver," the Bible calls it—probably served as a reservoir for the pure water that was used for the priests' ritual ablutions and for the purification of sacrificial animals.

If the circumference of the "molten sea" was exactly three times its diameter, clearly these figures have been rounded off. Assuming that they are otherwise accurate, the basin's capacity would have been about 15,000 gallons—"two thousand baths," the Bible says, a bath being in this case a Hebrew liquid measure equal to about 7½ gallons—and it would have weighed well over thirty tons. Even if these dimensions are exaggerated by a factor of several cubits, the "molten sea" must have been a genuine showpiece of Phoenician technology. The First Book of Kings mentions that Hiram of Tyre was also responsible for all the "basons" and other vessels in the Temple. Casting a 15,000-gallon caldron in a single piece seems like a formidable, if not impossible, project even for the Phoenicians, but the Bible gives a fairly clear idea how this could have been done: "In the plain of Jordan did the king cast them [the vessels, presumably under Hiram's supervision], in the clay ground between Succoth and Zarthan." In other words, the dried clay of the riverbed was used as a mold into which the molten brass was poured. It would be a simple enough matter to make a few test borings in the riverbed between Succoth and Zarthan to find traces of this enormous, and very messy, undertaking—if we had any idea of where these places actually were.

The "molten sea," like the other wonders of King Solomon's reign, was destroyed when the armies of King Nebuchadnezzar of Babylon sacked Jerusalem about 350 years later:

> . . . the brasen sea that was in the house of the LORD, the Chaldeans brake, and carried all the brass . . . to Babylon.
>
> —JEREMIAH 52:17

However much the authors of First and Second Kings may have exaggerated the minutely described splendors of the Temple—and of Solomon's palace, which is mentioned only in passing but which must have been no less costly and magnificent—it is clear enough that Solomon's treasury was utterly empty by the time these projects were completed. All of King David's legacy had been used up, and even the resourceful Solomon had run out of ways of squeezing taxes and tribute out of his subjects. His chief creditor, Hiram of Tyre, was becoming more and more insistent. Solomon finally came up with a scheme for paying him off that would not involve an actual outlay of cash: he offered to cede twelve cities in Galilee to the kingdom of Tyre. Hiram went out to inspect his new domain and was not pleased with what he saw:

> . . . What cities are these which thou hast given me, my brother? And he called them the land of Cabul ["dirty," "desolate"] unto this day.
> And Hiram sent to the king sixscore talents of gold.

—I KINGS 9:13–14

It seems perfectly natural for Hiram to complain that Solomon was trying to stick him with a tract of worthless desert real estate, but why did he express his displeasure by sending off almost five hundred pounds of gold bullion? Someone has clearly been tampering with this passage—perhaps a scribe who thought that it looked much better for Solomon to receive a princely treasure than a final collection notice. But we can restore the sense here by shifting the tense of the verb: "Hiram *had* sent Solomon 120 talents of gold [in addition to all the materials that were used in the construction of the Temple]." Or, in modern commercial parlance, "Hiram sent Solomon *a bill for* 120 talents of gold"—because he refused to accept the wasteland of Cabul as payment of the original debt.

But of course Solomon's most ambitious venture into the field of international relations was not his partnership with Hiram but his "affinity" with Egypt and his marriage with Pharaoh's daughter—the first of a harem of seven hundred foreign princesses and three hundred concubines, though not all these were purely marriages of diplomatic convenience. The splendid house that Solomon built for his first wife, with a porch of cedar beams "like unto his own," is mentioned several times in the First Book of Kings. At one point we are told that:

> . . . Pharaoh's daughter came up out of the city of David unto her house which Solomon had built for her: then did he build Millo.

—I KINGS 9:24

(Millo, by the way—which literally means "the filling in"—was a ring of fortifications that ran around the original walls of the city of Jerusalem.) It was not simply out of diplomatic courtesy that Solomon maintained a separate establishment for his first wife, evidently:

> *But King Solomon loved many strange [that is, foreign] women, together with the daughter of Pharaoh, women of the Moabites, Ammonites, Edomites, Zidonians, and Hittites.*
>
> —I KINGS 11:1

Solomon's weakness for these exotic beauties, and for their pagan gods as well, scandalized the priests of Israel, for this sort of dalliance was explicitly forbidden by the laws of Moses:

> *Neither shall he [the king] multiply wives to himself, that his heart turn not away: neither shall he greatly multiply to himself silver and gold.*
>
> —DEUTERONOMY 17:17

Even if we decide to reduce the number of Solomon's wives by the usual factor of ten, this ambiguous commentary from a nineteenth-century German encyclopedia certainly seems to be accurate:

> *As he grew older, Solomon was so worn down by his foreign wives that he was no longer free to practice his religion as he chose; rather, he allowed himself to be seduced into joining them in the practice of their heathen rites.*
>
> —Brockhaus-Bilderlexikon, 1841

"Worn down" presumably refers to the gradual erosion of his willpower rather than just physical exhaustion, but in either case, the point is well taken.

The most famous of these distinguished foreigners to arrive at

189

Solomon's court was the Queen of Sheba. Her visit was not the ceremonial prelude to another royal wedding—she returned to her own country in fairly short order—and her purpose in coming to Jerusalem seems rather mysterious. The Bible says that she had simply heard of Solomon from afar and was eager to test his wisdom with "hard questions." Later tradition has turned this brief encounter into one of the great romances of ancient times, inspired no doubt by the sultry *Arabian Nights* atmosphere of the entire episode and such vaguely suggestive observations on the part of its authors as:

> . . . *she communed with him of all that was in her heart.*

> —I KINGS 10:2

and

> . . . *Solomon gave unto the queen of Sheba all her desire, whatsoever she asked.* . . .

> —I KINGS 10:13

The former emperors of Ethiopia, most notably Haile Selassie, "the Lion of Judah," claimed to be descended from the son of Solomon and Sheba (her name, according to Arab folklore, was Bilkis). And some writers have imagined that the "black but comely" beauty in the Song of Solomon was none other than the Queen of Sheba, so there may be something in this after all.

Whatever the reason, the Queen of Sheba traveled over one thousand miles to visit King Solomon. Her kingdom, which modern scholars prefer to call Saba, was in present-day North Yemen, at the southeastern tip of the Arabian Peninsula. Archaeologists in this century have uncovered many impressive relics of ancient Saba; then, for a time, no more light was shed on the Sabaeans because the Yemeni government was not well disposed toward foreign visitors, and more than one team of

190

archaeologists had had to leave the country in a hurry to avoid being shot as spies. Only recently has excavation begun again. (For our immediate purposes, this lapse is no great loss, because the written inscriptions on the Sabaeans seem to go back only to about 800 B.C., at least a century after the Queen of Sheba's visit to Solomon.)

The Bible's brief description of the queen's journey contains quite a bit of intriguing information:

> *And she came to Jerusalem with a very great train, with camels that bare spices, and very much gold, and precious stones . . .*

> —I KINGS 10:2

The "very great train" seems likely enough, for Saba was a prosperous country, the terminus of the main trade route from India and the Orient. The primary local products were "balm" and "spices"—frankincense, in other words, which was used in virtually every temple in the ancient Near East to mask the stench of animal sacrifices on the altar. (A brief digression: The use of incense was forbidden in the early Christian church because of its obvious pagan associations, and then revived in the Middle Ages, because the ambient aromas in a medieval cathedral must have been almost overwhelming.)

A camel caravan would have been the only practical way for the queen and her retinue to cross the long stretches of desert between Yemen and Jerusalem. The Sabaeans were great camel breeders and camel trainers, because these animals were essential to the conduct of their extensive overland trade with the countries of the eastern Mediterranean. Likely the Queen of Sheba had some other purpose in mind besides an exchange of courtesies and "hard questions." One possible explanation might be that her visit to Jerusalem was more of an economic summit meeting than a romantic tryst, and that the provocative phrase "Solomon gave unto the Queen of Sheba all her desire" was the

191

biblical equivalent of a joint communiqué expressing both parties' satisfaction at the conclusion of a mutually beneficial trade pact.

Despite all these secular distractions, Solomon, along with David, continued to be regarded as the living embodiment of the faith of the Old Testament, even in the late apocryphal books of Ecclesiasticus (not to be confused with Ecclesiastes) and the Wisdom of Solomon, which was composed during the last few centuries before Jesus. Solomon was also supposed to have been the author of some works less edifying than the Song of Solomon and Ecclesiastes. The so-called Testament of Solomon and Solomon's Seventh Seal, which mail-order publishing houses and occult bookstores still occasionally offer for sale, are, like the "lost books of Moses," forgeries concocted by early medieval alchemists, numerologists, cabalists, and other dabblers in the black arts and have long since been discredited.

Until the nineteenth century the biblical claim that Solomon "spake three thousand proverbs: and his songs were a thousand and five" was also taken at face value. Today, though we are inclined to be more skeptical, it also seems clear that Solomon's real cultural legacy was far greater than that. Thanks to him, the poetry and philosophy of other Near Eastern cultures were incorporated into the Bible once again and, as in the past, often enriched with a new spiritual significance. Solomon was the first to have a genuine, unprejudiced appreciation of the cultural achievements of Israel's neighbors, and if the royal road to cultural enlightenment also led straight to the harem, that is only a tribute to Solomon's discernment in choosing his wives. It also speaks well for Solomon that his eagerness to acquire the spiritual treasures of "the nations" was dictated simply by personal taste, not by any desire to imitate or impress—the upstart ruler's usual motive in picking up a smattering of foreign culture.

Although Solomon's wisdom is often referred to in the First Book of Kings and elsewhere, we are given only one specific example of a Solomonic judgment in an actual civil case. Two harlots appear before the king, each claiming that the other's child "died in the night: because she overlaid [smothered] it," each claiming to be the mother of the surviving child. Solomon orders that the child be divided in half, with a sword, to satisfy both claimants. The harlot who cries out, "Give her the living child, and in no wise slay it," is awarded custody. "She is the mother thereof."

A different aspect of daily life at Solomon's court is illustrated by the following verses from First Kings:

> *And Solomon's provision for one day was thirty measures [kor]*
> *of fine flour, and threescore measures of meal,*
> *Ten fat oxen, and twenty oxen out of the pastures, and an*
> *hundred sheep, beside harts, and roebucks, and fallow deer, and*
> *fatted foul.*
>
> —I KINGS 4:22–23

A *kor* was about eight bushels, by the way, and even including the thousand wives and concubines, plus an unspecified number of courtiers and hangers-on, we have to conclude that Solomon set an admirably high standard of conspicuous consumption.

In spite (or more probably because) of this largess, Solomon's empire was about to crumble by the end of his life. The priests condemned him for his indulgent interest in foreign cults. Farmers and artisans hated him as a tax-gouger and an oppressive taskmaster. His viceroys had set themselves up as independent princelings, happily plundering the public treasury or plotting against their enfeebled monarch. After decades of imperial peace, the army was discontented and bored by monotonous garrison life. And the king's vassals and tributaries in neighboring countries, who were certainly aware of all this, saw no reason to maintain even the pretense of allegiance to a ruler who had lost the allegiance of his subjects.

It does say a great deal for Solomon's prestige that he was not dethroned or assassinated on the spot, like so many of his successors. His chief political rival, Jeroboam, who later proclaimed himself king of the breakaway state of Israel, conducted his intrigues from the safety of his Egyptian exile, and all the forces of confusion and chaos that were shortly to overwhelm Solomon's empire were unleashed only at the moment of his death.

> . . . but the LORD was not in the fire: and after
> the fire a still small voice.

> —I KINGS 19:12

The Second Book of Kings: The Beginning of the End

Scarcely any of Solomon's successors died in their beds; most of them were murdered or killed in battle. After the eleventh chapter of the First Book of Kings—which ends with the death of Solomon—through the end of Second Kings we are thrown back into a primitive world of blood feuds and tribal violence.

While Solomon's heirs squabbled over their inheritance of Judah, the ten northern tribes chose their own king and established a new capital at Samaria. Five kings reigned over the northern kingdom of Israel in a space of ten years; all but one was assassinated.

About the only one of those early kings who is not a complete nonentity was Omri, a veteran warrior who was acclaimed king by the army after the previous king had been assassinated and his successor had been discarded after reigning a mere seven days. The Bible says very little about him, except that he "did worse than all that were before him"—that is, he tolerated or even encouraged the worship of pagan gods. Omri founded the Israelite capital of Samaria, and he was evidently a good enough tactician to pick out a site that dominated the surrounding plain and could easily be defended against a far superior force. Omri's fortifications at Samaria, the ruins of which can still be seen, later proved strong enough to withstand a siege of thirty years, though the Bible dismisses all this with the observation that "he bought the hill Samaria . . . for two talents of silver, and built on the hill." He apparently made more of an impression on his contemporaries than on the authors of the Old Testament, because the Assyrian chronicles were still referring to Israel as "the land of Omri" 150 years later, and he was the only one of those ephemeral early kings who succeeded in founding a dynasty.

The rest of the First Book of Kings deals primarily with the reign of Omri's son, Ahab. Here, fortunately, the dramatic interest picks up quite a bit, not so much because of Ahab himself as because the biblical account of his reign is dominated by two powerful, strong-willed personalities: Queen Jezebel, the daughter of the king of Tyre and Sidon, and Elijah, the greatest of the prophets of the Lord since Samuel.

Ahab, like his predecessors, is made out to be a pretty despicable character, completely overawed by his villainous consort, though he comes close to redeeming himself (in the eyes of the reader, perhaps, if not the authors) by dying bravely in battle against the Arameans ("the Syrians," the Bible calls them). Before the battle is joined, however, he makes a strange suggestion to his ally, the king of Judah:

> . . . I will disguise myself, and enter into the battle; put thou on my robes. . . .
>
> —I KINGS 22:30

This sounds like malingering, pure and simple; but what Ahab apparently has in mind is a tactical ruse: the Judean troops will bear the brunt of the Aramean first wave while Ahab holds his troops in reserve for a flanking attack when the Aramean charge is spent. This is what happens at any rate. When Ahab sees the allied troops wavering, he presses forward in his chariot to rally them and is hit by an Aramean arrow that penetrates the joints of his armor—a very lucky shot, or as the Bible calls it, "a bow drawn at a venture."

Ahab orders his charioteer to take him back behind the lines to safety, and "the battle increased." We can imagine the dispirited Israelites beginning to give ground, the Arameans regrouping for their final assault. At this point Ahab's valor gets the better of his discretion. Choosing to ignore the fact that jolting along over rough ground with an arrowhead in his belly is likely to prove both excruciating and fatal, he wheels around, and propped up by his charioteer and perhaps with the reins lashed around his body ("stayed up in his chariot," the Bible says), he leads a counterattack against the Arameans.

"By even," when the battle breaks off, the Arameans are in retreat, the armies are dispersing, and Ahab is dead in a pool of blood on the floor of his chariot. The wicked King Ahab turns out to be a hero after all—and in good company, for the same heroic feat later turns up in the Spanish chivalric epic *El Cid*, as well as in several Scottish ballads in which the wounded warrior stoically proclaims: "I'le lay me doune and bleed awhile, and then I'le rise and ffight agayne."

After Ahab's body is brought back to Jerusalem,

> . . . *[they] washed the chariot in the pool of Samaria; and the dogs licked up his blood; and they washed his armour.* . . .

—I KINGS 22:38

This last phrase is another of the King James translators' attempts to make sense of a passage that (until recently) was totally incomprehensible. Luther's literal translation—"and

196

young girls washed themselves in his blood"—turns out to be correct. This does not refer to some exotic Oriental perversion but to a ritual of the cult of Baal in which temple prostitutes were sprinkled with (or washed themselves in) the blood of a sacrificial animal. Elijah has already foretold that dogs will lick Ahab's blood; the devotees of Baal apparently interpreted Ahab's death as a sacrifice to a rival god.

Queen Jezebel, whose father was a priest of Baal, was the great patroness of his cult in Israel, and thus the mortal enemy of the prophet Elijah and Elisha, his disciple. Not surprisingly, the authors of the Books of Kings have almost nothing good to say about Jezebel, though she seems to have been a remarkable woman: intelligent, decisive, and god-fearing (the wrong god, unfortunately). She had persuaded Ahab to build a temple to Baal in Samaria, and the cult of Baal remained the state religion of Israel throughout most of her long reign. Even though she relentlessly persecuted the prophets of Jahweh, the pious authors of the Old Testament still allowed her, as they did Ahab, a final moment of dignity and heroism on the day of her death. Here, she gets word of the approach of King Jehu, a ferocious partisan of Elijah and his God:

> And when Jehu was come to Jezreel, Jezebel heard of it; and she painted her face, and tired [dressed] her head, and looked out at a window.
>
> —II Kings 9:30

She calmly prepares herself for death, and when Jehu finally appears at the palace gate, she greets him with regal disdain:

> Had Zimri peace, who slew his master?
>
> —II Kings 9:31

(Zimri was the regicide who ruled for seven days before Omri took the throne, and his name had become a byword for treachery and bad faith.)

In other words, Jezebel is deliberately goading this hot-tempered religious fanatic into killing her on the spot. Jehu calls out to "two or three [of her] eunuchs" to throw her out the window, which they do, "and he trode her under foot. And when he was come in, he did eat and drink." (While Jehu is inside the palace at his victory feast, Jezebel's body is eaten by dogs, thus fulfilling another of Elijah's prophecies.)

This was a holy war, waged with casual brutality on both sides, and Elijah's campaign against "idolatry" and "witchcraft" was no less relentless than Jezebel's attempt to exterminate the prophets of Yahweh. The name Elijah means "Yahweh is my God," which just about says it all.

Under powerful monarchs like David and Solomon, the prophets had retreated into the background, but in the anarchic days of the two kingdoms they came back into their own, not only as the messengers of God's word but as his champion in the bloody arena of politics. Elijah was a master of what is sometimes called "the propaganda of the deed"—a kind of holy terrorist, in other words. On one occasion he publicly challenged the prophets of Baal to prepare a sacrifice to their god while he prepared a sacrifice to Yahweh on an adjacent altar. When Elijah's sacrifice was consumed by fire from heaven, the onlookers were convinced that Yahweh was the one true God, and they fell upon the prophets of Baal (with some encouragement from Elijah) and massacred them.

To restore the Israelites' respect for the covenant and the laws of Moses that they have forsaken, Elijah makes a symbolic journey to Mount Sinai (here called Horeb), where Moses received the Law. Elijah makes his way to Mount Horeb as a lonely fugitive, not with great fanfare and "in the sight of the people" as Moses did. But the fact that Elijah stands on the spot where Moses stood and spoke with God cannot have failed to make a certain impression:

And, behold, the LORD *passed by, and a great and strong wind rent the mountains, and brake in pieces the rocks before the* LORD; *but the* LORD *was not in the wind: and after the wind an earthquake; but the* LORD *was not in the earthquake:*

And after the earthquake a fire; but the LORD *was not in the fire: and after the fire a still small voice.*

And it was so, when Elijah heard it, that he wrapped his face in his mantle, and went out, and stood in the entering in of the cave.

—I KINGS 19:11–13

Powerful words. Here the reader was expected to pause and reflect for a moment, and we are clearly in the presence not just of the Lord but of great literature as well. What is especially striking about this passage is how far the Israelite conception of their God has evolved from the earlier nature gods (like Baal) or even the God of Moses, who appears on Mount Sinai in a tremendous cloud of fire and smoke. The God of Elijah, whose name is so holy that it cannot be pronounced and whose form cannot be captured in any graven image, still has the power to command these phenomena, of course, but he is not *in* them. He is omnipresent, and he may even choose to manifest himself in the softest whisper, the "still small voice."

Elijah's biography was first written down only fifty years after his death, and surprisingly many parallels are found between the lives of the prophet and his successor, Elisha, and the life of Jesus as described in the New Testament: the miracles, the way in which Elijah chooses his disciple, and particularly his final ascension into heaven:

. . . behold, there appeared a chariot of fire, and horses of fire, and parted them both [Elijah and Elisha] asunder; and Elijah went up by a whirlwind into heaven.

—II KINGS 2:11

199

Elijah and Moses are the only Old Testament prophets who are mentioned by name (and who actually make an appearance) in the New Testament: Matthew describes how the disciples saw Jesus on a mountaintop conversing with Elijah and Moses, a miraculous event that is referred to as the Transfiguration.

Elijah comes upon Elisha while he is plowing his father's fields and calls him as his disciple with a familiar gesture:

> . . . *and Elijah passed by him, and cast his mantle upon him.*

> —I KINGS 19:19

As we recall from the Book of Ruth, this means that Elijah is putting the younger man under his protection—adopting him, in effect. This explains his admonition to Elisha when he asks permission to run back and kiss his parents good-bye (which is a little garbled in the King James version):

> . . . *Go back again [that is, "Go, but come back quickly!"]: for what have I done to thee?*

> —I KINGS 19:20

Elijah has cast his mantle over Elisha, and now the disciple must leave his father's house to follow his master.

The miracles worked by Elisha have a familiar ring to them (even to those of us who are not so well versed in the Old Testament):

Elisha walked on water—rather, he parted the waters of the Jordan and walked across the riverbed, dry-shod . . .
He made tainted water fit to drink . . .
He replenished a poor widow's oil jar . . .
He raised her son from the dead . . .
He fed a multitude with only twenty loaves . . .
He healed a leper . . .
He caused "iron to swim"—to float, in other words . . .

ADAM AND EVE DRIVEN OUT OF THE GARDEN OF EDEN
(*From the Doré Bible*)

THE TOWER OF BABEL (*From the Doré Bible*)

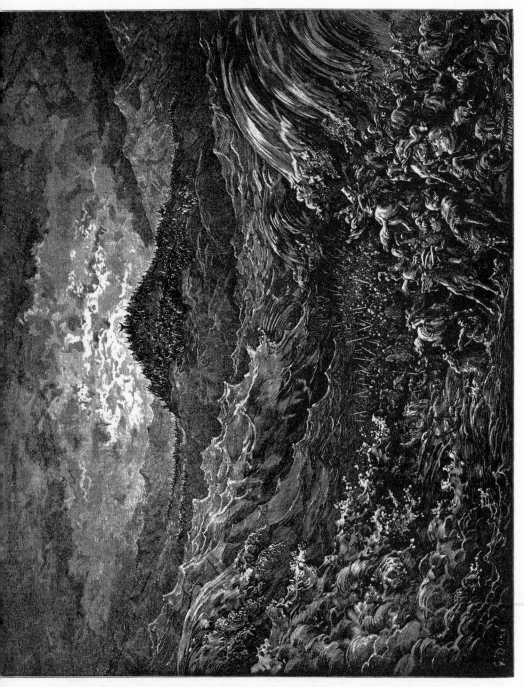

THE WATERS OVERWHELMING THE EGYPTIAN CHARIOTS
DURING THE EXODUS (*From the Doré Bible*)

JAEL KILLING SISERA WITH A TENT STAKE (*From the Doré Bible*)

JOSEPH INTERPRETING PHARAOH'S DREAM (*From the Doré Bible*)

THE ANGEL DESTROYING SENNACHERIB'S ARMY (*From the Doré Bible*)

ESTHER ACCUSING HAMAN (*From the Doré Bible*)

ELEAZAR SLAYING THE ELEPHANT (*From the Doré Bible*)

THE NATIVITY (*From the Doré Bible*)

THE APOSTLES PREACHING THE GOSPEL (*From the Doré Bible*)

MAPS

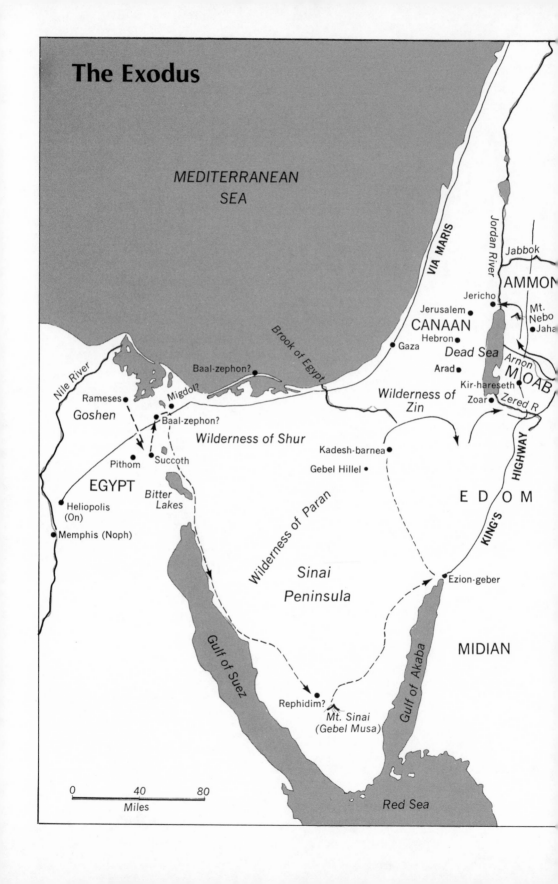

The Exodus

MEDITERRANEAN
SEA

Nile River

Brook of Egypt

Baal-zephon? •

Rameses •

Goshen

Migdol?

Baal-zephon? •

Succoth

Pithom •

EGYPT

*Bitter
Lakes*

Heliopolis
(On) •

Memphis (Noph) •

Wilderness of Shur

Kadesh-barnea •

Gebel Hillel •

Wilderness of Paran

*Sinai
Peninsula*

Rephidim? •

Mt. Sinai
(Gebel Musa)

VIA MARIS

Jordan River

Jabbok

AMMON

Jericho •

Jerusalem •

CANAAN

Hebron •

• Gaza

Dead Sea

Arad •

*Wilderness of
Zin*

Kir-hareseth •

Zoar •

Arnon

MOAB

Zered R.

Mt.
Nebo
Jaha

EDOM

*KING'S
HIGHWAY*

Ezion-geber •

Gulf of Suez

Gulf of Akaba

MIDIAN

Red Sea

0   40   80
Miles

Conquest of Canaan

0   25   50
Miles

MEDITERRANEAN

SEA

Kishon River

Damascus

Dan

Arameans

Lake Huleh

Tyre

Hazor

Merom

Sea of Galilee

BASHAN

Achshaph   Hamath

Aphek

Mt. Tabor

Plain of Esdraelon

Ramoth-gilead

Dor   Megiddo

Jezreel   Valley of Jezreel

Beth-shean

Mt. Gilboa

Jabesh-gilead

Taanach

Bezek

GILEAD

Jordan River

Tirzah

Mt. Ebal

Shechem

Mahanaim

Mt. Gerizim

C   A   N   A   A   N

VIA MARIS

Aijalon River

Aphek

Shiloh

AMMON

Joppa

Beth-horon

Bethel

Gilgal?

Rabbah

Mispeh

Ai

Gibeon

Michmash

Jericho

Gibeah

Ashdod

Gezer

Jerusalem

Mt. Nebo

Ekron

Gath

Bethlehem

Philistines

Ashkelon

Jarmuth

Gaza

Eglon   Lachish

Hebron

En-gedi

Dibon

Debir

Gerar   Ziklag

MOAB

Arad

Beersheba

Kir-hareseth

KING'S HIGHWAY

Zoar

EDOM

AMALEK

Kadesh-barnea

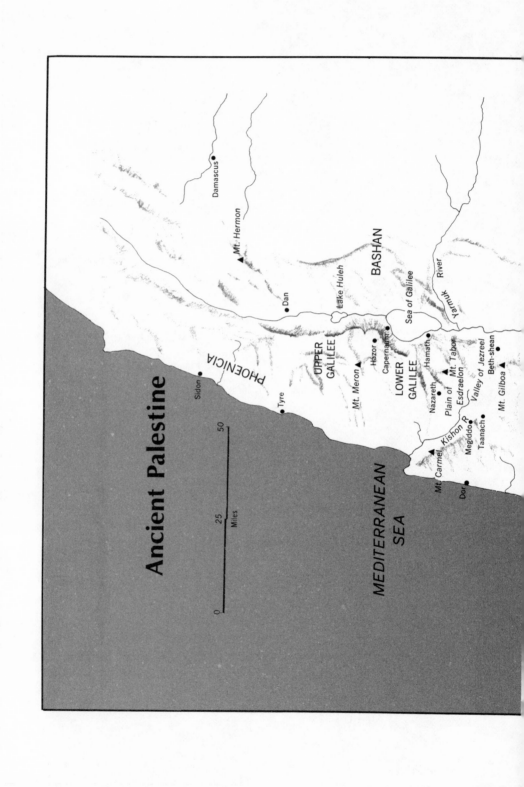

Ancient Palestine

0   25   50
Miles

MEDITERRANEAN
SEA

PHOENICIA

Sidon

Tyre

Damascus

Mt. Hermon

Dan

Lake Huleh

BASHAN

Sea of Galilee

Yarmuk River

UPPER
GALILEE

Mt. Meron

Hazor

Capernaum

LOWER
GALILEE

Hamath

Nazareth
Mt. Tabor
Plain of
Esdraelon
Valley of Jezreel
Beth-shean
Mt. Gilboa

Kishon R.

Mt. Carmel
Megiddo
Taanach

Dor

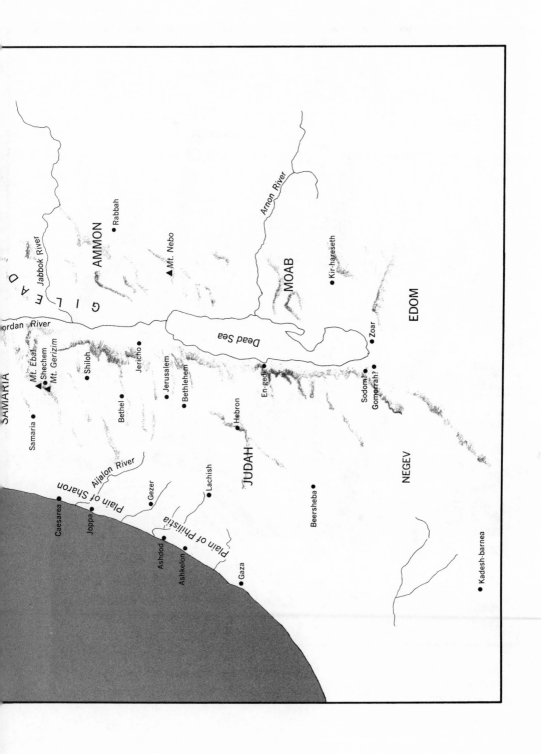

SAMARIA

Mt. Ebal
Shechem
Mt. Gerizim

Samaria •

Bethel •

Shiloh •

Jericho •

Jerusalem •
Bethlehem •

Hebron •

JUDAH

Lachish •

Gezer •

Caesarea •

Joppa •

Plain of Sharon

Ashdod •
Ashkelon •

Plain of Philistia

Gaza •

Beersheba •

NEGEV

Kadesh-barnea •

En-gedi •

Sodom? •
Gomorrah? •

Zoar •

Dead Sea

Jordan River

Jabbok River

G I L E A D

AMMON

Rabbah •

Mt. Nebo

Arnon River

MOAB

Kir-hareseth •

EDOM

Aijalon River

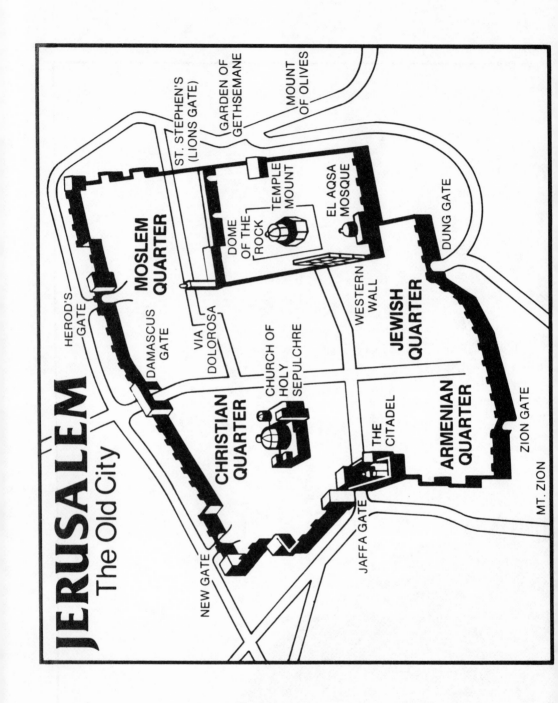

JERUSALEM
The Old City

MOSLEM QUARTER

CHRISTIAN QUARTER

JEWISH QUARTER

ARMENIAN QUARTER

ST. STEPHEN'S (LIONS GATE)

GARDEN OF GETHSEMANE

MOUNT OF OLIVES

TEMPLE MOUNT

DOME OF THE ROCK

EL AQSA MOSQUE

DUNG GATE

HEROD'S GATE

DAMASCUS GATE

VIA DOLOROSA

WESTERN WALL

CHURCH OF HOLY SEPULCHRE

THE CITADEL

NEW GATE

JAFFA GATE

ZION GATE

MT. ZION

All these sound very much like the miracles attributed to Jesus in the New Testament (with perhaps a faint echo of Moses as well). And, as with many of the Christian saints, Elisha's healing ministry continued even after his death; miracles were later reported at the site of his tomb:

> And Elisha died, and they buried him. And the bands of the Moabites invaded the land at the coming in of the year.
>
> And it came to pass, as they were burying a man, that, behold, they spied a band of men [Moabites]; and they cast the man into the sepulchre of Elisha: and when the man was let down, and touched the bones of Elisha, he revived, and stood up on his feet.
>
> —II KINGS 13:20–21

But like his master, Elisha is as much a political strategist as a miracle worker. He continued Elijah's holy war to restore the worship of Jahweh (and exterminate the worshipers of Baal), and it was Elisha who chose Jehu to carry out the second part of this program. (Elijah had been ordered by the Lord on Mount Horeb to anoint Jehu king of Israel, but he neglected to do so for reasons that are not explained.) In this case Elisha chooses to work from behind the scenes; he sends a stand-in, "one of the sons of the prophets," to take Jehu "into the inner chamber" of his house, where he pours the oil on Jehu's forehead and gives him his marching orders—"Thou shalt smite the house of Ahab"—in secret.

It is easy enough to see why the prophets might have been reluctant to entrust the kingdom to a bloodstained ruffian like Jehu (though he is best remembered as a daredevil chariot driver; as the Hebrew text says, "he driveth like a madman"). As it turns out, though, Jehu wins most of his great victories by treachery— "subtilty," the King James calls it. He kills Ahab's son, King Joram, when Joram comes out of his fortress to parley with him. He invites the worshipers of Baal to an enormous sacrificial feast

217

and then orders his troops, "Go in, and slay them; let none come forth." He succeeds in wiping out all of Ahab's family, ending with Jezebel, and most of the royal house of Judah, who had consorted with Ahab, Joram, and Jezebel. One writer has described Jehu as "the instrument of a special purpose," and if so, admittedly he was an especially blunt instrument.

After the death of Elisha, the monotonous procession of "wicked kings" that "did evil in the sight of the Lord" begins all over again. Israel and Judah are in total chaos and obviously ripe for conquest; the only questions are when, and by whom?

As it happens, both kingdoms are destroyed by the same external enemy: the Assyrians. The northern kingdom of Israel, which borders directly on the Assyrian Empire, is the first to fall. Judah manages to hold out for another two hundred years. The siege and destruction of Samaria, the northern capital, are naturally viewed by the authors of the Second Book of Kings as God's judgment on its inhabitants, because they have failed to keep his commandments and have given themselves up to idolatry, as well as to all manner of witchcraft and sorcery.

Assyria, the realm of Assur, was an enemy the Israelites had not encountered before. Until recently it was thought that the original Assyrian state was a relatively small tract of the northern Mesopotamian plain, roughly between the cities of Assur and Nineveh. In 1979, when archaeologists at the University of Tübingen published their translation of 124 newly discovered cuneiform tablets, it became clear that the southern boundary of this kingdom was far to the south, on the river Khabur, a tributary of the Euphrates. In other words, the Assyrian kingdom was almost twice as big as had previously been thought. This question is somewhat academic, though, because a later dynasty of aggressive Assyrian monarchs embarked on an ambitious program of conquest that eventually overwhelmed the entire Fertile Crescent.

The tightly organized Assyrian armies devised new tactics and new weapons of war that assured their virtual invincibility for several hundred years. A series of Assyrian bas-reliefs in the British Museum illustrates in vivid detail the battles and siege operations which brought this great Assyrian empire into being.

First, the Assyrian sappers established a bridgehead. They constructed a pontoon bridge of inflated hides so that the heavy equipment—the enormous timbers for the siege towers—could be brought across without bogging down on the sandy banks of the river. These siege towers were assembled overnight and wheeled into position against the enemy fortifications; now, the Assyrian archers posted in the upper galleries could rake the enemy ramparts with a concentrated field of fire.

Iron-shod battering rams swung from chains attached to the lower crossbeams of this fighting platform. As the battering rams were brought into play against the city wall, sappers armed with wet hides tried to extinguish the firebrands and other incendiary devices that the enemy had flung down on the timbers of the siege tower.

Catapults laid down an accurate barrage of stone projectiles to drive the defenders from their ramparts before the assault troops advanced with scaling ladders to storm the city walls.

When a gate was successfully stormed or a wall breached, the cavalry were brought up for the final assault. The cumbersome chariots of former times had been replaced by mounted horsemen, who could maneuver much more easily in the narrow, barricaded streets. Finally, after the city capitulated, scribes with tablets and styluses made a careful inventory of the severed heads of the defenders, which were piled in heaps outside the walls.

One thing that we are not told by the Assyrian battle reliefs and inscriptions is how such formidable armies could be provisioned and supplied with fresh water in the field. When King Jehoahaz, routed by the Arameans, was left with "but fifty horsemen, and ten chariots, and ten thousand footmen," even such a skeleton force would still go through at least six tons of

219

food and forage per day. Because no supply trains or quartermasters followed the armies on their campaigns, the soldiers must have lived off the fields, pastures, and granaries of the surrounding countryside. And if the supply problem was acute for an invading army in the field, we can imagine how much worse things must have been for the defenders of a beleaguered city.

When the Arameans attacked Samaria in the time of Elisha, the Bible reports that

> . . . they besieged it, until an ass's head was sold for fourscore pieces of silver, and the fourth part of a cab [half a pint] of dove's dung for five pieces of silver.
>
> —II KINGS 6:25

In King Solomon's time 150 silver shekels was the price of a purebred Egyptian war-horse. In the black market of besieged Samaria it cost 85 shekels for a few shreds of carrion and a handful of weeds (which is what "dove's dung" seems to have been). As if that weren't bad enough, the ass was an unclean animal whose flesh was forbidden by the laws of Moses. The Samaritans, however, long past caring about such things, had even resorted to cannibalism. Another grisly anecdote from the same passage—a kind of ghoulish parody of the judgment of Solomon—makes this all too clear: A woman appeals to the king against her neighbor, who has tricked her into killing and cooking her son. But she complains: "I said unto her on the next day, Give thy son, that we may eat him: and she hath hid her son" (II Kings 6:29).

The Arameans finally raised the siege and went home, and it was the Assyrians who successfully stormed Omri's supposedly impregnable fortress in 721 B.C. The inhabitants of Samaria were driven into captivity, and the city was resettled by foreign captives from Babylon and elsewhere in the Assyrian Empire. The exiles who eventually returned to Samaria over the course of the next few centuries were no longer regarded by their southern compatriots as true Israelites at all, but as mongrels and outcasts. This is the original point of the parable of the Good Samaritan in the New Testament and why the Samaritan woman who meets Jesus at the well asks him sardonically:

> . . . *How is it that thou, being a Jew, askest drink of me, which am a woman of Samaria? for the Jews have no dealings with the Samaritans.*

> —JOHN 4:9

The kingdom of Judah had become a tributary state of the Assyrians, but twenty years later King Hezekiah of Judah entered into a secret diplomatic pact with two other restive vassals of Assyria, the pharaoh of Egypt and the king of Babylon, and raised the standard of rebellion. Hezekiah knew well enough that he would not be able to meet the Assyrians in open battle and that Jerusalem would have to withstand a siege. He set his engineers the task of digging a tunnel to ensure a supply of fresh water from the spring of Gihon outside the city walls.

The tunnel of Siloam, almost eighteen hundred feet long, was cut from both ends simultaneously and with such precision that the two work gangs met underground at the appointed spot, even though the shaft describes a shallow curve with a sharp bend in the middle (so designed, according to legend, to avoid the sepulchers of David and Solomon, though so far archaeologists have not found any evidence of this). Though the famous inscription which describes the "boring through" of the tunnel "one hundred cubits below the ground" was discovered, accidentally, only in 1881, the Bible does mention that Hezekiah diverted the spring of Gihon and "made a pool, and a conduit, and brought water into the city" (II Kings 20:20).

Hezekiah's rebellion against the Assyrians did not go nearly so smoothly. The Egyptians and the Babylonians proved to be no help at all, and the famous (or notorious) Assyrian king Sennacherib invaded Judah, overran forty-six walled towns, and despoiled the Judean stronghold of Lachish. (This was evidently not the worst tribulation the ancient city would have to endure; archaeologists have discovered mass graves containing over two thousand charred skeletons from a later level of occupation.)

At this point Hezekiah relents and offers to pay Sennacherib any amount of tribute he cares to suggest. Sennacherib names his terms—three hundred talents of gold and thirty talents of silver:

> And Hezekiah gave him all the silver that was found in the house of the LORD, and in the treasures of the king's house.
> At that time did Hezekiah cut off the gold from the doors of the temple . . . and from the pillars which Hezekiah . . . had overlaid, and gave it to the king of Assyria.

—II KINGS 18:15–16

Nevertheless, Sennacherib decides to send his armies against Jerusalem. Naturally he wants to spare himself the trouble of taking the city by storm, if the same results can be achieved by other means. Three of Sennacherib's captains arrive, with a large army at their backs, and begin to parley with three officers of Hezekiah's household. First, they point out, quite accurately, that as far as Pharaoh is concerned, "thou trustest upon the staff of this bruised reed . . . on which if a man lean, it will go into his hand, and pierce it . . ." Then they make a decisive offer that shows Hezekiah's men that they are very well informed about their master's depleted order of battle:

> . . . give pledges to my lord the king of Assyria, and I will deliver thee two thousand horses, if thou be able on thy part to set riders upon them.

—II KINGS 18:23

This is just verbal sparring so far. The Assyrians know perfectly well that the Judeans are not about to be intimidated by unctuous threats, or by Sennacherib's atrocities or his monstrous engines of war. The Judeans are convinced that Jahweh will not abandon them as their allies have done, and that they have nothing to fear from the Assyrians as long as they are strong in their faith. The Assyrian spokesman very shrewdly tries to turn this conviction to his own advantage:

> *Am I now come up without the* LORD *against this place to destroy it? The* LORD *said to me, Go up against this land, and destroy it.*

> —II KINGS 18:25

This shows how well the Assyrian—his name is Rabshakeh, by the way—really understands the Judean mentality and the Jewish view of history: there would clearly be no point in resisting the Assyrians if they have been sent by God to scourge the people for their sins. This sort of inflammatory talk is bound to have an effect, if not on Hezekiah's officers, then certainly on the people of the city, who have been listening intently to the Assyrian envoys harangue from the city walls.

> *Then said [Hezekiah's officers] . . . Speak, I pray thee, to thy servants in the Syrian language [Aramaic]; for we understand it: and talk not with us in the Jews' language in the ears of the people that are on the wall.*

> —II KINGS 18:26

This provides the perfect opening for Rabshakeh's next remarks. He points out, quite graphically, that he has not been sent to talk to Hezekiah and his household, but to the people of Jerusalem, for it is they who will have to endure the worst horrors of the siege:

Hath my master sent me to thy master, and to thee, to speak
these words? hath he not sent me to the men which sit on the
wall, that they may eat their own dung, and drink their own piss
with you?

—II KINGS 18:27

The Assyrians have obviously mastered all the classical
propaganda openings: your leaders have betrayed you, Rabshakeh tells the people of Jerusalem, it is you who will suffer for
their folly, and (an inspired bit of theological brainwashing) even
your God has abandoned you, and in any case, no other god has
ever saved his people from the armies of Sennacherib. This must
have been the normal prelude to a siege, because bas-reliefs from
Nineveh show Assyrian warriors with speaking tubes, shaped
exactly like modern carnival barker's megaphones, no doubt
broadcasting the same sort of threats and blandishments that
Rabshakeh did before the walls of Jerusalem:

Let not Hezekiah deceive you: for he shall not be able to deliver
you out of his [Sennacherib's] hand . . .
Make an agreement with me by a present [a gift of tribute],
and come out to me, and then eat ye every man of his own vine,
and every one of his fig tree, and drink ye every one the waters of
his cistern: . . .

—II KINGS 18:29,31

No question of Hezekiah's jamming seditious enemy broad-
casts or confiscating private receiving sets; he simply instructs his
people to pay no attention:

But the people held their peace, and answered him not a word:
for the king's commandment was, saying, Answer him not.

—II KINGS 18:36

The end of the story is something of an anticlimax. Sennacherib raises the siege, and Hezekiah's trust in the Lord is finally rewarded—though the Bible's explanation of how this came about is not very satisfying from a purely historical point of view:

> *And it came to pass that night, that the angel of the* LORD *went out, and smote in the camp of the Assyrians an hundred fourscore and five thousand: and when they arose early in the morning, behold, they were all dead corpses.*

—II KINGS 19:35

(The last clause is not even very satisfying from a syntactical point of view.) We might interpret this to mean that there was an outbreak of plague in the Assyrian camp, or we might speculate that Sennacherib raised the siege because he had pressing business elsewhere; his earlier encounter with the rebellious Pharaoh had been inconclusive, and perhaps he was worried about leaving an undefeated Egyptian army on his flank. Whatever the reason, Jerusalem was delivered from the Assyrians. A short time later, Hezekiah receives a delegation from his ally, the king of Babylon—who so far has not been of any use to him whatsoever. This is ostensibly a courtesy call, because the king of Babylon "had heard that Hezekiah had been sick." Apparently Hezekiah is still not at the top of his form; he fails to notice that the Babylonian envoys are really trying to sound out the economic, financial, and above all military resources of his kingdom—espionage with diplomatic cover, in other words. Hezekiah is completely taken in, unfortunately, and

> . . . *there was nothing in his house, nor in all his dominion, that Hezekiah shewed them not.*

—II KINGS 20:13

The prophet Isaiah at least sees through all this immediately, and even though Babylon was not a great military power in those days, he prophesies that no good will come of it:

> Behold, the days come, that all is in thine house, and that which thy fathers have laid up in store unto this day, shall be carried into Babylon: nothing shall be left, saith the LORD.

—II KINGS 20:17

Hezekiah, like many a later statesman, is content to be left with peace in his time: "Is it not good, if peace and truth be in my days?" Isaiah turns out to be right, of course, though we don't necessarily have to assume that a later editor added this prediction to enhance his reputation as a prophet. A farsighted political observer in 700 B.C. might certainly have predicted the breakup of the Assyrian Empire—especially after Sennacherib's last campaign—and the rise of Babylon.

The story of the last days of Judah is pretty much a repeat performance of Sennacherib's invasion, this time without a last-minute reprieve from an angel of the Lord. First, Judah becomes a vassal state of Babylon. Judah rebels—refuses to pay tribute, in other words—and concludes a secret alliance with Egypt. In 587 B.C. the Babylonian King Nebuchadnezzar II sends out a punitive expedition which takes Jerusalem, pillages and destroys the city, and carries off most of the population—those who might have some military or economic potential—into captivity:

> But the captain of the guard left of the poor of the land to be vinedressers and husbandmen.

—II KINGS 25:12

We are never told, in the Bible or anywhere else, what actually happened to the Israelites who were carried off by their Assyrian conquerors; hence, "the Ten Lost Tribes of Israel." The deportation of the tribes of Judah is much better documented and does not seem to have been as systematic as the Book of

226

Kings implies. The "poor of the land" who were left behind in Judah may have included as much as two-thirds of the population. The Babylonian Exile of the Judean power elite, which lasted for over fifty years, is mentioned in only a few scattered references in the Bible. Fortunately, this fragmentary record has been supplemented by a cache of Babylonian clay tablets discovered by the German archaeologist Robert Koldewey. These provide us with a detailed account of the Judean campaign and its aftermath, a monument to Nebuchadnezzar's triumph and to bureaucratic diligence. For example, the Second Book of Kings ends with the terse and uninformative account of King Jehoiachin of Judah's honorable captivity at the Babylonian court:

> And his allowance was a continual allowance, given him of the king, a daily rate for every day, all the days of his life.
>
> —II KINGS 25:30

In fact, all the Judean captives were royal pensioners who received a specific ration that varied according to the social standing of the recipient; the Babylonian scribes recorded these arrangements with pedantic exactitude. King Jehoiachin received eight *sila* of oil over a given period while "eight men of Judah" had to be content with a mere four *sila* among the whole lot of them.

> But wild beasts of the desert shall lie there; and their houses shall be full of doleful creatures, and owls shall dwell there, and satyrs [wild goats] shall dance there.
>
> —ISAIAH 13:21

The traveler who drives out to Babylon on the fine modern highway from Baghdad may not find "dragons in their pleasant palaces," or many other traces of "the beauty of the Chaldees' excellency," but eroded heaps of brick and the flooded excava-

227

tion site of the famous ziggurat. (Half a mile or so down the road, in the village of Hillah, you can still see Babylonian bricks in a much better state of preservation; they have been thriftily incorporated into the houses of the villagers for many centuries.)

In Nebuchadnezzar's time "the glory of the kingdoms" was a great city of about 400,000 inhabitants, dispersed over an area of about two hundred square miles. Many of its residential buildings were four stories tall. The great avenue that led through the Ishtar Gate was over fifteen yards wide, paved with limestone blocks and red-and-white checkered tiles and lit by oil lamps at night. The greatest of Babylon's glories, the Hanging Gardens, were constructed by Nebuchadnezzar II, on the roof terraces of his palace. Even the natural stone for the terraces must have been imported at great expense; the roof was specially insulated with lead sheathing, reed mats, and bitumen. The luxuriant branches of the trees and shrubs hung out over the windowless facade of the palace; hence the name Hanging Gardens. According to legend, this horticultural wonder of the world was built for Queen Semiramis (who may or may not have existed); in fact, however, the gardens were an extravagant wedding gift for Nebuchadnezzar's beloved wife, Amytis, who was originally brought to Babylon as a captive after her father, Kyaxeres, was defeated and killed in battle. The gardens—perhaps as much as twelve thousand square feet in area—were intended to re-create the green hills of Amytis's Persian home-land on the marshy plains of Babylon—a touching and magnifi-cent gesture, even in the circumstances. (This pleasant illusion was perpetuated, to some extent, inside the palace as well, where the water that was brought up for the garden by a system of waterwheels was recirculated to cool the interior rooms, even when the temperature outside reached 120 degrees.)

The laborers who built Nebuchadnezzar's palaces, temples, and fortifications were all war captives, like the Judeans, who had been brought to Babylon from every corner of his empire.

Certainly the most eloquent expression of the Judeans' bitter memories of exile can be found in the famous opening lines of Psalm 137:

> *By the rivers of Babylon, there we sat down, yea, we wept, when we remembered Zion.*
> *We hanged our harps upon the willows in the midst thereof.*
> *For there they that carried us away captive required of us a song; and they that wasted us required of us mirth. . . .*

It was during the Babylonian Exile that the first manuscripts of the Old Testament were written, and these became both a symbol and an instrument of Jewish unity and cohesiveness in exile. Also in Babylon the first Jewish houses of worship were established in which the scrolls of the prophets were read aloud to the congregation. Only Hebrew was permitted to be spoken in these sacred precincts (Aramaic was the everyday language of the Babylonian Jews), but they came to be known by the Greek name, *synagogue.*

After Nebuchadnezzar's death the Babylonian Empire began to disintegrate rapidly. Nebuchadnezzar himself, at least according to the Bible, had taken to walking on all fours and eating grass "like a beast of the field," which must have impaired considerably his effectiveness as a statesman. His successor was a nonentity; the last king of Babylon was an upstart courtier who was unceremoniously put off his throne when Cyrus of Persia—he preferred to be called "the Great"—marched into the city during a state banquet. There was no resistance; the Babylonians welcomed Cyrus as a liberator. (This was only twenty-three years after Nebuchadnezzar's death.)

One of Cyrus's first official acts was to issue an edict of religious toleration—a remarkable break with precedent for a Near Eastern potentate. The images of foreign gods which had been brought back as battle trophies to adorn Nebuchadnezzar's palace were returned to their temples. Cyrus must have felt particularly sympathetic toward the Judeans, who were not only allowed to return to their homelands with the other captive peoples but commanded to rebuild the Temple at Cyrus's expense (Ezra 6:4). The treasures of Solomon which had been carried off by the "Chaldeans" were restored to the returning exiles.

You might imagine that Cyrus's edict was followed by great jubilation among the exiles and a triumphant exodus out of Babylon; but after all, fifty years had already gone by. Many of the exiles were too old to entrust themselves to the rigors of such a journey to a dimly remembered homeland. The majority were too young to have known any homeland but Babylon, and they preferred to stay in that prosperous, cosmopolitan city. All in all, scholars believe that only about 10 percent of the Judean exiles—about fifty thousand people—finally found their way back to Judea.

> *We have trespassed against our God, and have taken strange wives of the people of the land: yet now there is hope in Israel concerning this thing.*
>
> —EZRA 10:2

The Book of Ezra and the Book of Nehemiah: The Restoration of Jerusalem

The biblical account of Cyrus's edict and the exiles' return to Judea can be found in the opening chapters of the Book of Ezra. Ezra himself, "a ready scribe in the law of Moses" and a direct descendant of the high priest Aaron, however, did not arrive in Jerusalem until over sixty years after the rebuilding of the Temple, about 450 B.C. Ezra and his younger contemporary Nehemiah were the spiritual and political leaders of a later generation of returning exiles who dedicated their lives to the restoration of the people's faith in Yahweh and the laws of Moses and to the restoration of the city of Jerusalem to its former greatness.

Before Ezra himself appears on the scene, the Book of Ezra gives a concise account of the rivalry between "the children of the captivity" and the remnants of the nation of Israel—the Samaritans—whose intrigues temporarily put a stop to the reconstruction of the Temple. In chapter 5, which is far and away the best from a literary point of view, the climax of these events is presented through a dramatic exchange of letters between the local Persian authorities and the great King Darius, in which the original edict of Cyrus is emphatically confirmed. The origins of this conflict (see Ezra 4:2–3) may seem a little obscure: the Samaritans offer to help the exiles rebuild the Temple; "the fathers of Israel" bluntly refuse this offer, probably because they suspect that the Samaritans' real motive in all this is to ensure that Jerusalem will not be restored so thoroughly that it will eclipse Samaria as the chief city of the region.

Ezra carried this exclusionist tendency even further; his strict interpretation of the laws of Moses results in what is, in effect, a policy of racial and religious apartheid. Mixed marriages were forbidden (which was nothing new, at least in theory), and Ezra went so far as to insist that all existing marriages between "the children of the captivity" and "the children of the land" should be dissolved, and that their "outlandish" wives and children should be banished from Judea:

> *Now therefore let us make a covenant with our God to put away all the wives, and such as are born of them . . . and let it be done according to the law.*

> —EZRA 10:3

Nehemiah was even more insistent on this point:

And I contended with them, and cursed them, and smote certain of them, and plucked off their hair, and made them swear by God, saying, Ye shall not give your daughters unto their sons. . . .

—NEHEMIAH 13:25

Ezra (probably) subscribed to the prevailing theory that it was the Israelites' disastrous fascination with the cult of Baal that brought about the destruction of the two kingdoms, a theory that may well have been confirmed by his experience of life in pagan Babylon. In any case, the magnanimous example of Cyrus of Persia seems to have made absolutely no impression on these two stiff-necked strict constructionists, whose intolerance seems to have been as disturbing to some of the authors of the Old Testament as it is to us today.

We do not get a very clear picture of Ezra as a personality; the man himself is almost entirely obscured by his great passion for the Law. Quite the reverse with Nehemiah—a masterful leader whose phrases ring out like commands. He writes exclusively in the first person (except for a few historical flashbacks) and is obviously proud of his accomplishments, almost to the point of arrogance. He complacently relates how he refused to draw his salary as governor of the Persian province of Judea "because of the fear of God," how he set out a table every day for the citizen volunteers who rebuilt the walls of Jerusalem. "Think upon me, my God," he adds, "for good, according to all that I have done for this people," or, after he has reorganized the finances of the Temple and generally set the Lord's house in order— "Remember me, O my God, concerning this, and wipe not out my good deeds . . ."

Nehemiah has good reason to take this lofty tone, because, as he explains quite early on, in Persia he was a courtier, "the king's cupbearer," and in those days when a dose of poison and a bribe for the king's chamberlain were almost invariably the

232

prelude to a coup d'état, this was a position of the highest trust. Jerusalem, on the other hand, was something of a hardship post, and "the rulers of the land" had a great deal of trouble recruiting settlers to repopulate the once-magnificent city of David. Nehemiah describes how

> . . . the rest of the people also cast lots, to bring one of ten to dwell in Jerusalem the holy city, and nine parts to dwell in other cities.
>
> And the people blessed all the men, that willingly offered themselves to dwell at Jerusalem.

—NEHEMIAH 11:1–2

(This blessing could probably be paraphrased in the contemporary idiom as "Better you than me.")

Between reminiscences of his career as a decisive and highly conscientious administrator, Nehemiah appears in a different guise, as a puritan preacher denouncing the everyday ungodliness of the people. The Sabbath breakers got off with a rebuke and a warning ("If ye do so again, I will lay hands on you"), but the usurers are treated to a full-fledged sermon (Nehemiah 5:1–13), which is a genuine pleasure to read. Naturally, Nehemiah does not fail to mention that the usurers at first were left speechless, then promised to mend their ways while "the congregation said, Amen, and praised the Lord." (Amen—"so be it"—does not have any explicitly religious connotations until the New Testament. Here it simply means that a decision has been reached, a bargain struck—the verbal equivalent of a nod and a handshake, or the removal of a shoe.) After he has dealt with the pagan merchants who have profaned the Sabbath and the hapless Judeans who have been fraternizing with the ungodly, Nehemiah ends his memoirs with a final reminder to the Lord: "Remember me, O my God, for good."

In neither style nor substance are the Books of Ezra and

Nehemiah in the same class with the greatest books of the Old Testament. They were probably composed sometime during the fourth century B.C., at the same time as First and Second Chronicles, possibly even by the same author. As we have already seen, the Books of Chronicles are nothing more than a tendentious reworking of the Books of Kings, with the themes of guilt and expiation—and the ruling idea of the hand of God as the dominant force in human history—much more prominently presented. Just skimming over a few pages should be enough to show how the turbulent history of the two kingdoms has been rewritten as a moral tract for a politically more tranquil age; the intensity and immediacy of the Books of Kings have been smothered in the dust of the scholar's study.

> *Now therefore give God thanks: for I go up to him that sent me; but write all things which are done in a book.*
>
> —TOBIT 12:20

Ripping Yarns: The Apocryphal Books of Tobit and Judith, and the Book of Esther

Several books that appeared in the Septuagint, the Greek translation of the Old Testament, were excluded from most of the Masoretic manuscripts of the Hebrew Bible. Though they were included in a separate section of the original editions of the King James, they are often not found in modern Protestant versions of the Old Testament either. The Book of Tobit, or Tobias, follows Nehemiah in the Catholic Bible, however.

Tobias, the Dreamer

Though Tobit may well be a second-rate production from the standpoint of literature and revealed truth, it can also be regarded as a minor classic of naive fantasy, a direct ancestor of Isaac Bashevis Singer's Yiddish stories in which the homey details of everyday life are unexpectedly blended with strange supernatural encounters with demons and evil spirits. The historical background and geographical setting of the Book of Tobit are almost entirely fanciful; the story, which is probably based on a much more ancient folktale called "The Grateful Dead," is all that really matters.

Tobias, a pious Jew of Nineveh, has been accidentally blinded when "sparrows muted warm dung into [his] eyes" while he was sleeping next to a wall where they had made their nests. Faced with the prospect of destitution, he sends his son, Tobit, off to Rages (Teheran) in Persia to recover some money he had left in safekeeping with a kinsman years before. Tobit sets off, accompanied by his dog and a hired guide (actually the angel Raphael in disguise). On the way, while bathing in the Tigris, Tobit is almost eaten alive by an enormous fish. Raphael advises him to save the liver and gall of the fish, which can be dried and burned to "make a smoke" that will drive off any evil spirits they might encounter on their journey.

This turns out to be excellent advice, of course. When they arrive in Rages, Raphael arranges a match between Tobit and Sara, the daughter of his father's kinsman. The only problem is that Sara has already been married seven times, though she is still a virgin—"the evil spirit Asmodeus" has devoured all the other bridegrooms on their wedding night. Tobit burns the fish's liver and handily disposes of Asmodeus, and—not to prolong the suspense—the fish's liver turns out to be the very thing that will cure his father's blindness.

A later scene, in which Raphael reveals himself in his glory to

Tobias and his family, was a favorite subject of another master who was fascinated by the contrast between the mundane and the miraculous: Rembrandt. The theme of Tobias and the angel inspired at least half a dozen paintings and engravings in which the radiance of the angel's corona fills the murky Dutch interior of Tobias's cottage with blinding light.

A copy of the long-lost Hebrew original of the Book of Tobit was discovered among the Dead Sea Scrolls in the 1950s. The Hebrew text—it has still not been published—apparently differs substantially from the Greek of the Septuagint, and it may even be better. Nevertheless, the Book of Tobit is worth the effort of reading in English, in either the Catholic Bible or the King James Apocrypha (published as a separate volume by Oxford University Press); if you prefer a modern translation, there are the Jerusalem Bible, the New English Bible, and many others.

Judith, the Heroine

The apocryphal Book of Judith is known to us only from the Greek version of the Septuagint; the Hebrew original has still not come to light. As with the Book of Tobit, the historical background is sketchy (Nebuchadnezzar is referred to as the king of the Assyrians, for example), though the theme of the Book of Judith is essentially patriotic and political.

The story line is disarmingly simple: Judith is a beautiful widow who saves her native city of Bethulia from an invading Assyrian army. She exchanges her widow's weeds for her most seductive finery and presents herself in the Assyrian camp. The Assyrian general, Holofernes, invites her to join him in his tent for an evening of carousal; she accepts, and later that night, after Holofernes has passed out—"he drank much more wine than he had drunk at any one time since he was born"—Judith hacks off his head with a sword and returns home with her bloody trophy safely tucked away in a bag.

The story of Judith has obvious dramatic possibilities, as even Luther was quick to recognize; "a fine, stirring, serious tragedy," he called it. The German playwright Friedrich Hebbel adapted this lurid tale for the nineteenth-century stage by introducing a love interest between Judith and Holofernes and thus an interesting conflict: Judith is torn between her tender feelings as a woman and her homicidal duty as a patriot. (Various stage and silent-film versions of Hebbel's play, most of them called *Judith of Bethulia*, were enormously popular in England and America.)

Still, the story of Judith does sometimes rise above the level of Victorian melodrama and is worth reading, not only for such curious archaeological details as the mosquito netting on Holofernes's bed but for an occasional passage like the following one, in which Judith eloquently rebukes the elders of Bethulia, who have decided that they would rather surrender to Holofernes than "die for thirst" in the besieged city:

> *And now who are ye that have tempted God this day, and stand instead of God among the children of men?*
>
> *And now try the Lord Almighty, but ye shall never know any thing.*
>
> *For ye cannot find the depth of the heart of man, neither can ye perceive the things that he thinketh: then how can ye search out God, that hath made all these things, and know his mind, or comprehend his purpose? Nay, my brethren, provoke not the Lord our God to anger.*
>
> *For if he will not help us within these five days, he hath power to defend us when he will, even every day, or to destroy us before our enemies.*
>
> *Do not bind the counsels of the Lord our God: for God is not as man, that he may be threatened; neither is he as the son of man, that he should be wavering.*
>
> *Therefore let us wait for salvation of him, and call upon him to help us, and he will hear our voice, if it please him.*

—JUDITH 8:12–17

It seems ironic that such a fervent affirmation of the faith of the Old Testament should have been banished from Hebrew and Protestant Bibles as an "uninspired" imitation of the real thing.

Esther, the Queen

The Book of Esther, on the other hand, is a tale of romance and revenge that has found a secure place for itself in the canon (right after Nehemiah in the Protestant Bible, after Judith in the Catholic Bible), even though its theme is purely patriotic and not the slightest bit religious (God is not mentioned once, except in a few apocryphal passages that were added to the Septuagint to remedy this omission). The author simply describes how a beautiful Jewish girl becomes the queen of Persia and frustrates a plot to massacre all the Jews in the Persian Empire. The Jewish festival of Purim commemorates Esther's heroism and her compatriots' narrow escape from annihilation—though it may be the other way around, that the story was invented to provide an explanation, or a plausible pretext, for a popular holiday whose origins are otherwise mysterious.

The setting is the court of Xerxes I ("Ahasuerus") of Persia, at Susa ("Shushan"), and some authorities believe that the story of Esther was originally a Persian folktale that has not been preserved or was never written down. The name Esther itself is Babylonian and has clear affinities with the pagan goddesses Ishtar and Astarte, the Semitic equivalent of Venus. (This is only an assumed name, by the way; Esther's Hebrew and real name, Hadassah, is mentioned once and quickly forgotten.)

The Book of Esther was probably written a century or two after the "third year of his [Ahasuerus's]" reign (around 520 B.C.), when these events allegedly took place, though the author's account of the great king's drunken antics and the intrigues of his wicked minister is certainly vivid enough. As the story begins, Ahasuerus has been feasting with his courtiers for seven days.

. . . when the heart of the king was merry with wine, he commanded . . . the seven chamberlains. . . .

To bring Vashti the queen before the king with the crown royal, to show the people and the princes her beauty: for she was fair to look on.

—ESTHER 1:10–11

In other words, he wants Vashti to parade before his drinking companions wearing nothing but her royal diadem. Vashti, who is presiding over a more decorous "feast for the women in the royal house," haughtily refuses to set foot out of the harem; Ahasuerus is furious.

This prologue may reflect the Persians' reputation as the great drunkards of the ancient world (or simply the tradition that Purim was the one day of the year on which pious Jews were actually encouraged to get drunk). Persian women apparently did enjoy a certain measure of independence; they did not wear veils, for example, and widows were accustomed to settle their husband's business affairs themselves (which to the Jewish author of the Book of Esther must have seemed an equally outlandish pagan excess). In this case, Ahasuerus's councilors agree that Vashti's insubordinate refusal is likely to set an unhealthy precedent.

For this deed of the queen shall come abroad unto all women, so that they shall despise their husbands in their eyes. . . .

—ESTHER 1:17

Ahasuerus decrees that "every man should bear rule in his own household" and commands his officers to assemble all the fairest young virgins of the empire in his palace. (Esther's uncle Mordecai arranges for her to take part in this beauty pageant.) After a twelve-month period of "purification"—actually an exhaustive course of beauty treatments involving "oil of myrrh

. . . sweet odours, and with other things"—Esther is selected as Vashti's replacement.

And the king loved Esther above all the women, and she obtained grace and favour in his sight. . . .

—ESTHER 2:17

At this point this frothy romantic comedy suddenly becomes a more conventional biblical drama of plot and counterplot, malicious villainy (on the part of Haman, the king's chief minister), and righteous vengeance (on the part of Esther and the Jews of Persia). The conflict escalates swiftly: Mordecai snubs Haman, Haman decrees that all the Jews in the empire shall be destroyed (on the thirteenth of the month of Adar, the first day of Purim); Esther (who has so far concealed her Jewish origins) prevails on the king to countermand the decree and to hang Haman on the gallows he has prepared for Mordecai, and to give the Jews free reign to avenge themselves on Haman's co-conspirators:

Thus the Jews smote all their enemies with the stroke of the sword, and slaughter, and destruction, and did what they would unto those that hated them.

—ESTHER 9:5

After seventy-five thousand of his subjects have been dispatched, Ahasuerus asks Esther if there is another favor he can grant her. Only one, she replies: let the massacre continue for another day. Ahasuerus, who seems to have forgotten all about being the master in his own house, indulgently agrees, which is why the festival of Purim is a two-day holiday.

In those days went there out of Israel wicked men, who persuaded many, saying, Let us go

240

and make a covenant with the heathen that are
round about us. . . .

—I MACCABEES 1:11

Rebellion and Resurrection: The First and Second Books of the Maccabees

Only First and Second Maccabees can be found in the Catholic Bible, the New English Bible, and the King James Apocrypha, though there were originally two more books in the Septuagint, neither of which has much to do with the historical Maccabees (to whom we shall get shortly). Third Maccabees is a legendary story, probably derived from a non-Jewish source, which describes how the Jews of Alexandria were miraculously saved from being trampled to death by elephants in the arena of one of the Ptolomies, circa 200 B.C. Fourth Maccabees is a philosophical treatise on the superiority of reason over physical passion. Both are considered to be pseudepigraphical ("false inscriptions"), which is one rung lower than apocryphal, and it is really no great loss that they have been excluded from both the Catholic and the Protestant Apocrypha.

This leaves us with the Maccabees themselves. At first there was only one Maccabee, Judah, who was given the nickname Makkabah ("the hammerer") because of his prowess in battle. Later the name was also applied to the rest of the family—his father and four brothers—and finally to the entire guerrilla army that they led against the Seleucid rulers of Judea. The Seleucids were the descendants of Seleuceus Nikator, one of Alexander the Great's generals, and more than a century later—in 167 B.C.— they still ruled over a considerable empire that stretched from the Syrian coast to beyond the Caspian Sea.

The cause of the Maccabean rebellion was not simply political—after all, Judea had been ruled by various foreign powers for over five hundred years—but religious and cultural. Antiochus Epiphanes, the current occupant of the Seleucid throne, had outlawed the worship of Yahweh in Judea. He intended to substitute the cult of the Greek gods (among whom he included himself), which was the state religion of the Seleucids' empire. The final provocation was the pillaging of the Temple by a band of Hellenized Jews who set up "the abomination of desolation"—an altar to Zeus—in the sanctuary. But as this holy war continued, it also became a war of conquest, as holy wars have a tendency to do. By the time the Maccabees had finished, about 135 B.C., they had conquered almost all the territory that had once been ruled by King David and forced their new Gentile subjects—many of whom converted to Judaism—to pay tribute.

The idea of the Maccabean rebellion is stirring enough—a fanatically brave band of rebels taking up arms against a mighty empire—but the Books of Maccabees themselves are pretty heavy going, and it takes quite a bit of patience to wade through so much patriotic gore. What is really interesting in all this is not the formalized, Book of Judges–style battle reports—exchange of envoys, insolent defiance, great slaughter, spoils divided among the widows and orphans—but the occasional passing references to the conflict between two cultures, which was the real cause of the rebellion.

For example, it is clear that the Hellenistic Greek culture of the Seleucids has a certain appeal for the more sophisticated urban Judeans—"wicked men who persuaded many" to "make a covenant with the heathen." To begin with, they built a "place of exercise"—a Greek gymnasium—"at Jerusalem, after the custom of the heathen," and perhaps more significantly, "that made themselves uncircumcised, and forsook the holy covenant" (I Maccabees 1:15). In this context, we should probably interpret "they made themselves uncircumcised" to mean that they no longer circumcised their children, because any artificial attempt to conceal this vital social distinction would probably have made them even more conspicuous. And because no one wore jock straps or jogging shorts in a Greek gymnasium (*gymnos* means "naked" in Greek), the first generation of backsliders from the holy covenant would have been hard pressed "to hide their loyalties," as one writer delicately puts it, and probably had to endure a great deal of locker-room taunting from the Greeks and Hellenized Syrians who made up the Seleucid ruling class.

The introduction of the Hellenistic cult of the body beautiful is mentioned later in II Maccabees 4:12–13, where we are told that it was the upstart high priest Jason who built the gymnasium beside the city wall and also "brought the chief young men under his subjection, and made them wear a hat."

> *Now such was the height of Greek fashions . . . through the exceeding profaneness of Jason, that ungodly wretch. . . .*

The hat in question was the wide-brimmed, low-crowned straw hat which farmers wore in ancient Greece to keep off the sun and rain. These had long since gone out of fashion in the metropolitan Greek cities but were apparently still all the rage in the provinces. This sounds like a harmless affectation, comparable to the current urban fad of wearing overalls or cowboy boots. But as far as the authors of Second Maccabees, and the Maccabees themselves, were concerned, even the slightest attempt to bridge the enormous cultural gap that separated the Judeans from their Hellenistic overlords was simply "whoring after the gods of the heathen" all over again, which had destroyed the godly kingdom of David and Solomon.

After the desecration of the Temple, the Maccabee brothers and their father "fled into the mountains" to escape persecution.

> *Then many that sought after justice and judgment went down into the wilderness, to dwell there: . . .*
>
> —I Maccabees 2:29

This sounds as if the Maccabees are heading in one direction and their followers in another; actually, both are going "up," in the literal, geographical sense, to the mountains above Jerusalem. But in biblical terms, anyone who left Jerusalem, the city of Yahweh and the site of his Temple, was descending to a lower (spiritual) elevation, and thus "going down" from Jerusalem.

The Maccabees' army was organized along strictly traditionalist lines; they even refused to fight on the Sabbath (at least at first), and their recruitment policy followed the law of Moses to the letter. There was no such thing as a conscientious objector, of course:

> *But as for such as were building houses, or had betrothed wives, or were planting vineyards, or were fearful, those he commanded that they should return, every man to his own house, according to the law.*

> —I MACCABEES 3:56

But after a particularly disastrous engagement in which the elder Maccabee is killed, the brothers reluctantly agree to shed heathen blood on the Sabbath, if necessary, and the rest of the war, at least as described in First and Second Maccabees, is thoroughly conventional. The only instance of really colorful reporting occurs in I Maccabees 6, a description of the Syrian elephant corps forming up for battle:

> *And to the end they might provoke the elephants to fight, they shewed them the blood of grapes and mulberries.*

> *Moreover they divided the beasts among the armies, and for every elephant they appointed a thousand men, armed with coats of mail, and with helmets of brass on their heads; and beside this, for every beast were ordained five hundred horsemen of the best.*

> *These were ready at every occasion: wheresoever the beast was,*

and whithersoever the beast went, they went also, neither departed they from him.

And upon the beasts were there strong towers of wood, which covered every one of them, and were girt fast unto them with devices: there were also upon every one two and thirty strong men, that fought upon them, beside the Indian that ruled him.

—I Maccabees 6:34–37

None of the other superweapons that were deployed against the Israelites, including the Aramean chariot armies and the siege engines of the Assyrians, were ever described in such vivid detail. This passage reads as if it were written by a trained military historian rather than by a patriotic rhapsodist (or a terrified eyewitness, for that matter). The sequel—in which Eleazar, the younger brother of Judah Maccabee, single-handedly brings down one of these monsters—is narrated with the same dry precision:

Wherefore he ran upon him courageously through the midst of the battle, slaying on the right hand and on the left, so that they were divided from him on both sides.

Which done, he crept under the elephant, and thrust him under, and slew him: whereupon the elephant fell down upon him, and there he died.

—I Maccabees 6:45–46

Eleazar had found the elephant's weak spot, where it was unprotected by its armor and its hide was relatively thin. Unexpectedly, though, the Maccabees are not encouraged by Eleazar's epic feat, and the Syrians do not fall back in a rout. It is the Maccabees who retreat, and Antiochus goes on to pillage Jerusalem. This episode, at least, has the ring of real history.

Actually the First Book of Maccabees is an extremely valuable source of the history of the period. Second Maccabees, roughly

245

comparable to the Books of Chronicles, is basically a parallel account of some (though not nearly all) of these events, emphasizing the spiritual rather than the patriotic aspects of the Maccabean rebellion. In that respect, there is an important concept that appears here for the first time—and that may be a large part of the reason the Books of Maccabees kept their precarious place in the Christian Bible. This is the idea of the resurrection of the flesh and of a life after death, which is mentioned twice in Second Maccabees. In the first instance, Judah Maccabee collects two thousand silver drachmas and sends them to the Temple in Jerusalem:

> . . . *to offer a sin offering, doing therein very well and honestly, in that he was mindful of the resurrection.*

> —II MACCABEES 12:43

The second instance comes at the end of what in later periods of history would be called "an act of martyrdom," or an atrocity tale in modern parlance. Seven young Jews have been tortured to death before their mother's eyes, and, as is usual in such accounts, we are not spared any of the details. To summarize briefly, they are flayed alive, scalped, their "utmost parts" are hacked off, and their dismembered but still living bodies are "fried in the pan," one after another. The reason for this is that they have refused to eat "swine's flesh" in defiance of the laws of Moses, and the Seleucid king, Antiochus, has decided to make a particularly gruesome example of them.

Modern biblical scholars are inclined to believe that this episode, like many others in Second Maccabees, is a pious legend, invented to illustrate the inhumane cruelty of the "Greeks" and the bravery and steadfastness of the Jews who resisted them. (The presence of the mystical number seven tends to support this interpretation.) In earlier times, though, the story was taken at face value, and the seven courageous brothers were duly inscribed on the roll of blessed martyrs of the Catholic Church, where they still remain, along with several other pre-Christian and non-Christian saints and martyrs. The explanation for this unusual state of affairs can be found in two of the brothers' dying speeches, addressed to their tormentor, King Antiochus:

> *And when he was at the last gasp, he said, Thou like a fury takest us out of this present life, but the King of the world shall raise us up, who have died for his laws, unto everlasting life.*
>
> *So when he [the fourth brother] was ready to die he said thus, It is good, being put to death by men, to look for hope from God to be raised up again by him: as for thee, thou shalt have no resurrection to life.*

—II MACCABEES 7:9, 14

Thus, they died in the hope of the resurrection and eternal life, which is clearly a Christian concept, even if these particular martyrs were very early Christians indeed, because they died for their beliefs, and "for his laws," at least 150 years before the birth of Jesus. This is certainly the most striking demonstration we have encountered so far of how deeply the fundamental tenets of Christianity are rooted in the faith of the Old Testament.

> *Surely I would speak to the Almighty, and I desire to reason with god.*

—JOB 13:3

The Poetic Books

The Book of Job: Reasoning with God

Job's real name was Iyyob ("where is the father?"), and he lived in the land of Uz, which means he was not an Israelite at all but an Edomite (possibly), or at any rate an inhabitant of the desert steppeland to the northeast of Canaan.

The broad outlines of Job's story are familiar enough: he endures his calamities and his comforters, the slaughter of his family, the ruin of his household, sore boils and loathsome afflictions, all with the patience of Job. But finally, even this "perfect, upright," God-fearing man becomes impatient with the complacent platitudes of his comforters. He begins to doubt that God is just, and he demands to know why a righteous man such as himself should have met with such an undeservedly disastrous fate.

God's answer comes in the form of a series of questions, all of which have the same basic thrust: How can a mere mortal expect to understand the ways of the Lord?

The Book of Job is a coherent, psychologically developed story, told with great poetic power. It is also a challenging and highly problematical work—"the Matterhorn of the Bible," one scholar has called it—and more has been written about it than about any other book of the Old Testament. The reason for this has not so much to do with Job, or even with God, but with the third major character in this drama: Satan.

Satan—"the Adversary"—has brought all this misery about on his own initiative, to test the strength of Job's faith, though God has given him explicit permission to do his worst because he has an equal stake in the outcome. Satan has made a bet with God, in effect, that Job will curse God if he is stripped of all his "substance." God agrees to this: "Behold, all that he hath is in thy power" (and later, when Job passes his first trial, "Behold, he is in thine hand," and Job is stripped of everything else, except his life). Goethe borrowed the idea of a wager between God and Satan for the "Prologue in Heaven" of his great poetic drama *Faust*, in which Satan's oblique proposal is paraphrased more directly in these words:

What will you wager that you will still lose him
If you let me lead him gently along with me?

The Faust myth shares the central preoccupation of the Book of Job: the tragedy of a man suspended between God and Satan, between good and evil. And the Book of Job poses the greatest problem of faith: if God is good, and God is all-powerful, why is there so much evil in the world (or any at all, for that matter)? Or, to put it in terms of the original cast of characters, if Satan can do only what God allows him to, why does Satan have so much power over mankind? The Devil makes his first appearance as a theological problem, and it is hard to imagine how theology could have gotten along without him. Even the most blameless man, the Book of Job tells us, can be brought low by the power of Satan. It is a comparatively short step from the idea of diabolic temptation to that of diabolic possession, exorcism, and "casting out demons." The Catholic Church (as well as many Fundamentalist Protestant groups) still proclaims the existence of Satan as an article of faith—though a survey conducted by the Buchert Institute suggests that fewer than 11 percent of practicing Catholics in West Germany actually believe he exists.

Whether he does or not, we do have a very good idea of where he came from, at least as far as the Book of Job is concerned. During the Babylonian Exile the Jews came into contact with a religion that was as different from the cult of Baal, with its celestial pantheon of a dozen or more gods, as it was from their own monotheistic cult of Yahweh. This was the Persian religion, in which all earthly and heavenly events were seen as the outcome of the constant warfare between two gods, the gods of light and darkness, of good and evil. Man was continually forced to choose between the two, and thus it was the dualistic teachings of Zoroaster, the great Persian prophet, that provided the open back door through which Satan slunk into the Bible.

The concept of God that appears in the Book of Job also represents a new development. As we have seen, Moses' God is still closely associated with the more dramatic forces of nature; Elijah's God is present only in the silence that follows the storm, "the still small voice"; and the God of Nehemiah is simply a tabulator (a personal computer, we might say) of good deeds (input) and their earthly rewards (output). Job is the first to realize—as he has good reason to—that God is not just a celestial insurance agent who provides full health-and-accident coverage for his devotees. This is a frivolous way of expressing a very important concept, one that has an even more important concept underlying it: not only does man need God, God needs man also. In particular, God needs men like Job, who ask troublesome questions but who finally submit wholeheartedly to his incomprehensible will.

The Book of Job is one of the most intellectually provocative and one of the most beautifully written books of the Bible. The grandeur of its style and the rhythm of its language perfectly match the greatness of the theme, one that finds innumerable echoes throughout Western literature:

> *Call now, if there be any that will answer thee; and to which of the saints wilt thou turn?*

> *And when I cried out, which of the host of angels heard me?*

(The first of these quotations is the first verse of chapter 5 of the Book of Job; the second, the opening line of Rainer Maria Rilke's *Duino Elegies*, written near the beginning of this century, some two thousand five hundred years later.) The passages in chapters

40 and 41 in which the Lord likens himself to the great beasts Leviathan and Behemoth certainly bear comparison with Shakespeare in terms of the power and originality of the imagery:

> *Canst thou draw out leviathan with an hook? or his tongue with a cord which thou lettest down?*
>
> *Will he make many supplications unto thee? will he speak soft words unto thee?*
>
> *Wilt thou play with him as with a bird? or wilt thou bind him for thy maidens?*
>
> *Shall the companions make a banquet of him? shall they part him among the merchants?*
>
> *Behold, the hope of him is in vain: shall not one be cast down even at the sight of him?*
>
> *None is so fierce that dare stir him up: who then is able to stand before me?*

—JOB 41:1, 3, 5, 6, 9, 10

In short, you are strongly encouraged to read the Book of Job, the first of the "poetic" books of the Old Testament (as distinct from the historical and pseudohistorical books and the writing of the prophets). This category includes several other examples of what is often called Wisdom Literature—Proverbs, Ecclesiastes, and the apocryphal books of Ecclesiasticus (less confusingly known by its Hebrew title, the Book of Jesus Son of Sirach) and the Wisdom of Solomon, as well as the Israelite hymnbook—the Psalms—and that unexpected erotic classic, the Song of Solomon.

> *As the hart panteth after the water brooks, so panteth my soul after thee, O God.*

—PSALMS 42:1

The Psalms: Play Skillfully with a Loud Noise

The Book of Psalms—the Psalter, as it used to be called—is a collection of 150 commemorative songs and hymns of praise (which are arranged in a slightly different order in the Protestant and Catholic Bibles). The original Psalms—and there must have been an enormous number of them—were written (or could be suitably rewritten) to commemorate specific occasions, though when they were written and by whom we really don't know. It is clear at least that they were songs (*psalmas* in Greek) that were meant to be sung to the accompaniment of a lyre or some other stringed instrument (*psalterion*, hence Psalter). The last of the Psalms evokes the entire temple orchestra:

> *Praise him with the sound of the trumpet:*
> *praise him with the psaltery and harp.*
> *Praise him with the timbrel and dance:*
> *praise him with stringed instruments and organs.*
> *Praise him upon the loud cymbals:*
> *praise him upon the high sounding cymbals.*
> *Let every thing that hath breath*
> *praise the* LORD. *Praise ye the* LORD.

—PSALMS 150:3–6

(The "organ" was probably a much simpler reed instrument; Luther calls it a "shawn," which was a medieval ancestor of the oboe.) "Praise ye the Lord" in the original text is simply *Hallelujah* (*jah* is a shortened form of *Yahweh*, as in *Elijah* and *Adonijah*, both of which mean "the Lord is God"), which was already part of the call-and-response pattern of the Hebrew liturgy.

The mysterious subtitles that are attached to some Psalms were added by later editors, as attributions of authorship (not necessarily reliable) or as performance instructions for the Temple musicians (usually incomprehensible)—"To the chief musician on Neginoth upon Sheminoth" and the like. These have been retained in some modern editions of the Bible out of force of habit and very sensibly omitted in others.

Only slightly less obscure are such passages as

Purge me with hyssop, and I shall be clean: wash me, and I shall be whiter than snow.

—PSALMS 51:7

Hyssop is not, as this passage seems to imply, a brand-name laxative or detergent, but an aromatic herb; sprigs of hyssop were used to sprinkle water over a sacrificial offering as part of the ritual of purification.

Some of the Psalms are hymns of hatred and revenge, elaborate maledictions that may sound totally repellent to the modern ear. Many of these are especially difficult to ignore, because some of the most beautiful Psalms—137, "By the rivers of Babylon," is a good example—are songs of both consolation and (by contemporary standards at least) pathological bloodlust. Still, it seems doubtful that anyone would want to throw out the entire collection just to get rid of a few disagreeable reminders of our collective past—including songs that accompanied the early Christians into the arena and Cromwell's armies into battle, and that gave many victims of tyranny in our own century the strength and courage to endure their final hours.

Both Protestants and Catholics have tried to reinterpret the Psalms as Christian allegory, not always with the most satisfactory results. Thus, "Zion" becomes the Church, "the king of Israel" the Messiah, and "the Temple" the Crucifixion—though it must be admitted that the captions that the King James translators provided to explain the Christian allegory of the Song of Solomon are quite a bit more farfetched, to say the least. Many surprising parallels between the Psalms and the New Testament, however, show how deeply ingrained the language and imagery of the Psalms had become in traditional Jewish culture by the time the New Testament was written. All four Evangelists quote the Psalms, but there are many more striking ways in which dramatic phrases and everyday mannerisms mentioned in the Gospels seem to refer back to the Psalms. For example, Matthew describes Pontius Pilate handing Jesus over to the people with what seems to be a stoical Roman gesture:

> . . . he took water, and washed his hands before the multitude, saying, I am innocent of the blood of this just person. . . .

> —MATTHEW 27:24

But Psalm 26, attributed to King David, makes a similar allusion to the ritual cleansing of the priest's hand before a sacrifice:

> I will wash mine hands in innocency: so will I compass thine altar, O LORD.

> —PSALMS 26:6; see also PSALMS 73:13

This may simply be coincidence, but the later episodes of Jesus' passion contain an increasing number of explicit allusions to the Psalms. All four Gospels describe how the Roman soldiers cast lots for Jesus' garment at the foot of the Cross. John points to this as the fulfillment of the Psalms' prophecy of the torments that will be endured by the Messiah:

> They part my garments among them, and cast lots upon my vesture.

> —PSALMS 22:18

Jesus' last words on the Cross, as variously reported by Luke and Mark, are also taken verbatim from the Psalms:

> Into thine [thy] hands I commend my spirit.

> —PSALMS 31:5; LUKE 23:40

The Old Testament

My God, my God, why hast thou forsaken me?

—Psalms 22:1; Mark 15:34

*Whoso diggeth a pit shall fall therein: and he
that rolleth a stone, it will return upon him.*

—Proverbs 26:27

The Book of Proverbs: The Wise Shall Inherit Glory

The Book of Proverbs is attributed in the text itself to King
Solomon (except for the last two chapters, which are said to be
by a certain "Agur" and "King Lemuel," otherwise unidenti-
fied). In fact, as we now understand it, these proverbs (which are
largely concerned with worldly success rather than spiritual
advancement as an end in itself) were not written by King
Solomon, nor do they really belong to the Hebrew tradition of
Wisdom Literature. The Book of Proverbs, as the title certainly
implies, is simply a collection of commonsense maxims and
pithy sayings from all the cultures of the ancient Near East.

A few are memorable, eloquently and poetically expressed
(especially Agur's contribution in chapter 30). The majority are
prosaic examples of what in a less venerable context would be
called the conventional wisdom, on a level somewhere between
Poor Richard and Dear Abby. Some of these wise sayings are
empty tautologies, like:

A faithful witness will not lie: but a false witness will utter lies.

—Proverbs 14:5

This proverb is repeated several times, with slight variations:

*A wise son maketh a glad father: but a foolish son is the
heaviness of his mother.*

(Why not the other way around?) And unfortunately the dividing line between wisdom and folly is not all that easily drawn. "Solomon," for example, is a strict prohibitionist:

> *Look not thou upon the wine when it is red, when it giveth his colour to the cup, when it moveth itself aright [when it goes down smoothly].*
> *At the last it biteth like a serpent, and stingeth like an adder.*
> *Thine eyes shall behold strange women, and thine heart shall utter perverse things.*
> *Yea, thou shalt be as he that lieth down in the midst of the sea, or as he that lieth upon the top of a mast.*
>
> —PROVERBS 23:31–34

"Lemuel," on the other hand, is much more discriminating: kings and princes should definitely not drink on duty, "lest they . . . pervert the judgment of any of the afflicted," but "strong drink" is to be encouraged as an opiate for the masses:

> *Give strong drink unto him that is ready to perish, and wine unto those that be of heavy hearts.*
> *Let him drink, and forget his poverty, and remember his misery no more.*
>
> —PROVERBS 31:6–7

One subject dealt with exhaustively in the Book of Proverbs is the folly of consorting with "strange women" (bored housewives in particular). "Solomon" describes, in the soft-core pornographic style that has become traditional for such harangues, an encounter between a "young man void of understanding" and a predatory adulteress, whose husband is off somewhere on a business trip:

And, behold, there met him a woman with the attire of an harlot, and subtil of heart.

So she caught him, and kissed him, and with an impudent face said unto him,

Therefore came I forth to meet thee, diligently to seek thy face, and I have found thee.

I have decked my bed with coverings of tapestry, with carved works, with fine linen of Egypt.

I have perfumed my bed with myrrh, aloes, and cinnamon.

Come, let us take our fill of love until the morning: let us solace ourselves with loves.

For the goodman is not at home, he is gone a long journey:

He hath taken a bag of money with him, and will come home at the day appointed.

—PROVERBS 7:10, 13, 15–20

He also draws an interesting distinction between the prostitute (merely a financial drain) and the adulteress (a fatal obsession):

For by means of a whorish woman a man is brought to a piece of bread: and the adulteress will hunt for the [his] precious life.

—PROVERBS 6:26

In Luther's translation the difference is even more clear-cut: "For the price of a harlot is as much as a half a loaf of bread." But whether this passage means that the unfortunate philanderer will only be half a loaf the worse for it, or that (as in the King James) he will be despoiled of everything but his last crust, prostitution is clearly the lesser of these two particular evils.

In general, women come off pretty badly in the Book of Proverbs, which is full of misogynistic remarks like "The contentions of a wife are a continual dropping [as irritating as a leaky roof]" and "As a jewel of gold in a swine's snout, so is a fair woman which is without discretion." Perhaps the editor of this

257

anthology was trying to make amends when he added the proverbs attributed to King Lemuel—"the prophecy that his mother taught him"—which bring the Book of Proverbs to a close with a belated tribute to "the virtuous woman."

"And who knoweth whether he shall be a wise man or a fool?"

—ECCLESIASTES 2:19

The Book of Ecclesiastes: Kohelet the Fatalist

Perhaps the most remarkable thing about this remarkable book is that it is in the Bible at all. Its almost unrelievedly pessimistic and despairing tone seems to contradict the teachings of all the other books of the Old Testament. The few traces of the standard Old Testament orthodoxy—"Fear God, and keep his commandments"—appear to have been added by later editors to make this maverick "Book of the Preacher" conform at least nominally to the rest of the canon.

The Hebrew title of Ecclesiastes is The Words of Kohelet ["the teacher of the assembly"], the Son of David, the King of Jerusalem, which was enough to persuade Luther and the King James panel, among others, that its author must have been none other than King Solomon. Since then, scholars have decided on stylistic grounds that Ecclesiastes could not have been written by Solomon or by any of his contemporaries; the author's intense pessimism strongly reflects the prevailing philosophical outlook of the Hellenistic era, and "the words of Kohelet" were probably not written much before 250 B.C.

The famous opening line of Kohelet's sermon, "Vanity of vanities, saith the preacher, all is vanity," have often been tampered with by later translators, but never really improved upon—"all is futility," "all is emptiness," and even "nothing is really worthwhile." (The Hebrew word that is translated "vanity" means something like "a gust of wind.") In any case the meaning is clear:

> *For in much wisdom is much grief: and he that increaseth knowledge increaseth sorrow.*

> —ECCLESIASTES 1:18

This suggests only one conclusion:

> *Wherefore I praised the dead which are already dead more than the living which are yet alive.*
> *Yea, better is he than both they, which hath not yet been, who hath not seen the evil work that is done under the sun.*

> —ECCLESIASTES 4:2–3

For the living are trapped in an endless cycle of injustice and oppression:

> *If thou seest the oppression of the poor, and violent perverting of judgment and justice in a province, marvel not at the matter: for he that is higher than the highest regardeth, and there be higher than they.*

> —ECCLESIASTES 5:8

Kohelet is a fatalist who believes that any attempt to tamper with the predetermined order of the world will only make things worse:

> *For who knoweth what is good for man in this life, all the days of his vain life which he spendeth as a shadow? . . .*

> —ECCLESIASTES 6:12

We are not rewarded for our labors, either in life or in death, but because there is no comfort and no hope, we should simply

259

resign ourselves to the world as we find it and take pleasure where we can; despair is just as vain and empty as longing for a better world:

> *Live joyfully with the wife whom thou lovest all the days of the life of thy vanity, which he hath given thee under the sun, all the days of thy vanity: for that is thy portion in this life, and in thy labour which thou takest under the sun.*
>
> —ECCLESIASTES 9:9

Even if you don't find Kohelet's fatalistic world view especially attractive, he is well worth reading for the sheer power and beauty of his language. Read chapter 12 of Ecclesiastes, a grim prophecy of the "evil days" of old age which carry us ever closer to the "long home" of the grave. Every phrase rings out like the stroke of a death knell—but this crescendo of destruction and dissolution is finally resolved with a few words of conventional graveside piety (probably supplied by a nervous editor):

> *Then shall the dust return to the earth as it was: and the spirit shall return unto God who gave it.*
>
> —ECCLESIASTES 12:7

It may have been this same editor who added the last few verses, in what is evidently an attempt to neutralize the heretical brilliance of Kohelet's sermon by turning his own irresistible rhetoric against him:

> *And further, by these, my son, be admonished: of making many books there is no end; and much study is a weariness of the flesh.*
> *Let us hear the conclusion of the whole matter: Fear God, and keep his commandments: for this is the whole duty of man.*
>
> —ECCLESIASTES 12:12–13

Stay me with flagons, comfort me with apples:
for I am sick of love.

—SONG OF SOLOMON 2:5

The Song of Solomon: I Have Compared
Thee, O My Love . . .

By now even the theologians admit that the Song of Solomon (also called the Song of Songs, or the Canticle of Canticles) is a collection of Hebrew, Egyptian, and Mesopotamian love lyrics, all dealing explicitly with the theme of erotic love and not, as was once supposed, a metaphorical celebration of "the mutual love of Christ and his Church." Many of these songs appear to have been composed long before the time of Solomon; very similar lyrics have also been discovered in papryus texts and on cuneiform tablets.

After reading a verse or two of the Song of Solomon one can easily see why the commentators would have been hard pressed to justify including this erotic anthology in the Bible on strictly religious grounds. The *Handbuch zur Bibel* (Handbook of the Bible), which appeared in 1969, offers this disingenuous explanation: "The pleasures of the marriage bed, which include a component of frankly erotic love, are all part of the procreative drive which replenishes and invigorates God's people and which represents the fulfillment of his commandment, Be fruitful and multiply." In fact, the Song of Solomon is exclusively concerned with the raptures of "frankly erotic love," expressed in startlingly original and imaginative metaphor, and has nothing whatsoever to do with the pleasures of the marriage bed or the joys of parenthood.

The Song of Solomon really does not require much in the way of commentary, though it might be worth noting that several of these ancient love lyrics are among the earliest

261

examples of what came to be called the pastoral tradition, that is, the celebration of love in the great outdoors. Compare

> *Behold, thou art fair, my beloved, yea, pleasant: also our bed is green.*
> *The beams of our house are cedar, and our rafters of fir.*

> —SONG OF SOLOMON 1:16–17

with the love songs of the Elizabethans—Shakespeare's "Under the Greenwood Tree" or Marlowe's "Come live with me and be my love"—or with the more straightforward sentiments of the medieval troubadour:

> *Under the linden tree*
> *Out on the heather*
> *My love and I made our bed together.*
> *You will still see*
> *Should you happen to pass,*
> *Where we broke the blossoms and crushed the grass.*

> —WALTER VON DER VOGELWEIDE, circa 1250

> *But the souls of the righteous are in the hand of God, and there shall no torment touch them.*

> —WISDOM OF SOLOMON 3:1

Ecclesiasticus and the Wisdom of Solomon: From Proverbs to Plato

These two apocryphal books are extremely late productions, or imitations, of the Hebrew school of Wisdom Literature. The Wisdom of Solomon, a revolutionary work in many ways, as we shall see, was actually written at least a century later than Ecclesiasticus (or, the Book of Jesus Son of Sirach), but because it was once supposed to have been written by Solomon himself, it comes before Ecclesiasticus both in the Catholic Bible (after the Canticle of Canticles) and in the Protestant Apocrypha (after the Book of Judith and the apocryphal Additions to Esther).

This Jesus ben Sirach, we are told, "did imitate Solomon, and was no less famous for wisdom." Unfortunately, the Solomon he chose to imitate was not the author of Ecclesiastes but the sententious old drone of the Book of Proverbs. What Jesus ben Sirach is interested in is not so much the getting of wisdom as the cultivation of respectability and regular habits:

> *Sound sleep cometh of moderate eating: he riseth early, and his wits are with him. . . .*
> *And if thou hast been forced to eat, arise, go forth, vomit, and thou shalt have rest.*

> —ECCLESIASTICUS 31:20–21

His denunciations of "loose women" are colorful, but predictable:

> *The grace of a wife delighteth her husband, and her discretion will fatten his bones.*

> —ECCLESIASTICUS 26:13

And he seems to have the veteran hypochondriac's strangely ambivalent attitude toward the medical profession:

> *Honour a physician with the honour due unto him for the uses which ye may have of him: for the Lord hath created him. . . .*
> *He that sinneth before his Maker, let him fall into the hand of the physician.*

> —ECCLESIASTICUS 38:1, 15

You are not likely to miss very much by skipping over the wisdom of Jesus ben Sirach, but the Wisdom of Solomon is well worth reading. The contrast between the two books is interesting. Ecclesiasticus really represents the end of a long tradition, the Wisdom of Solomon the beginning of another, which is still very much alive.

The anonymous author, who lived in Alexandria around 50 B.C., was probably the first to try to reconcile the teachings of the Old Testament with the speculative philosophy of the Greeks. This is understandable, because Alexandria was the great intellectual center of the Hellenistic world, and he knew perfectly well that his readers would not think very much of the wisdom of Solomon or the faith of Moses unless they had Plato and Aristotle to back them up.

The style of the Wisdom of Solomon may be a little earnest and plodding, but the author's approach to the problem is truly ingenious. The search for enlightenment, which is the goal of both the righteous Jew and the philosophic Greek, can lead only to God, he concludes, for God is the source of all true wisdom. In Plato's philosophical system the only true reality is the world of pure forms; any material object is merely the imperfect reflection of a universal *idea*, as Plato calls it. Our author relates the Jewish conception of an omnipresent, immaterial God to the Platonic concept of a universal idea—"the spirit of wisdom" or "the Spirit of the Lord," he calls it. Thus, the Wisdom of Solomon anticipates the next fifteen hundred years or so of Western religious thought, in the course of which the original biblical declaration of faith, "And God created the heavens and the earth," would finally be restated in the language of classical philosophy: "The universe is an idea in the mind of God."

Not surprisingly, some other concepts that we think of as exclusively Christian make their first appearance in the Wisdom of Solomon: the resurrection (here linked to the Greek idea of the immortality of the soul), the Last Judgment, and the idea of a heavenly reward for a virtuous life on earth. The Wisdom of Solomon may have a special relevance to our own age, because its essential message seems to be that knowledge is not necessarily the same thing as true understanding. The apparent conflict between religion and science, and the more elusive possibility that we might be able to reconcile them, is the subject of this passage from an article written in 1970 by a Polish cleric named Karol Wojtyla, now better known to the world as Pope John Paul II:

> *I recall a long conversation I once had with a prominent research scientist, a very fine man, who said to me, "Both from the standpoint of my scientific method and your way of looking at things as well, I am an atheist. So when the subject of proofs of the existence of God comes up, I feel that I cannot take part in the discussion. As a scientist, I simply cannot see how such a thing could be possible." But this same man once sent me a letter in which he confessed in all honesty, "Whenever I find myself confronted with the majesty of nature, of a mountain landscape, I feel certain that He exists"—which precisely echoes the words of the Book of Wisdom [the Wisdom of Solomon]; "for the first author of beauty hath created them." When this scientist and his colleagues find themselves exclaiming over the grandeur of these works of nature, they might also bear in mind how much greater He who created them must be.*

> *Therefore the* LORD *himself shall give you a sign: Behold, a virgin shall conceive, and bear a son, and shall call his name Immanuel.*
>
> —ISAIAH 7:14

The Prophets

We think of a prophet as a visionary, someone who is wise enough or inspired enough to see into the future. Professional seers and soothsayers abounded in the ancient world, in Egypt, Assyria, and Athens, just as they did in the Middle Ages and in our century. And the more esoteric and ambiguous the prophecy, the more highly regarded it was likely to be; the Delphic Oracle in antiquity and Nostradamus in more recent times are the most famous examples of this.

Though this kind of prophecy does figure in the Old Testament—when Isaiah fortells the destruction of Babylon, for example—this is not really what the word *prophet* primarily means in the Old Testament. In ancient Israel a prophet was simply a spokesman, someone who *spoke for* someone else (which is what *prophētēs* means in Greek). In everyday contexts a prophet might be engaged to speak on behalf of a client who, like Moses, "was slow of speech" or had difficulty expressing himself in public. The prophets of the Old Testament were speaking on behalf of their God, of course, and the prophetic message is generally introduced by a phrase like "Then the word of the Lord came unto me" or simply "Thus saith the Lord."

The prophetic tradition lasted for over five hundred years, and there were hundreds of prophets altogether, who exerted a powerful influence, directly and indirectly, on the political and spiritual life of Israel. Whenever Israel lapsed into political disarray or social decadence—which is to say primarily during the period of the two kingdoms—the prophets flourished. They often risked their lives by denouncing social abuses, and like most other men of goodwill in troubled times, they almost invariably antagonized the state, the religious establishment, and society as a whole.

The words of the prophets were not even written down until after the Babylonian Exile. There are seventeen prophetic books in the Protestant Bible; the Catholic Bible includes an eighteenth book, Baruch, which Protestants and Jews consider apocryphal. Twelve of these are called "minor prophets," but this term simply refers to the relative length of the texts rather than to literary quality or spiritual stature. (Judging by those criteria, Lope de Vega, who is said to have written over two thousand plays, would have to be considered a major dramatist, and Shakespeare, with only thirty-eight, a minor one.)

The great theme of the prophetic books is the coming of the Messiah, the promised Redeemer of the nation of Israel. The concept of the Messiah is very old and was also known among the Persians and Assyrians. Only the Jews, however, regarded the coming of the Messiah as an absolute certainty and a corroboration of the belief that their people had been singled out by God. Some difference of opinion existed, though, about whether the Messiah would be a new King David or a great spiritual leader like Moses; both Judah Maccabee and Zerubbabel, the priest who led the first wave of returning exiles out of Babylon, were thought by some to have fulfilled the Messianic prophecies, at least for a time.

A great many passages in the prophetic books are confusing at best and at worst completely baffling. The authors have a tendency to switch from the present to the past or the future tense, or from the singular to the plural, in mid-sentence. (This is sometimes the fault of the early translators, who had not really mastered some of the finer points of Hebrew grammar.) And there are a great many obscure topical allusions that scholars have still not succeeded in deciphering and probably never will.

The earliest of the prophets who has a book all to himself is Jonah. His story, including the famous three-day journey in the belly of the "great fish," is really a classic of humorous understatement. If you haven't read the Book of Jonah since Sunday school, take another look; its author is a master of the pregnant pause, and he gives his readers plenty of time to react to his last comic effort before he springs the next one.

The story of Jonah begins seriously enough. The Lord

commands Jonah, "Arise, go to Nineveh, that great city, and cry against it; for their wickedness is come up before me." Jonah simply takes to his heels; the author does not take the trouble to explain that a Jewish prophet might be understandably reluctant to show up in the pagan Assyrian capital with a message of doom and destruction.

Jonah decides to avoid both the Assyrians and the Lord by taking ship for Tarshish, but—and this is the only part of the story that most of us remember—the Lord prepares a raging tempest and a great fish to intercept him. The great fish spits him out on the shore, just three days' journey from Nineveh, and Jonah sets off, chastened but probably still grumbling, to deliver his prophecy, "Yet forty days, and Nineveh shall be overthrown."

Strangely enough, Jonah's mission is a complete success, the Assyrians repent, and the Lord decides that Nineveh should be spared after all. Jonah is furious; he claims that he knew all along that Nineveh would never be destroyed, which was the reason, he says, that he had refused to go in the first place, "when I was yet in my country." Jonah goes off to the desert to sulk—and to wait hopefully for Nineveh to be destroyed after all. The Lord causes a castor plant (a "gourd" in the King James) to sprout overnight to give Jonah a patch of shade to sit in; then he sends a worm "and it smote the gourd that it withered." Jonah takes this as another personal affront; he begins to complain bitterly. The Lord listens patiently, then asks Jonah, "Doest thou well to be angry for the gourd?" Yes, Jonah replies, "I do well to be angry, even unto death."

Unlike Job, who really does yearn for death after all his undeserved tribulations, Jonah is merely being petulant, like a child who threatens to hold his breath until he turns blue. This gives the Lord (or rather the author) the perfect opportunity to deliver a crushing rejoinder, which, like the rest of the Book of Jonah, is at most half serious, as the last line makes very clear:

> *Then said the LORD, Thou hast had pity on the gourd, for the which thou has not laboured, neither madest it grow; which came up in a night, and perished in a night.*
>
> *And should not I spare Nineveh, that great city, wherein are more than sixscore thousand persons that cannot discern between their right hand and their left hand [children and other innocents]; and also much cattle?*
>
> —JONAH 4:10–11

This certainly ranks alongside the passage in Genesis in which Abraham haggles with his God to save his nephew's native city from destruction as one of the most delightful scenes in the Old Testament—only this time it is the prophet, not the Lord, who plays the straight man.

The Book of Jonah is certainly the most accessible of the prophetic books, and one of the shortest as well. All the others are worth reading selectively—you probably won't want to read through Ezekiel or Jeremiah at a single sitting—because they all contain haunting passages of great poetic beauty, passionate declarations of faith and social justice (as well as the characteristic denunciations of the sins of the people and prophecies of doom for the enemies of Israel).

Isaiah is the master stylist of the prophets, and Christian readers may be especially intrigued by his descriptions of the sufferings endured by the Messiah, which closely parallel the Gospels' account of the Passion of Jesus.

> *But he was wounded for our transgressions, he was bruised for our iniquities: the chastisement of our peace was upon him; and with his stripes we are healed.*
>
> *All we like sheep have gone astray; we have turned every one to his own way; and the LORD hath laid on him the iniquity of us all.*

He was oppressed, and he was afflicted, yet he opened not his mouth: he is brought as a lamb to the slaughter, and as a sheep before her shearers is dumb, so he openeth not his mouth.

—ISAIAH 53:5–7

Isaiah was a great scholar and a respected political councilor of several kings of Israel. (You may recall that it was Isaiah who blew the cover of the Babylonian secret agents in II Kings 20.) Most of the Book of Isaiah was actually written by his disciples or his "school" over the next few hundred years. Some of the later additions are obscure or uninspired. Others are worthy of the master himself, notably chapter 40, which provided several texts for Brahms's *German Requiem* and Handel's *Messiah*; this chapter contains some of the most memorable lines in the Old Testament, including "The voice of him that crieth out in the wilderness," "And every valley shall be exalted," and "All flesh is as grass."

The prophet Micah, who preached in Judah at about the same time as Isaiah, was a much less polished article, a fiery backwoods-evangelist type rather than a cultivated Temple scholar, though he describes himself in much more graphic terms:

Therefore I will wail and howl, I will go stripped and naked: I will make a wailing like the dragons and mourning as the owls.

—MICAH 1:8

He denounces the corruption and rapacity of the Judean ruling classes in especially pungent language:

. . . Is it not for you to know judgment?
Who hate the good, and love the evil; who pluck off their skin from off them, and their flesh from off their bones;

270

Who also eat the flesh of my people, and flay their skin from off them; and they break their bones, and chop them in pieces, as for the pot, and as flesh within the caldron.

—Micah 3:1–3

But his particular targets were the "seers and diviners" who deluded the people with false prophecies of hope. Though Micah predicted the imminent downfall of both kingdoms, much of his own prophecy is devoted to the coming of the Messiah—but only after the people have been redeemed by suffering and captivity. The Messiah will be born of the House of David, and in the original city of David, which was not Jerusalem but a small village a few miles to the south, the birthplace of King David:

But thou, Bethlehem Ephratah, though thou be little among the thousands [districts or townships] of Judah, yet out of thee shall come forth unto me that is to be ruler in Israel; whose goings forth have been from of old, from everlasting.

—Micah 5:2

If Micah's historical prophecies are relatively straightforward, Daniel's put even Nostradamus to shame. More has been written about them than any other prophetic book, because the Book of Daniel is highly symbolic—it includes a great many of the mysterious beasts and arcane emblems we will encounter later on in the Book of Revelations—very difficult to interpret, and very original as well. The Book of Daniel contains the only Old Testament vision of the Apocalypse, in which (another innovation) the entire history of the ancient Near East is interpreted as the preparation for the establishment of God's kingdom on earth. The early Christians especially cherished the more familiar story of Daniel in the lions' den as the great Old Testament example of constancy in the face of persecution, and three cities, Venice among them, claimed to have preserved the relics of the prophet Daniel.

Whether there really was a prophet called Daniel ("God is my judge") is not clear. Some scholars believe the biblical account of his life to be authentic—that he was a young Judean who was brought as a captive to Babylon. But the Book of Daniel exhibits such a great diversity of literary styles (several chapters are even written in Aramaic) and literary genres that it was most probably compiled by many different authors over a period of several centuries.

The Book of Daniel in the Catholic Bible also includes the edifying moral tale of Susanna and the Elders, which is actually a very neatly plotted detective story (called the History of Susanna in the King James Apocrypha). Two "ancients of the people" (common-pleas judges, we would call them) have been watching a beautiful young woman named Susanna strolling in her husband's garden, so attentively that "their lust was inflamed toward her." Once they have confessed their guilty passion to each other, all their scruples suddenly vanish. They decide that the only possible way that their yearning for this pious matron can be satisfied is by a bit of sexual blackmail. They conceal themselves in the garden, Susanna appears on schedule, and, the day being hot, she immediately dismisses her maids and undresses for her bath.

> Now when the maids were gone forth, the two elders rose up, and ran unto her, saying,
>
> Behold, the garden doors are shut, that no man can see us, and we are in love with thee; therefore consent unto us, and lie with us.
>
> If thou wilt not, we will bear witness against thee, that a young man was with thee: and therefore thou didst send away thy maids from thee.

Then Susanna sighed, and said, I am straitened on every side: for if I do this thing, it is death unto me: and if I do it not, I cannot escape your hands.

It is better for me to fall into your hands, and not do it, than to sin in the sight of the Lord.

With that Susanna cried with a loud voice: and the two elders cried out against her.

—SUSANNA 19–24

Susanna is convicted of adultery (with the hypothetical young man) on the strength of the elders' testimony, but Daniel interrupts this raucous kangaroo court by rebuking the people for failing to interrogate the witnesses properly. He takes over the role of examining magistrate himself, questions the two elders separately, and catches them out in a fatal contradiction: one says they were hiding under a "mastick tree," the other under a "holm tree" (a pistachio and an oak, respectively). The elders are condemned for bearing false witness, Susanna's honor is restored, and

From that day forth was Daniel had in great reputation in the sight of the people.

—SUSANNA 64

Malachi is the last of the prophetic books—the last book of the Old Testament in the Protestant Bible—though there never was a prophet called Malachi. Malachi ("my messenger") was the pseudonym chosen by its unknown author, which the early translators mistakenly assumed to be his real name.

This mistake has a great deal of symbolic truth behind it, though, as all the prophets might have been called Malachi; it was they who preserved the message that Yahweh had entrusted to Moses through a thousand years of Israel's troubled history.

According to the Hebrew tradition, this nameless prophet who called himself Malachi was the last of these messengers to be inspired directly by God. From then on (about 400 B.C.), and particularly after the Maccabees' revival of the kingdom of David, faith was no longer a matter of revelation—"Thus saith the LORD"—but of interpretation and, inevitably, disagreement. The two great forces for unity—the scrolls of the Law and of the prophets, and the prophecies of the coming of the Messiah—also inspired a profusion of warring sects and false messiahs, the most successful of whom (from the point of view of the Jewish priestly establishment) was Jesus.

In the last thirty years or so, we have heard a great deal about one of these Jewish splinter groups, the Essenes, a band of ascetics who followed the Maccabees into the wilderness to preserve the purity of their faith from the Syrian oppressor, and later from the profane squabbles of their fellow Jews.

As early as the fifteenth century it was suggested that Jesus and his disciples were simply a later breakaway sect who had brought the teachings of the Essenes back from the wilderness and proclaimed their master to be the Messiah. Scholars had already suspected that there was an essential continuity between the Old and New Testaments; all that was lacking was proof.

The discovery of the Dead Sea Scrolls at Qumran, two hundred years later, raised this question once again, and more urgently this time, because it seemed very likely that the missing evidence had at last been found.

Jesus must actually have been an Essene, since his teachings are steeped in Essene morality.

—FREDERICK THE GREAT, letter to
D'ALEMBERT, October 18, 1770

PART III

THE ESSENES: THE CHILDREN OF LIGHT AND THE TEACHER OF RIGHTEOUSNESS

Blessed are they who have remained poor for the spirit's sake.

—DEAD SEA SCROLLS

In the early morning of June 11, 1956, a report came in over the wire services that was clearly the stuff of which a night editor's dreams are made:

2000 YEAR OLD DIRECTIONS TREASURE SITE DISCOVERED 200 METRIC TONS GOLD AND SILVER STOP INSTRUCTIONS PRECISE ENOUGH PERMIT RECOVERY STOP POSSIBLE TREASURE SOLOMONS TEMPLE FINALLY FOUND STOP

According to the instructions referred to in this breathless dispatch (which purported to be the text of a telegram sent from one archaeologist to another), the treasure was located in the vicinity of Jerusalem, between Mount Gerizim and the ancient cities of Nablus and Hebron, which narrowed the exploration site down to a radius of less than fifty miles. More precise hints were included—"In the cistern in the court with the colonnade, in one corner of the pavement, in a hole opposite the topmost opening, nine hundred talents . . ." and "In the cistern below the eastern wall, in a hole cut from the cliffside, six hundred silver bars . . ."

This was more than a quarter of a century ago, and Solomon's

277

treasure has still not been found. The original wire-service report might seem a little suspect, because it came out during what British journalists call the "silly season"—June, July, and August—when real news is scarce and editors are most likely to give in to the impulse to run a story on the latest doings of the Loch Ness monster and when UFO sightings have the best chance of making headlines.

In fact, this report emanated from a highly reliable source: an international team of scholars and specialists who were working on the monumental project of recovering, restoring, and reassembling the thousands of surviving parchment and papyrus fragments of the Dead Sea Scrolls. Americans, Englishmen, Frenchmen, Germans, Poles, Israelis, and Jordanians, mountain climbers, military officers, chemists, infrared photographers, and paleographers (experts on ancient handwriting) were all involved in this project. The work is still going on and is likely to continue for a great many years more.

The stop-press item about the treasure map was inspired by an inscription discovered inside two large and badly corroded rolls of copper; the scribes evidently thought that this information was important enough to be entrusted to a costlier but much more permanent medium than parchment or papyrus. The scrolls were carefully cut open (it was impossible to unroll them) with a special device that had been constructed for exactly that purpose at the University of Manchester. The moment the three-thousand-character message had been deciphered, Professor John M. Allegro sent a telegram to the head of the research team in Jerusalem, and the treasure hunt was under way. Unfortunately, the landscape had changed so much after two thousand years that the site could not be identified without a systematic search, which, given the political situation on the Israeli-Jordanian border, was clearly impossible.

We might want to interpret this as a kind of parable of the search for the real significance of the Dead Sea Scrolls—there are plenty of tantalizing clues, but the treasure (in this case, evidence of a direct connection between the doctrines of the Essenes and the teachings of Jesus) remains elusive, even after a quarter-century.

The scrolls themselves were discovered in 270 different caches, many of them almost inaccessible; this is where the mountain climbers came in. Nearby were the ruins of what was originally thought to have been a Roman fortified camp. There was no natural source of water for this sprawling complex of thirty barracks rooms, however, which might easily have sheltered two hundred people. Instead, water was brought down from the mountains through a series of conduits cut from the rock and stored in enormous underground cisterns—far more water than would have been needed to supply the ordinary needs of two hundred Roman legionnaires, except in the event of an extended siege. In that case the besieging force could easily have cut the conduits that fed the cisterns.

The scrolls supplied the answer to this puzzle. This "Roman camp," which has since been completely excavated, was actually the site of the Essene community of Qumran, the home of the Essene spiritual elite, ascetics who spent their days in prayer and meditation, in copying and expounding the sacred texts. Qumran was very much like a medieval monastery, though there were other Essene communities all over Judea whose members were not celibate and who were not bound by the strict rule that was practiced at Qumran, which required, among other things, that the brothers symbolically wash their sins away in the Qumran "baptistry" three times every day.

As you probably know, the phrase "Dead Sea Scrolls" is something of a misnomer; most of the Qumran texts have survived only as tiny fragments. Many of those that scholars acquired from Bedouin dealers (who quickly cornered the market as soon as the original finds were announced) are no larger than a fingernail. The more enterprising Bedouins even began tearing up more or less intact parchments and papyruses and selling them off piecemeal as soon as they realized that the buyers would pay just about any price they cared to name for a scrap that had even a trace of writing on it. After all, what was at stake was a treasure that was worth a good deal more than all the shekels and ingots of Solomon's temple—over a hundred manuscripts of the books of the Old Testament that are a good thousand years older than the Masoretic texts on which our translations of the Bible are based.

But the original expectations that the entire Old Testament would have to be rewritten proved to be totally unfounded. The differences between the Masoretic texts (see Part I) and the Dead Sea Scrolls are surprisingly insignificant.

Over six hundred separate Qumran texts have come to light so far; they can be roughly grouped into three categories:

1. Copies of all books of the Old Testament (except the Book of Ruth). The Book of Tobit, which is generously represented, was apparently a great favorite with the Essenes (though probably more because of Tobit's vision of the New Jerusalem than because of the story of the magic fish and the demon Asmodeus).

2. Miscellaneous secular writings—medical treatises and horoscopes, the plan of the treasure cache, and the special calendar that the Essenes used. They rejected the Jewish lunar calendar then in common use (because it was the work of man) and divided the year into weekly cycles based on the Sabbath. This may eventually be of some value in fixing the chronology of the New Testament, which is based on a similar cycle of Sabbaths and festivals.

3. Spiritual writings, hymns, and regulations governing the Qumran community itself, including the initiation process and the sequence of daily prayer. Texts in this category, rather than the biblical manuscripts, have caused the greatest sensation, because they contain many phrases that also occur in the New Testament, or very close parallels to them. In at least one case

(quoted at the beginning of this section) the Essene version is quite a bit clearer. Instead of Matthew's "Blessed are the poor in spirit," the Qumran text reads "Blessed are they who have remained poor for the spirit's sake [for the sake of enlightenment]." (Incidentally, a manuscript from Cave IV at Qumran, not yet completely translated, appears to be an Essene version of the entire Sermon on the Mount—at least, every phrase begins with "Blessed are they," though it may be some time before we know how close the parallel really is.)

The Essenes' initiation process seems to have been very selective and very strict. The chosen candidates were admitted into the community for a probationary period, then subjected to a preliminary test before they could take part in the daily baptismal rites; then, after passing a second test, they joined the inner circle of initiates who met twice a day for a communal meal, which was (roughly speaking) a combination eucharist and silent prayer meeting.

Qumran was not just a community of scribes and scholars, however. The Essenes were a militant order, similar in many ways to the Knights Templar and the other crusading orders of the Middle Ages, who were fully prepared to fight and, if necessary, to die for their convictions. Essenes were probably among the last defenders of the famous stronghold of Masada, not far from Qumran, who took their own lives rather than surrender to the Romans after the first great Jewish rebellion in A.D. 73. You may recall from the preceding chapter that the earlier prophecies of the Messiah portrayed him as either a great teacher and lawgiver like Moses or a mighty warrior like David. All the Essenes (and not just the fighting ascetics of Qumran) believed there would be *two* Messiahs: one who would renew the faith of Israel, and another who would drive out the Roman legions by force of arms.

The community of Qumran was organized along strict hierarchical lines. Their spiritual and temporal leader was called

"The Teacher of Righteousness"; one of the masters who bore this title is said to have been crucified, though this is not mentioned in any of the Qumran texts that have been published so far. All important decisions were made by a council of three initiates and twelve laymen. (The number twelve has nothing to do with Jesus' twelve disciples, except indirectly; both were chosen in symbolic memory of the twelve tribes of Israel.)

The Romanized Jewish historian Flavius Josephus, who took part in the first Jewish rebellion and claimed to have been a student of the Essenes, has left us this account of the beliefs of a more typical Essene community, which was not subject to the stern monastic discipline of Qumran. Even so:

> . . . they shun all the pleasures as an abomination, and they regard continence and resistance to the passions as the only true virtue. . . . They take in the children of others, as long as they are of tender years and still receptive to teaching. . . . It is their unalterable conviction that the flesh is subject to decay and that the material body is ephemeral, but that the soul, being immortal, endures forever.

(Despite their contempt for the physical body, by the way, the Essenes were famous not only as teachers but as healers—which may have been what the word Essenes originally meant—and were especially noted for their vast knowledge of herbal medicine.)

The Essenes and their teachings were known only from secondary sources until the nineteenth century, but there was enough in Josephus and other ancient writers to convince Voltaire (and his sometime disciple, Frederick the Great) that Christianity was merely a continuation of the teachings of the Essenes. Even before the discovery of the Qumran texts, the similarities were striking (especially to those, like Voltaire, who were not terribly well disposed toward Christianity to begin with), though not necessarily convincing.

The Essenes took part in a ritual meal during which they felt themselves to be in communion with God and his angels.

The Essenes taught that poverty, chastity, and humility were the first prerequisites of a life of righteousness, that we should love our enemies as well as our neighbors, and that our sins could be washed away (if only temporarily) through the ritual of baptism.

Thanks to the Qumran texts, a few more possible parallels have come to light: the council of twelve, the Essenes' ascetic pilgrimages into the desert (reminiscent of Jesus' forty days and forty nights in the wilderness). But even with this new evidence, the controversy continues in more or less its original form. None of the Qumran texts that have been published so far can be cited as incontrovertible proof that Christianity was just Qumran writ large, or that the New Testament is merely a postscript to the scrolls of the Teacher of Righteousness. At this point the postscript school may seem to have a slight edge, though, so it seems only fair to present a few of the opposing arguments. Note that none of the evidence is really in dispute here (there is not so much of it that we can afford to waste it); it is merely a question of which facts (or plausible suppositions) you choose to cite and how you would like to interpret them.

In general, the Jesus-was-original school takes the position that although many broad similarities exist between Essene and Christian teachings and practices, these differ in many important particulars.

First, the Essene "communion" was not offered to the entire community of believers but only to a small group of initiates. Cripples and invalids were excluded (as they were from participation in certain Temple rituals under the laws of Moses); women were excluded as well, "so as not to drive away the angels."

Second, there is the question of the twelve disciples and the Qumran council of twelve. (We already know that the number itself is not significant.) In addition, the Teacher of Righteousness was much more of an absolute hierarch than Jesus—it is difficult to imagine him washing the feet of *his* disciples, for example. More important, Jesus' message was intended not just for the twelve tribes of Israel (as symbolized by the disciples), but for all the peoples of the earth. The Teacher of Righteousness preached that only the Essenes, "the holy remnant of Israel," would be saved from universal destruction.

Third, although both the Essenes and Jesus refused to acknowledge the authority of the traditional priesthood of the Temple, their motives in doing so were entirely different. The Essenes rejected the empty formalism of the established church (so to speak), but only because they hoped to restore the pure and uncorrupted faith of their forefathers: the laws of Moses. Jesus, on the other hand, proclaimed that the old law had been superseded by a new covenant. This is certainly the most fundamental difference between the teachings of Jesus and of the Essenes, or of any other Jewish sect. The final points—the journey into the wilderness, and the poverty, or "primitive communism," of Jesus and his disciples—probably have a common origin in the tradition of the Old Testament prophets (Moses' forty-year trek across Sinai in the first case); evidently many other wandering ascetics and preachers in that period shared their possessions and lived out of a common fund of alms and donations.

The postscript school's most persuasive argument is based on the many remarkable parallels between the Gospels and the Qumran texts. Their opponents clearly can't dismiss these as easily, though they do try to limit severely the scope of this argument. These parallels, they maintain, simply demonstrate that *some* of the authors of *two* of the Gospels—Matthew and John—seem to have been familiar with the teachings of the Essenes and that they borrowed key phrases and striking metaphors from the Essene writings. John was long thought to have been the Evangelist who was the most heavily influenced by Greek religious and philosophical thought. The Qumran texts at least have shown that John need not have studied at the feet of an Athenian sage to have adopted the image of the conflict between light and darkness as a symbol for the struggle between good and evil. The title alone of one of the more important scrolls makes this clear—"The War Between the Children of Light and the Children of Darkness" (the work that is the source of the Essene version of "Blessed are the poor in spirit").

In him [God] was life; and the life was the light of men.

—JOHN 1:4

I am the light of the world: he that followeth me shall not walk in darkness, but shall have the light of life.

—JOHN 8:12

John also speaks (not in the Gospel but in the first of the two "general epistles" that are traditionally attributed to him) of "the spirit of truth" and "the spirit of error," two phrases that have also turned up in the Qumran *Manual of Instruction.* It is not always that easy to tell the difference between John, when he is writing in his "Greek" philosophical vein at least, and the Essenes:

It is God who has established all things, and without him nothing comes to pass.

—QUMRAN TEXTS

All things were made by him; and without him was not any thing made that was made.

—JOHN 1:3

What are we to make of all this? In fact, the most reasonable

285

conclusion seems to be the one proposed by the adherents of the Jesus-was-*not*-an-Essene school: some of the authors of the Gospels (there were a great many more than four) had come into contact, directly or indirectly, with the teachings of the Essenes. But this does not necessarily mean that Jesus himself actually used these Essene symbols and phrases. At the moment, even the most ardent champions of the postscript school will have to be content with this, though they would certainly be the first to point out that there are more than twenty thousand scroll fragments in the Israel Museum in Jerusalem that have still not been sorted or catalogued, much less translated. And for all we know, other scrolls may still be hoarded by a canny Bedouin dealer or moldering in some undiscovered cave in the Dead Sea cliffs. Archaeologists, who are accustomed to thinking in terms of centuries and millennia, have learned to be patient about such things, and there may well be some decisive new development awaiting us in just a few decades.

Still, one prominent New Testament figure we haven't yet considered may very well have been an Essene, at least at some early phase of his career, is John the Baptist. After all, John was an ascetic who dressed in "raiment of camel's hair," fed on roasted locusts (as did the Essenes), and spent almost all his life in the wilderness—more specifically, he preached and baptized his followers on the banks of the Jordan, at a bend in the river that is actually within sight of the monastery of Qumran.

True, John the Baptist departed from the strict Essene doctrine in one important respect, because the Essenes regarded baptism as an essential daily ritual of purity rather than a permanent remission of sin. It is tempting to speculate that John served his novitiate at Qumran or some other Essene community and then struck out on his own to preach his slightly unorthodox version of the original Essene creed, like the wandering Essene preachers who are mentioned by Josephus and other contemporary writers. (The differences among these early accounts make it clear that the Essene doctrines were a great deal more flexible than the Qumran document would suggest.)

That Jesus came to be baptized by John and spoke of him as the greatest "among them that are born of women" (Matthew 11:11) even inspired a new Jewish sect, which lasted until the second century A.D., whose members regarded John as the true Messiah and Jesus merely as one of his disciples. (It may also be worth mentioning, though, that a certain number of John's followers may have been attracted to him for financial reasons rather than because of his great personal charisma. The officially sanctioned alternative to baptism would have been a pilgrimage to Jerusalem and a costly Temple sacrifice, a price that many repentant sinners may have been unwilling to pay.)

Unfortunately, the Bible tells us very little about John's ministry in the wilderness, though we are given a sketchy account of his dramatic martyrdom at the hands of the tetrarch Herod. (The missing details have been enthusiastically supplied by poets, artists, and composers from the early Greek icon painters to Oscar Wilde and Richard Strauss.) According to the Bible, John was imprisoned because he denounced Herod for his bigamous marriage with his brother's wife, Herodias. Her daughter—Josephus tells us that her name was Salome—danced before the king so bewitchingly that he offered to grant her any favor she cared to ask for, "unto the half of my kingdom." Prompted by her mother, she asked for "John the Baptist's head in a charger" instead. (The interesting possibility that she was passionately in love with John was first suggested by Oscar Wilde's *Salome*, which in turn inspired Strauss's opera and the famous Dance of the Seven Veils.)

John the Baptist figures primarily in Strauss's opera as a disembodied voice (and later on as a disembodied head). He plays a more substantial role in the Gospels as "the voice of one crying in the wilderness" (a phrase from Isaiah that was frequently quoted by the Essenes) who foretells the imminent arrival of the Messiah:

There cometh one mightier than I after me, the latchet of whose shoes I am not worthy to stoop down and unloose.

—MARK 1:7

The Church later rewarded John's humility; he is the only one of the saints who has two feast days; the anniversaries of his birth (June 24) and of his martyrdom (August 29) as well.

Whether John the Baptist will ever be proved to be the missing connection between the mysterious Teacher of Qumran and the teachings of Jesus, this much at least is clear: John was the last of the biblical prophets to foretell the coming of the Messiah, the living bond between the Old Testament prophets, longing for deliverance and the restoration of their faith, and the New Testament Evangelists' conviction that their prophecies had been fulfilled by a new covenant between God and man, the beginning of a new epoch in the history of the world.

The beginning of the gospel of Jesus Christ . . .

—Mark 1:1

PART IV

THE NEW TESTAMENT

Meanwhile the basic paradox remains that the historic Jesus, so far as we can know him, was not directly responsible for either the success or failure of Christianity. When he was resurrected, he was indeed transfigured by his followers. He became the Christ, a Greek word he was unacquainted with. He was sent abroad to strange peoples, to compete with their mystical savior gods. . . .

—Herbert J. Muller

The historical and prophetic books of the Old Testament (counting First and Second Maccabees) provided us with an almost continuous record of twelve centuries of Jewish history. In contrast, the New Testament is exclusively concerned with the events of a single century, the life of Jesus and (roughly) the first three generations of the early Church. Before we go any further, let us take a brief look at the history of the New Testament itself.

To begin with, the word *Gospel* (Old English *godspell*, "good story") is simply a translation of the Greek word *evangelion* ("good tidings"). *Evangelion* originally referred to the *reward* that was paid to the messenger, the evangelist, who brought the message; later it came to mean the good news itself. A Roman inscription celebrating the birth of Octavian (the future Emperor Augustus) in 63 B.C. refers to the *evangelion,* or as we might say, the blessed event. Strangely enough, the word *evangelist* is occasionally used in the Gospels to mean something a little different: an authoritative witness, someone whose testimony is entirely reliable.

The New Testament is a collection of twenty-seven books (a little less than a third of the Bible): the four Gospels, the Acts of the Apostles, twenty-one letters (epistles), and the Book of Revelation. All were originally written in Greek, and at least nineteen of them were not written by the men whose names they bear. The Gospels are thought to have been written by several different authors; and however accurate the testimony of these Evangelists may have been, it is far from certain that any of them was actually an eyewitness to the events he describes.

In fact, the letters that are traditionally (and in some cases correctly) attributed to Paul are the earliest New Testament writings. The Gospels were composed a full generation later, Mark between A.D. 60 and 70, Matthew between A.D. 70 and 80, Luke about A.D. 85, John between A.D. 90 and 100.

As with the Old Testament, the distinction between canonical and apocryphal books was not all that sharply defined for quite some time. Finally, in A.D. 367, Bishop Athanasius of Alexandria settled this controversy in a pastoral letter which established the twenty-seven books that were to be read in the churches of his diocese. Within a century or two this list was accepted as authoritative all over the Christian world.

The Christian Bible was originally divided into chapters in the twelfth or thirteenth century. The present arrangement of verses was worked out by an English printer named Robert Stevens "while on a horseback journey from Paris to Lyon" in about 1550 (the first printed version appeared in 1560).

The Old Testament is referred to about 900 times in the New Testament, including about 250 direct quotations. In the very early New Testament texts, these quotations are usually inaccurate. This was because at that time the scrolls of the Jewish Bible were read aloud only in the synagogue and thus had to be recorded by hearsay. (Later scribes got around this problem by copying directly from the Septuagint.)

The earliest of these surviving texts date from the second century A.D. The oldest, the so-called Papyrus 52, which contains parts of two chapters of John, may date back to as early as A.D. 120—just twenty years or so after the lost original manuscript of the Gospel. Most of these papyrus fragments were found near the town of Oxyrhynchus (modern Behnesa) in Upper Egypt. This town has been a particularly rich hunting ground for archaeologists, not because the citizens of Oxyrhynchus were especially devout (many of the papyruses are manuscripts of Greek plays, magical charms, and other secular works), but because the dry desert climate preserved papyruses almost as if they had been in a museum display case. Many of these papyrus manuscripts were found in graves, but not as grave gifts or funeral texts in the early Egyptian style. The papyruses had been glued together to make a kind of heavy cardboard that was used as a coffin—once again, not for religious reasons but simply because there were not many trees in Oxyrhynchus.

The most famous complete manuscript copies of the Greek New Testament are the Codex Vaticanus and the Codex Sinaiaticus (the first is so called because it is in the Vatican Library collection; the second was discovered during the last century in the monastery at the foot of Mount Sinai). Both were copied sometime during the fourth century, not much more than two hundred years after the original manuscripts were written. This is really not much of a time lapse, when you consider that the earliest copies of Plato's *Dialogues* that have come down to us were produced almost fifteen hundred years after Plato's death.

New Testament scholars are doubly fortunate in that they

have an unprecedented abundance of material to work with—
almost four hundred manuscripts of the Greek New Testament.
This means that a careful comparison can be made of all the
common variant readings ("text families," as scholars say),
which makes it a great deal easier to weed out scribal errors and
misunderstandings and to restore the text that has come down to
us to something very close to its original form. Unfortunately,
the early Christians were much more casual about such things
than the Masoretes, but certainly no other book in history has
been picked over so carefully, letter by letter, so many times, by
so many devoted scholars. Starting in the Renaissance, over a
dozen increasingly elaborate critical editions of the Greek New
Testament have been prepared. Though the New Testament
may not quite be the most widely read book of all times, it is
certainly the most carefully edited.

Some of the problems involved with copying, translating,
or merely deciphering these early manuscripts can be graphically illustrated in one sentence. INTHOSEDAYSALMOS
TEVERYTHINGWASWRITTENINCAPITALLETTERSWIT
HNOPUNCTUATIONANDNOSPACESBETWEENWORDS.
Other problems for copyists arose from the use of abbreviations
(so that the words for "God" and "who" looked almost identical)
and, in dictation, from the fact that colloquial Greek pronunciation had gotten a little sloppy by the second century A.D., and so
the Greek words for "we" and "you" were pronounced in almost
the same way.

Purely mechanical problems like these are not too difficult to
deal with. A simple example can be found in Matthew 2:6, a
reference to Micah's prophecy of the birth of the Messiah that
originally began:

In Bethlehem, the land of Juda. . . .

The King James translators knew perfectly well that Bethlehem was not a "land" but a city and that obviously a word had been dropped:

In Bethlehem, in *the land of Juda. . . .*

(This seems pretty elementary, but even Luther overlooked it, and the same correction was not made in the German Bible until 1969.)

But the real problem for the translator is not just to make the Greek words correspond to the words in a modern language, but to make the meanings correspond. It has been said that the King James translation is actually better written than the Greek original—which is our good fortune. If, however, we are really interested in restoring the meaning of the original text, we may have to look elsewhere, at least occasionally. And, if necessary, we may have to sacrifice literary excellence for linguistic accuracy. Take the familiar Christmas carol text from Luke 2:14:

Glory to God in the highest, and on earth peace [not "peace on earth"], good will toward men.

This is a beautiful sentiment, but probably not what the original author had in mind. Saint Jerome translated this last phrase "peace on earth to men of good will," only a little closer to the Greek, which literally means something like "to men of satisfaction." This seems to be a slightly cryptic way of saying "to men with whom the Lord is satisfied, or well pleased." The New International Version of the New Testament has "peace on earth to men on whom his favor rests." So, then, the King James reading is actually an elegant paraphrase of a sentence that sounds pretty cumbersome in English (and would look terrible on a Christmas card), but that is much closer to what the author of the Gospel actually wrote.

This is more a matter of style than of interpretation, really. But what happens when the translator is not entirely sure what the Greek text actually means? Probably the best-known example of this is a line from the Lord's Prayer:

Give us this day our daily bread.

The word translated as "daily" in the New Testament occurs only in this one place, but by careful comparison of textual variants from other manuscript traditions, it now seems likely that an "accurate" translation of the line would read something like "Give us our bread for tomorrow. . . ." This is offered only as a marginal reading in modern translations of the New Testament (primarily because no one knows exactly what it means). Once again, though most of us would certainly prefer the inspired misreading of the New Testament scholars, this is what the text of the Gospel "really" says.

This brings us to our next point: the desirability of interpretation when the text speaks for itself perfectly clearly. The tendency to help the reader too much—to provide too much commentary—is a common occupational frailty of the conscientious scholar. This does no great harm. The same certainly cannot be said for the kind of devious or disingenuous explanations that have been made for many biblical texts, solely designed (or so it seems) to obscure the actual meaning of the original. The classic example of this is Jesus' remark to his disciples in Mark 10:25:

It is easier for a camel to go through the eye of a needle, than for a rich man to enter into the kingdom of God.

You may have heard that "the Eye of the Needle" was the nickname of a particularly narrow gate in Jerusalem, with barely enough clearance for a fully laden camel, or even that *camel* should actually be *kamilos*, supposedly the Greek word for a ship's cable or a length of rope. In fact, this was much more likely to have been just a particularly vivid figure of speech, a little farfetched perhaps but perfectly comprehensible. It is difficult to avoid the feeling that what ingenious commentators are really looking for is a loophole just big enough for a rich man to squeeze his way through. (All their ingenuity seems to have gone to waste; the "rich man" whom the author of Mark is talking about was not just rich, he was also a smug, self-satisfied Pharisee, which is probably why Jesus seemed to be so eager to get rid of him.)

The last word on the subject of scriptural interpretation has already been spoken, a little over two hundred years ago, by the great Protestant theologian Friedrich Carl Oetlinger: "All these questions that still remain unanswered we must not try to resolve by interpretation alone. The time will come when we will find the answers." This was addressed to Oetlinger's eighteenth-century colleagues, true sons of the Enlightenment, who were determined to clarify every obscurity in the New Testament by the unaided exercise of pure reason. Today we have the scientific disciplines of archaeology and textual criticism to help us in our inquiries, and every archaeological find and every ancient manuscript that comes to light brings us that much closer to the historical truth of the New Testament.

From the beginning Christianity has been thought of as fixed in historical time, and because it is one of the youngest of the world's great religions, it is also more accessible to historical inquiry than any other. This in itself is part of its greatness—that it can be explored from the outside, not just studied as a body of sacred writings and traditions. The teachings of Jesus have a transcendent, timeless value, but the words and deeds of Jesus can be understood only in terms of the context of the time and place in which he lived.

> *He that rejecteth me, and receiveth not my*
> *words, hath one that judgeth him: the word that*

297

I have spoken, the same shall judge him in the last day.

—John 12:48

Jesus: The Man from Galilee

So far about seventy thousand biographies of Jesus have been written, not counting the Gospels. This is probably because we know so very little about his life. The dates of his birth and death are still a matter of conjecture, though one thing we can be certain of is that he was not born on December 25, A.D. 1.

Believers and nonbelievers can still agree that certain events that took place in a small corner of Palestine, within a radius of twenty miles or so, changed the course of world history, or, as Hegel concisely put it, "History ended and began with Jesus." Unfortunately, history—at least in the more prosaic sense of authentic, nonbiblical documentary sources—also seems to have ignored Jesus completely. There are no records of his trial, no authentic testimonial letters from a blind man whose sight he had miraculously restored (though a great many forgeries were circulated a few centuries later). As far as the Roman occupying authorities were concerned, Jesus was simply one of a great many agitators and troublemakers, too insignificant for the bureaucrats to bother with.

The earliest Roman sources in which Jesus is mentioned at all are accounts of the persecution of Christians under Nero and later emperors. The most detailed of them appears in the *Annals* of Tacitus (written about A.D. 115): "The name [Christians] derives from Christus, who was condemned by Pontius Pilate during the reign of Tiberius. This detestable superstition, which was suppressed for a brief time, has sprung up again and has spread not only through Judea, which was the source of the

298

contagion, but to Rome as well, where all the world's vileness finds a home and willing followers."

An earlier Roman historian, Suetonius, simply mentions that a certain "Chrestus" had been stirring up a great deal of trouble in Rome. Suetonius was sometimes careless about his facts, so it is not really clear whether "Chrestus" refers to Jesus' followers or his teachings, or to another prophet or agitator of some sort called Chrestus who was really in Rome at the time.

Josephus's account is much more positive. He extols Jesus as a miracle worker, even as the Messiah. But it seems curious that Josephus, a renegade Jew who was completely Roman in his outlook, would have had such enthusiastic praise for Jesus, and his passage on Jesus reads suspiciously like an early Christian interpolation.

In the Talmud and the writings of the rabbis, famous for their scholarly thoroughness, Jesus is understandably dismissed rather curtly as a sorcerer and rabble rouser whose five disciples healed the sick. And that, as far as the contemporary, nonbiblical sources are concerned, is that.

Not long after Jesus' death, many of the gaps in the Evangelists' accounts of his life were filled in with inventive legendary tales—of his childhood in particular, about which the Gospels tell us very little. These apocryphal stories, whose informational value is precisely nil, relate how the young Jesus modeled a flock of little birds out of clay, which immediately came to life and flew out of his hands, and other small-scale miracles, some of which he is said to have performed while still in Mary's womb.

The Surrealist artist Max Ernst has given us a glimpse of another unreported incident from Jesus' boyhood that is much better suited to the tastes of our own irreverent age. *The Virgin Spanks the Christ Child in the Presence of Three Witnesses* shows Mary, her hand ominously upraised, with the child bent over her knee, his bare backside already bright red. Mary's halo is still firmly in place, but Jesus' has tumbled onto the ground, and we can only imagine what childish misdemeanor he might have committed. When this painting was first exhibited in 1926, it caused a howl of protest, but today even seminary students can appreciate this vivid apocryphal genre scene.

A more authoritative source for the events of Jesus' later life, discovered twenty years later, was the so-called Thomas Gospel. This purports to have been written by the disciple "Doubting Thomas," who had to be convinced that Jesus had actually risen from the dead. His name means "the twin" in Aramaic, though no explanation of this is provided in the Gospels.

Manuscripts of this Gospel had been circulating since the early Middle Ages, but their authenticity was always suspect until 1946, when a fourth-century Coptic manuscript of the Thomas Gospel was discovered in Nag Hammadi in Egypt, near the tombs of the pharaohs at Luxor. This gave the Thomas Gospel a respectable pedigree, and it may in fact be one of the earliest records of the teachings of Jesus. Simply a collection of his sayings, it lacks any connecting narrative or commentary by the author. The Thomas Gospel generally coincides with the canonical Gospels' record of the words of Jesus, though a few of the *logia* (sayings) that appear only in the Thomas Gospel may be useful in interpreting a few of the more problematical passages in the New Testament. (Professor Oetlinger's prophecy that we would eventually come to understand these things better has been at least partially fulfilled.)

For example, take this verse from Luke, which Kierkegaard called the most troubling and the most difficult of all of Jesus' teachings:

> *If any man come to me, and hate not his father, and mother, and wife, and children, and brethren, and sisters, yea, and his own life also, he cannot be my disciple.*

> —LUKE 14:26

It seems as though Jesus is offering a bitter choice to his disciples. But Logion 101 of the Thomas Gospel adds a final sentence that does not appear in Luke and suggests a totally different interpretation:

> *And whosoever does not love his father and mother as I do, he will not be one of my disciples.*

So it seems that Jesus is not necessarily forcing his disciples to choose between their master and their families. He is simply announcing that he intends to accept no one as a disciple who is halfhearted or indifferent—"neither hot nor cold," as Paul says—and who cannot both love and hate, the full gamut of human emotions.

Reason lies behind the Evangelists' failure to give us so little information about Jesus' individual character and personality. We have to depend on occasional stray references to find out, for example, that he was fond of eating and drinking, even in low company (Luke 7:34), or that he could be a bit peevish when awakened from a sound sleep (Mark 4:38). The authors of the Gospels were not really interested in writing a biography of Jesus in the modern sense but in compiling an account of his life that was intended solely to strengthen and reaffirm the faith of the various congregations that made up the early Church. An especially critical need for this existed in the first century after Jesus' crucifixion, when the early Church was increasingly plagued by unrest and anxiety because the eagerly awaited Second Coming of Christ had been inexplicably delayed.

Because each of the Gospels was addressed to a different audience, they differ substantially in content and in overall viewpoint. The real question—because none of the authors of the Gospels was an eyewitness to any of these events or even a contemporary of Jesus—is where the Gospel information came from. Twentieth-century scholars have proposed many theories, the simplest and most widely accepted of which is called the two-source theory. According to this theory, the earliest Gospel, Mark, plus a hypothetical record of the sayings of Jesus (which scholars call the Q-document, from the German *Quelle*, "source"), formed the basis for the later Gospels.

All the Gospels stress a single essential point again and again (some more vigorously than others): that Jesus was indeed the Messiah whose coming had been foretold by the prophets. Both Jewish and Gentile Christians were well acquainted with the Old Testament (the Gentiles adopted the Septuagint as their sacred book), which is why two of the Gospels include the "begats,"—a detailed genealogy of Jesus which traces his lineage all the way back to "Adam, the son of God" (in Luke) and Abraham (in Matthew). Micah had foretold that the Messiah would come from Bethlehem, the birthplace of David; in the Gospels Jesus is born in Bethlehem, either because Mary and Joseph lived there already (as in Luke) or because they had returned from Nazareth to take part in the Roman census so that Joseph would be numbered among his kindred of the House of David.

This census has proved to be about as much of an ordeal for modern biblical scholars as it must have been for Mary and Joseph. A census of the entire Roman Empire was carried out every fourteen years, "that all the world should be taxed," as Luke explains. This particular census, he goes on to say, was carried out while Cyrenius (Quirinius) was governor of Syria (the Roman province that also included Palestine). The Roman records confirm that a senator called Publius Sulpicius Quirinius, surnamed Cyrenius, was dispatched to Syria in A.D. 6 (Josephus confirms that a census was taken in the year 6). So far, so good.

Both Matthew and Luke make it very clear, however, that Jesus was born during the reign of Herod the Great, the autonomous ruler of the Roman client state of Judea, and Herod died in 4 B.C., ten years before the arrival of Quirinius.

Quirinius seems to have been in the right place at the wrong time. Fortunately, however, scholars were able to resolve this deadlock by referring to Matthew's account of a more distinguished visitor to Judea in the year of Jesus' birth: the Star of Bethlehem.

As early as 1606 the astronomer Johannes Kepler had pointed out that a "grand conjunction" of the planets Jupiter and Saturn in the constellation Pisces had occurred in the year 7 B.C. This spectacle would have been visible from the latitude of Bethlehem, 32° N. These two giant planets had approached so close to each other that they appeared to be a single point of light; according to Kepler, this phenomenon could have been observed at three different times during the year—May 29, October 3, and December 4. The astrologers chimed in with what in the seventeenth century was considered to be conclusive proof of Kepler's discovery. Saturn, they explained, was the planet that governed Syria and Judea, Jupiter was the planet of imperial Rome, and thus of the ruler of the world. In Jewish tradition, the constellation Pisces was associated with the last age of human history and the coming of the Messiah.

The purely astronomical side of Kepler's theory remained unchallenged until 1977, when an article appearing in the highly reputable *Journal of the Royal Astronomical Society* suggested that the light that guided the Three Wise Men to Bethlehem was actually a supernova, an exploding star. According to Chinese and Korean astronomical records from A.D. 5, a remarkably bright star had appeared in March and continued to be visible for a longer period every night. And according to the British astronomers who proposed this theory, the supernova would have been visible in the night sky over Judea as well.

Yet whether this spectacular celestial event actually coincided with the birth of Jesus is another question entirely (which the astronomers wisely make no attempt to answer). These two events might well have been simply associated by tradition, or by the author of Matthew, who was writing about seventy-five years after the fact. It is even possible that Matthew's description of the Star of Bethlehem is nothing more than another allusion to the Old Testament prophecy of the advent of a powerful king of Israel.

> . . . there shall come a Star out of Jacob, and a Sceptre shall rise out of Israel. . . .
>
> —NUMBERS 24:17

Later Christian tradition has considerably embellished Matthew's account of the Three Wise Men who came "from the east to Jerusalem." They are said to have been Magi—Persian sages, skilled astronomers who had seen the star in the east and were the first to recognize Jesus as the true Messiah.

According to an earlier legend, they were three kings, Caspar, Balthazar, and Melchior, one of whom is represented as a black man in Renaissance paintings. For some reason, the Three Kings were thought of as the special protectors of miners, who scratched their names on the doorposts of their houses every New Year as a good-luck talisman. And after their relics were housed in a magnificent golden shrine in Cologne Cathedral, they became the patron saints of the city of Cologne (when this reliquary was opened, many years ago, it was found to contain the bones of three children).

In all fairness, though, it should be mentioned that Caspar, Balthazar, and Melchior once saved the Emperor Constantine's Church of the Nativity in Jerusalem from destruction. In 614 Jerusalem was conquered by King Khosrau of Persia, and most of the city was razed. The church, however, was indulgently spared because its outer walls were decorated with a fresco of the Three Kings, who were shown wearing Persian national dress.

The author of Matthew does not mention Caspar, Balthazar, and Melchior by name. He says nothing about their being kings at all, or even that there were three of them. Three kings *are* referred to in the Bible, though—about three hundred pages earlier, in a song of praise to King Solomon, which was later interpreted as a prophecy that the Messiah would receive tribute from the farthest countries of the earth:

> *The kings of Tarshish and of the isles shall bring presents: the kings of Sheba and Seba shall offer gifts.*
>
> *Yea, all kings shall fall down before him: all nations shall serve him.*

> —PSALMS 72:10–11

The actual date of Jesus' birth is not foretold in the Old Testament or even mentioned in the Gospels. The traditional date of December 25 was fixed by Pope Liberius in the fourth century. This date was a shrewd choice, because the Romans celebrated the ancient pagan festival of the winter solstice on the same day—which allowed the pagan celebration of the unconquerable sun to be absorbed by the Christian celebration of the triumphant Son of God.

Luke at least gives us an indirect hint about when Jesus' actual birthday might have been:

> *And there were in the same country shepherds abiding in the field, keeping watch over their flock by night.*

> —LUKE 2:8

In this particular part of Palestine, grazing animals were (and are) kept out in the fields only from Easter until November, when the rainy season began and they were brought back to their barns and sheepfolds. When the flocks were put out to graze, their stalls were rented to travelers for the night, which is how Mary and Joseph ended up in a stable when there was "no room for them in the inn." This doesn't necessarily mean that the inns were full to capacity. More likely, Mary, who was expecting to give birth at any moment, preferred a private room (even if it was in a stable) to the crowded common dormitory of an ordinary inn.

This is all assuming that the shepherds really were in the fields, of course; it would have been symbolically appropriate for the shepherds to have been the first to acclaim Jesus as the Messiah, because Christ was to be of the lineage of David, and David himself was originally a shepherd.

Matthew also makes an implied connection between Jesus and Moses, both of whom barely escaped a wholesale massacre of newborn male children. (And Joseph's flight into Egypt with his family is explicitly mentioned as the fulfillment of a prophecy that the Son of God would be called out of Egypt, actually a reference to the Exodus in Hosea 11:2.) There is no evidence to suggest that King Herod actually carried out such a massacre, but it fits in very neatly with the story of the Wise Men and is certainly in keeping with Herod's bloodstained record as an ambitious, unscrupulous despot. (Apart from murdering numerous political enemies, he also had his favorite wife decapitated, two of his sons garroted, and his brother-in-law drowned.) His subjects remembered him with particular loathing, because he had taken twelve prominent Judeans as hostages when he knew that he himself was about to die and had ordered them all killed in the arena of Jericho as soon as word came of his own death.

Both Matthew and Luke tell the story of the Nativity and the events leading up to it, though the account in Luke is the more familiar "Christmas story." Both Gospels report that an "angel of the Lord" instructed Joseph to name the child Jesus. Matthew adds the interesting detail that the angel also persuaded Joseph not to "put away" his pregnant bride, "for that which is conceived in her is of the Holy Ghost." (His original inclination was to divorce her—secretly, to avoid making her "a publick example.") The name Jesus is the Greek version of the Hebrew name Josua, which means "Yahweh is my help" and in the time of Jesus was probably pronounced "Yehoshua" or "Yeshua." This appears to have been a very common name; Josephus mentions ten men of that name who were contemporaries of Jesus.

It is still not clear whether Jesus actually came from Nazareth or the phrase "He shall be called a Nazarene" (Matthew 2:23) should be interpreted to mean that he was consecrated as a Nazarite—the Greek word used in the New Testament may mean one or the other, and perhaps one day we will know which one it is.

At any rate, it is clear that he was a Galilean, like Peter, who is recognized as one of Jesus' disciples in Jerusalem by his countrified Galilean accent, which the Jews of Jerusalem regarded as particularly comical and uncouth. The word *Galilee* itself means something like "land of the heathen," and, as you may recall, the desolate land of Cabul that Solomon tried to palm off on Hiram of Tyre was part of Galilee.

In Jesus' time the Galileans were mostly fishermen and craftsmen, and Jesus may have originally been a craftsman of some kind; Mark calls him "the carpenter" and Matthew "the carpenter's son." This does not mean that he was a cabinetmaker but a "builder" *(tekton)*, a word that referred to stonemasons or any other skilled craftsmen who were involved in what we would call construction work. Most of these skilled trades were passed on from father to son—as the Talmud says, "He who does not teach his son a handicraft is no better than a robber." Scholars have tried to prove that Jesus was a carpenter by citing references from the Gospels to house building and related activities (just as others have tried to show that Shakespeare must have been a courtier or a lawyer or a professional soldier). Unfortunately, it is just as easy to prove that Jesus was a fisherman, a cook, or even that he worked in a vineyard, by this same method.

One passage in Mark appears to indicate that Jesus was commonly regarded as illegitimate and that he was not an only child:

> *Is not this the carpenter, the son of Mary, the brother of James, and Joses, and of Juda, and Simon? and are not his sisters here with us?*

> —MARK 6:3; compare MATTHEW 13:55

The fact that Jesus is called the "son of Mary" and not "the son of Joseph" has been taken to mean that he was regarded as Mary's illegitimate son (and that Joseph's fears of making her a public scandal had been realized).

Jesus' brothers and sisters are mentioned seven times altogether in the Gospels, James more frequently than the others. Some authorities prefer to take this literally, and James, Juda, and Simon have sometimes been identified with the apostles James the Less, Judas, and Simon. Others are inclined to believe that the authors of the Gospels used the words *brothers* and *sisters* to mean something more like "members of the same generation of an extended family" (as they do in Hebrew), and that James, Juda, Simon, and the rest were more likely to have been Jesus' cousins.

Whether or not Jesus was an only child, we do know that he came from a relatively poor family. Luke describes how Joseph and Mary brought Jesus to be presented at the Temple in Jerusalem when he was forty days old, according to the laws of Moses (Leviticus 12:6), "And to offer a sacrifice according to that which is said in the law of the Lord, A pair of turtledoves, or two young pigeons" (Luke 2:24). In fact, the child's parents were required to sacrifice a lamb in addition to the pair of turtledoves, but this was apparently much too expensive a proposition.

A few verses later we are told that Jesus accompanied his parents to Jerusalem when he was twelve years old; they went "every year at the feast of the passover." A few days later he is discovered "sitting in the midst of the doctors [in the Temple], both hearing them, and asking them questions." A great many attempts have been made to prove that Jesus had already mastered Hebrew—the appropriate language for a scholarly symposium of this kind—and even Greek, as well as his native language, Aramaic. This was the common language throughout Judea in the time of Jesus. Hebrew, which had become extinct as a spoken language since the Babylonian Exile, was still used in the Temple; the priests were assisted by a special class of interpreters who repeated the words of the service in Aramaic for the benefit of the great majority of the congregation who had never learned Hebrew.

Several Aramaic words have a special meaning in the New Testament. *Abba* is translated as "Father" in the King James; this is the way God was customarily addressed in prayer (as Jesus does in the Garden of Gethsemene shortly before his arrest by the servants of the high priest Caiaphas). The Aramaic word is a diminutive, not a formal title, and is really closer to "Papa" than "Father" (just as the bishop of Rome was later called *Papa* by the early Christians). *Gulgulta* (*Gulgolath* in Hebrew, *Golgotha* in the New Testament) means "[the place of] the skull," the hill where Jesus was crucified, better known as Calvary; *calvaria* means the same thing in Latin. *Mammon* means "riches" or "money," though Jesus uses it ironically ("Ye cannot serve God and mammon") in exactly the same way that we might speak of "the almighty dollar."

As we have seen, the authors of the Gospels were writing with a single purpose in mind: to make it unmistakably clear that Jesus was the promised Messiah, the Son of God. Later generations have done their best to reinterpret Jesus as the reflection of the ideals of their own ages and the patron of their own particular causes. For the early Christians he was the Meek Lamb of God, in the Byzantine Empire the stern autocrat of the universe, and in the last few centuries he has reappeared as the honorary founder of the abolitionist movement, as business executive and pioneer of the public-relations industry, as both an ascetic and a sophisticated man of the world, as a revolutionary firebrand and anti-imperialist freedom fighter, and—not so very long ago—as the original long-haired nonconformist.

Certain scholars have even suggested that Jesus as he appears in the Gospels is actually a composite portrait of two different men, a miraculous healer and a resistance fighter. This seems to bring us dangerously close to reawakening the Jesus-as-an-Essene controversy, so perhaps this theory is best passed over in silence. It is easy to see how the Son of Man came to be all things to all men, because the authors of the Gospels were concerned only with reporting his teachings, his miracles, and his Passion—the events of his last days on earth. They were definitely not interested in compiling a complex, multifaceted portrayal of a historical person. After Luke's account of Jesus' visit to the Temple, there is a gap of at least eighteen years. We hear nothing of him until he is baptized in the Jordan when he "began to be about thirty years of age."

The fact that the Gospels also tell us absolutely nothing about what Jesus really looked like has only acted as a spur to the imaginations of artists for two thousand years. His portraits are all idealized representations, though in our eyes the ideals that they represent seem very far removed from the reality as we might like to imagine it. The blond, small-boned, delicate figure of Gothic and Flemish art hardly seems to correspond to our image of Rabbi Yeshua of Nazareth; still less the greenish-skinned, limping Jesus of the Greek Orthodox Church. This latter strange tradition insists that Jesus' left leg was much shorter than his right. Accordingly, the footrest on the crucifix is often slanted downward to match this asymmetry (which is mentioned in two or three apocryphal accounts of the life of Jesus, though not in the Gospels).

The Gospels tell us that Jesus spent the last three years of his wandering ministry in Galilee, where he visited no more than twenty small villages and towns. He returned to Jerusalem only for the last Passover feast, shortly before he was arrested and condemned to death. (John says that he visited Jerusalem at least three times during this period, which, according to him, amounted to only a single year.)

Galilee, apart from being Jesus' native province, also may have provided a comparatively safe refuge from his political enemies. Matthew mentions that "when Jesus had heard that John was cast into prison, he departed [from Judea] into Galilee." Later he also seems to have been hounded out of Nazareth, which inspired his famous remark that "a prophet hath no honour in his own country," and made his headquarters in the city of Capernaum, on the Sea of Galilee. This, as certain scholars have pointed out, was conveniently close to the Phoenician border, in case further persecutions should force him to flee a third time.

We might like to think of Jesus as surrounded entirely by adoring multitudes, at least during the earlier stages of his ministry, but in fact his messages seem to have been well received only among the "people of the land"—the villagers and peasants of Galilee, and perhaps the humbler citizens of Jerusalem and Capernaum. Virtually all of Jesus' teachings were regarded as profoundly antagonistic to the established doctrines of the two powerful Jewish sects—the Pharisees and the Sadducees—who made up the spiritual and social elite of Judea and Galilee.

The Sadducees, who are mentioned much less frequently in the New Testament, were in effect the Judean governing class, many of them conservative landowners, who worked out a peaceful accommodation with the Roman occupation forces, even willingly collaborated with them at times. Accordingly, they played an important, perhaps a dominant, role in the

Sanhedrin, the Jewish council of elders. The Sadducees were strict religious purists who recognized only the five books of Moses as divinely inspired. Caiaphas, the high priest who condemned Jesus to death, was a Sadducee. In his efforts to have Jesus' heretical teachings suppressed, however, he seems to have joined in a kind of ad hoc coalition with members of a rival sect, the Pharisees, even though in other respects—their political views especially—there were profound differences between them.

Pharisees means "they who have separated themselves." They were a kind of cultural nationalist faction who refused to have anything at all to do with the Romans. The Pharisees were even more scrupulous than the Sadducees in their strict observance of the laws of Moses, which is why they are so often portrayed in the Gospels as Jesus' adversaries and "tempters." The Pharisees were not merely a pack of ostentatious hypocrites—which is what the word *Pharisee* implies today—though their painstaking attempts to obey all the commandments (more than six hundred altogether) must have made them fairly conspicuous. For example, it was forbidden to speak to (or even look at) a woman in public, so many Pharisees went as far as to walk through the streets with their eyes closed whenever they suspected that they were about to meet with temptation. The high incidence of bruised foreheads and bloody noses among this extremist wing of the Pharisees won them the derisive nickname "the Bloody Pharisees."

A man like Jesus, who consorted freely with women and other undesirables, and who made inflammatory remarks like "The sabbath was made for man, and not man for the sabbath" (Mark 2:27), had clearly thrown down a challenge to the Pharisees' uncompromising piety that could not possibly be ignored.

All the various sects and factions we have encountered so far—the Essenes, the Sadducees, and the Pharisees—came to terms with the Roman occupation, in one way or another. A fourth sect, the Zealots, were determined to resist the Romans to the death. In Greek the word *zelotes* is much stronger than *zealot* is in English—*fanatic* is a little closer to the mark. The Zealots formed the militant cadre who led the rebellion against the Roman tenth legion which broke out almost forty years later, in A.D. 66, and was ruthlessly suppressed by Titus, the future emperor. After Titus's punitive expedition arrived to reinforce the Roman tenth legion, Jerusalem was taken and pillaged, the Temple was destroyed (A.D. 70), and the Zealots' guerrilla army was forced to retreat into the wilderness around the Dead Sea. (The monastery of Qumran was abandoned at about this time; the defenders of Masada held out until A.D. 73.)

Because one of Jesus' disciples was called Simon Zelotes (at least in Luke 6:15), it seems entirely possible that he was a member of this militant nationalist sect. It has also been suggested that Judas Iscariot was a Zealot. Perhaps, the reasoning goes, Judas had originally hoped that Jesus would be "the son of David" who would drive the Romans from Judea at the point of a sword. When Jesus failed to give the call to arms, Judas became bitterly disillusioned, "and from that time he sought opportunity to betray him" (Matthew 26:16).

For many are called, but few are chosen.

—MATTHEW 22:14

Jesus and His Disciples

And when it was day, he called unto him his disciples: and of them he chose twelve, whom also he named apostles;

Simon (whom he also named Peter) and Andrew his brother, James and John, Philip and Bartholomew,

Matthew and Thomas, James the son of Alphaeus, and Simon called Zelotes,
And Judas the brother of James, and Judas Iscariot, which also was the traitor.

—LUKE 6:13–16

How many original disciples there were, in addition to these chosen few, is never made clear in the Gospels, though there seem to have been quite a few second-degree disciples (which is mildly reminiscent of Qumran) as well:

After these things the Lord appointed other seventy also, and sent them two and two before his face into every city and place, whither he himself would come.

—LUKE 10:1

As we have seen, the number twelve is a symbolic commemoration of the twelve tribes of Israel, and seventy is just the mystical seven times ten—usually interchangeable with seventy-two (as with the traditional number of translators who prepared the Septuagint). Many of the early manuscripts of the New Testament have "seventy-two disciples," the reading that has been adopted in the New International Version.

The word *disciple* simply means "student." Anyone who wanted to study the Torah and the other sacred books would seek out a particular rabbi and, as the phrase was, "go into his teaching." Jesus sought out his own disciples, of course, and they were rather unlikely choices. Matthew was a "publican," which is usually translated as "tax collector" in modern English versions. More specifically, Matthew was an employee of one of the civilian contractors who collected the Roman excise tax on various kinds of merchandise and thus, in the eyes of most of his compatriots, was not only a traitor but probably a scoundrel as well.

Matthew, the repentant collaborator, is balanced by Simon Zelotes, the militant firebrand. John, the gentle "beloved disciple," is more than balanced by the bearish Simon Peter— though Jesus nicknamed John and his brother James "the sons of thunder" (Boanerges), so John may not have been as gentle as all that. Judas, the treasurer, was said to be a native of Iskerioth (Kerioth), which would have made him the only Judean of the twelve.

Of the Galilean contingent, John, James, Peter, and Andrew were all fishermen, though John's father, who had "hired servants" among the crew of his fishing boat, seems to have been comparatively prosperous. At least two of the apostles seem originally to have been disciples of John the Baptist. Several others—notably Philip and Bartholomew—were quiet, contemplative types who are barely mentioned in the Gospels.

On the fringes of this inner circle were a few female disciples as well, which certainly must have scandalized the Pharisees and has made their spiritual descendants in later centuries more than a little uneasy. In the Age of Faith the women who followed Jesus were thought of as the "mystical brides of Christ," the first nuns of the Christian church—and of course in our own Age of Rock, there are those who prefer to imagine them as groupies in the entourage of Jesus Christ Superstar. Not surprisingly, the Gospels give a slightly different explanation:

> . . . *and the twelve were with him.*
>
> *And certain women, which had been healed of evil spirits and infirmities, Mary called Magdalene, out of whom went seven devils,*
>
> *And Joanna the wife of Chuza, Herod's steward, and Susanna, and many others, which ministered unto him of their substance.*
>
> —LUKE 8:1–3

Mary Magdalene has become a great favorite with painters

315

and poets and various interpreters of the Gospels who prefer to
think of Jesus as a lusty, broad-minded man of the world. But
the idea that Mary Magdalene was a "repentant sinner"—a
reformed prostitute—has only very tenuous connections with the
few facts about her that are mentioned in the New Testament.
Magdalene probably means "from Magdala," which was a
Roman resort community not far from the famous mineral
springs at Tiberias. The words "Roman bath" conjured up all
sorts of disturbing visions in the early Christian mind, and the
conclusion seems to have been that Mary Magdalene was no
better than she should have been, otherwise, what was she doing
in a notorious haunt of vice like Magdala?

Luke also mentions in the previous chapter that "a woman in
the city which was a sinner" washed and anointed Jesus' feet
while he and his disciples were dining in the house of a Pharisee
at Capernaum. This unnamed "woman of the city" was assumed
to be none other than Mary Magdalene. The legend was further
enriched by the addition of another Mary, Mary of Bethany—
probably the sister of Lazarus, who also washed and anointed
Jesus' feet and "wiped his feet with her hair" on a later occasion
(John 12:3). This was the origin of Saint Mary Magdalene, who
was usually shown in medieval paintings as weeping pitifully
over the memories of her scarlet past. The charm of this pious
legend seems to have worn off after a while; our word *maudlin* is
simply the medieval English pronunciation of *Magdalene*.

The episode in which the anonymous "sinner" washes Jesus'
feet at the Pharisee's banquet in Capernaum is quite interesting.
At first it seems that she might possibly have been an *agent
provocateur* whom the Pharisee hired to discredit or simply
embarrass Jesus in front of the disciples. The Pharisee immediately points out that "if he were a prophet," he would have
recognized this woman for what she was and would never have
allowed her to touch him. Jesus' reply ends with the words

Her sins, which are many, are forgiven; for she loved much: but to whom little is forgiven, the same loveth little.

—LUKE 7:47

This verse is often quoted out of context, but it is very clear that the phrase "for she loved much" does not mean she has been especially generous with her favors in the past but that she has treated Jesus with much loving kindness on this particular occasion—in contrast to the Pharisee, who has shown himself to be a cold, ungenerous, and even treacherous host.

The word *love* in the New Testament always refers to the love between God and man; the Evangelists always use the word *agape* (spiritual love, sometimes translated as "charity" in the King James). The ordinary Greek word *eros*, which refers to physical love, is never used in the New Testament, though it is worth noting in this context that Jesus forgives the "sinner" of Capernaum for the sake of her faith and assures the skeptical disciples of John the Baptist that "the harlots and publicans" who have accepted his teachings will enter the kingdom of heaven before them.

The idea that Jesus could forgive even the most hardened sinners—the sort of thing that so "offended" his fellow citizens of Nazareth and "astonished" the other guests at the Pharisee's house in Capernaum—appears throughout the four Gospels, as proof that Jesus was indeed the Messiah. Forgiveness was no longer the exclusive province of the Temple priesthood, in other words, because the Son of God was present on earth.

Three of the Gospels bear the name of one of Jesus' disciples (the fourth, Luke, was a Gentile and a comparative latecomer), though it is almost certain that none of the Gospels was actually written until several generations later. This in itself does not diminish their value in any way; each of the Gospels was addressed to a different community of the early Church; each

317

has its own distinctive literary style and its own well-defined point of view.

There has always been a sort of vague suspicion that the Gospels are in some way redundant or superfluous, because they repeat and contradict one another in so many places. (The first attempt to straighten out this situation was made by a third-century heretic named Tatian, the latest by an American publishing house that is preparing a "Gospel Digest," where possible, with the help of a computer.)

In fact this diversity is one of the most remarkable things about the Gospels. An incident that one author clearly thinks is highly significant is barely mentioned by another, or even totally ignored. Events that are recounted in all four Gospels are given totally different interpretations by different authors. The Gospels do not provide us with a unified, ready-made picture of the life and teachings of Jesus but with a scattered, disorderly assembly of mosaic stones that we have to put together for ourselves.

> . . . *Suffer little children, and forbid them not,*
> *to come unto me: for of such is the kingdom of*
> *heaven.*
>
> —MATTHEW 19:14

The Gospel According to Saint Matthew

"The book of the generation of Jesus Christ, the son of David, the son of Abraham." So begins the Gospel of Matthew, the first of the four Gospels in the Bible, though it was probably the second to be written—sometime after the destruction of the Temple, about A.D. 70–80, ten years or so after the original Gospel, which is attributed to Mark.

Because the Apostle Matthew, who is called Levi in the older Gospels, was an excise collector at the customs house in Capernaum, scholars have naturally tried to demonstrate that the Gospel itself bears the traces of Matthew's bureaucratic temperament—all the words and deeds of Jesus recorded (particularly where numbers are involved) with the scrupulous, almost pedantic accuracy of a countinghouse clerk. Publicans, however, were not noted for their scrupulous accuracy (especially where numbers were involved), and it is quite certain that Matthew the publican was not the author of the Matthew Gospel.

It is true that the early Christians held this Gospel in the highest regard, because it does give the most detailed account of the deeds and the sayings of Jesus, which is how it came to be the first book of the New Testament. The traditional order of the Gospels has been retained in all but a very few modern translations of the Gospels, because Matthew provides the most natural transition between the Old and the New Testaments.

Matthew was written for the Jewish Christian community, and Matthew is thus especially eager to assure his readers that Jesus was the Messiah whose coming had been foretold by the prophets. The formula "that it might be fulfilled which was spoken by the prophets" recurs over and over; and because Matthew is a propagandist rather than just a scribal copyist, his quotations are often taken out of context or subtly altered to suit his own purposes. Matthew's fanciful "generation of Jesus Christ" begins with Abraham, and it is Matthew who introduces the stories of the "wise men from the east" and of the Massacre of the Innocents (which was prompted by the Wise Men's announcement to Herod that "the King of the Jews" had been born in "Bethlehem in Judea: for thus it is written by the prophet"). Matthew's interpretation of Jesus' ministry is neatly summed up in this verse from chapter 5:

319

*Think not that I am come to destroy the law, or the prophets: I
am not come to destroy, but to fulfill.*

—MATTHEW 5:17

Luke and Mark both mention Jesus' journey into the wilderness,
the symbolic reenactment of the Exodus. Characteristically,
though, only Matthew includes a scene in which Jesus is
tempted by the Devil—actually a rapid-fire interchange of Old
Testament quotations. (Every one of Jesus' replies contains the
phrase "it is written.")

Because the author of Matthew was forced to walk a very fine
line as a propagandist, he was always at great pains to proclaim
the message of Jesus without offending the religious sensibilities
of his Jewish Christian readers. After Jesus had chosen his
disciples, Matthew relates that

*These twelve Jesus sent forth, and commanded them, saying,
Go not into the way of the Gentiles, and into any city of the
Samaritans enter ye not.*
But go rather to the lost sheep of the house of Israel.

—MATTHEW 10:5–6

The other three Gospels do not mention this. John, in fact, even
describes how Jesus spent two days preaching among the
Samaritans (John 4:40) after his encounter with the Samaritan
woman at the well. Apparently Matthew felt that his Jewish
readers might be ready to accept Jesus as the Messiah, but that it
would be overoptimistic to expect them to discard their ancient
prejudice against the outcast Samaritans. It is true that this
restriction on the disciples' missionary activities seems to have
been revoked by Jesus after his Resurrection:

*Go ye therefore, and teach all nations, baptizing them in the
name of the Father, and of the Son, and of the Holy Ghost.*

—MATTHEW 28:19

But this sounds suspiciously like an addition by a later author, designed to bring Matthew into harmony with the truly evangelistic spirit of the other Gospels.

An early passage (considerably expanded and adapted from Mark 7:24) shows Matthew subtly implanting the suggestion in his readers' minds that Jesus was primarily (but not exclusively) the Messiah of "the house of Israel." A Canaanite woman (Mark calls her "a Syrophenician") approaches Jesus while he is preaching on the border of Tyre and Sidon and asks him to heal her daughter, who "is grievously vexed with a devil." (This may refer to epilepsy or almost any variety of mental illness.) At first Jesus simply ignores her (Mark does not mention this); then, when his disciples beg him to attend to her, "for she crieth after us," he replies:

> *I am not sent but unto the lost sheep of the house of Israel.*

> —MATTHEW 15:24

Mark does not mention this either, though the exchange is almost identical in both Gospels:

> *Then came she and worshipped him, saying, Lord, help me.*
> *But he answered and said, It is not meet to take the children's*
> *bread [the children of Israel], and to cast it to dogs [the heathen].*

> —MATTHEW 15:25–26

Jesus relents and agrees to heal the Canaanite woman's daughter after she humbly (and quick-wittedly) points out,

> *Truth, Lord: yet the dogs eat of the crumbs which fall from their*
> *masters' table.*

> —MATTHEW 15:27

It may seem that Matthew is catering rather shamelessly to the prejudices of his readers in passages like this. Yet this was actually an important part of his strategy as a propagandist: to give lip service to prevailing Jewish attitudes in order to proclaim Jesus' essential teachings even more clearly. Matthew explains to his readers that we should love our enemies as well as our neighbors (Matthew 5:44), and that, instead of "An eye for an eye, and a tooth for a tooth,"

> . . . I say unto you, That ye resist not evil: but whosoever shall smite thee on thy right cheek, turn to him the other also.

> —MATTHEW 5:39

This is the real message that Matthew was trying to put across, even if it involved a certain amount of diplomatic compromise on less important points of doctrine.

Today it may be difficult for us to realize how provocative, how really revolutionary, Jesus' message was in his own time. Even today such precepts as "Love your enemies" and "Turn the other cheek" may be fairly difficult to put into practice, but it is precisely this unrealistic, impractical body of ethical teachings that became the basis for an entirely new conception of morality.

For example, take the well-known text "Suffer little children . . . to come unto me," which usually gets a full-color insert page to itself in illustrated editions of the Bible. This doesn't sound the least bit seditious or heretical, but that is exactly what it was. The Jews of Jesus' time, like the other peoples of the ancient Near East, were pretty indifferent parents by modern standards, and their children grew up with very little in the way of adult supervision. A man who had sired a large family might be admired for his potency, but the individual qualities of his offspring would not be regarded as particularly to his credit (or discredit), because children were not really thought of as full-fledged human beings at all. The question of whether they were eligible to enter into the kingdom of God was a favorite topic of scholarly disputation among the rabbis. As far as Jesus was concerned, there was no question about it: "of such is the kingdom of heaven." And more than that:

> *Except ye be converted, and become as little children, ye shall not enter the kingdom of heaven.*

> —MATTHEW 18:3

This is a complete reversal of the doctrine that was taught in the synagogue: children could not really participate in Jahweh's covenant with his people or be accepted into his kingdom until they had grown up to be rational adults. The wandering preacher Jesus insisted that, on the contrary, rational adults would have to find their way back to the simple, unquestioning faith of childhood before they could expect to stand before the throne of God.

Jesus makes it very clear that he expected his hearers to take this precept very seriously indeed, because it is followed by one of the few real threats of punishment that appear in the New Testament:

> *But whoso shall offend one of these little ones which believe in me, it were better for him that a millstone were hanged about his neck, and that he were drowned in the depth of the sea.*

> —MATTHEW 18:6

This seems a heavy price to pay for such a trifling infraction, but the word *offend* here actually means something more like "cause to offend against God," or as the New International Version has it:

> *If anyone causes these little ones who believe in me to sin . . .*

According to one recent interpretation, the "little ones" are actually Jesus' disciples, who have humbled themselves "as this little child" before Jesus. And the threat is directed at those who might be inclined to corrupt them, to seduce them away from his teachings, or as a modern free translation puts it: "to destroy their childlike trust in me."

A little earlier on, the Pharisees are also condemned for their flashy, superficial piety:

> *But all their works they do to be seen of men: they make bread*
> *their phylacteries, and enlarge the borders of their garments.*

> —MATTHEW 23:5

The custom of wearing phylacteries (*tefillin*) during daily prayers and a fringed garment (*tallis*) still survives among observant Orthodox Jews. Phylacteries are small leather receptacles that contain slips of parchment inscribed with prayers from the Torah: One is worn on the forehead, attached by a thin leather strap; the other is bound around the upper arm (near the heart). The point here is that the Pharisees were more interested in conspicuous displays of piety than, as they claimed, in strict observance of the Law, and in this case they had succeeded in turning the ritual associated with daily prayer into a meaningless exercise in spiritual one-upmanship.

In his role as a propagandist who was appealing primarily to an audience of Jewish Christians, the author of Matthew, more than any of the other three Evangelists, is the special scourge of the Pharisees. His literary style, ordinarily quite dry and precise, bristles with indignation and inventive turns of phrase whenever he interrupts his narrative to denounce this "generation of vipers," the "blind guides," and the "whited sepulchres" who were Jesus' principal adversaries. His tone alternates between thundering invective:

> *Woe unto you, scribes and Pharisees, hypocrites! for ye compass*
> *sea and land to make one proselyte, and when he is made, ye*
> *make him twofold more the child of hell than yourselves.*

> —MATTHEW 23:15

—and a mischievous strain of satire, as when he has Jesus refer to

Ye blind guides, which strain at a gnat, and swallow a camel.

—MATTHEW 23:24

(This apparently refers to the custom of straining wine through a fine mesh, like cheesecloth, to filter out the impurities; modern versions are inclined to say "strain *out* a gnat and swallow a camel.")

As might be expected, Matthew assumes a more detailed knowledge of Jewish customs on the part of his readers than the other Evangelists tend to do. The curious story of the tribute money provides a good enough example of this:

And when they were come to Capernaum, they that received tribute money came to Peter, and said, Doth not your master pay tribute?

—MATTHEW 17:24

The New International Version helpfully explains "tribute money" as "the temple tax." Before you skip ahead to the curious part of the story (Matthew 17:27), you might be interested to know that:

1. A two-drachma piece (*didrachma*) was a coin minted in Tyre that was worth somewhere between one and two dollars.

2. By law the temple tax could be paid only in Tyrian coins, and it was the business of the famous moneychangers in the Temple to change the Greek and Roman coins that were the everyday currency in Judea into Tyrian drachmas, a service for which they received a hefty 4 percent commission.

3. The temple tax was paid every year by all adult Jewish males; only priests were exempt, which is probably why the tax collectors asked Peter if his master paid tribute—that is, was he a bona fide priest?

Jesus offers to pay the temple tax for both of them, "lest we should offend them." He instructs Peter to go to the sea (of Galilee) "and cast an hook, and take up the fish that first cometh up; and when thou has opened his mouth, thou shalt find a piece of money [a stater, equal to four drachmas] . . ." (Matthew 17:27). The stater is an especially nice touch, because there were not many *didrachmas* in circulation (like two-dollar bills), and a stater, or *tetradrachma*, was a much more common coin—even, apparently, in the mouths of fishes.

Jesus expresses a more ambiguous attitude toward the payment of state—rather than church—taxes in a much better-known passage in chapter 22. Here the Pharisees, who are trying, as usual, to catch him out in an inconsistency or a political indiscretion, ask Jesus: "What thinkest thou? Is it lawful to give tribute [taxes] unto Caesar, or not?" If he says yes, he will come off sounding like a collaborator. And if he says no, the Pharisees will be able to denounce him to the Roman authorities. Thus Jesus asks for a "penny," a Roman coin stamped with Caesar's likeness, and gives his famous reply, "Render therefore unto Caesar the things which are Caesar's; and unto God the things that are God's" (Matthew 22:21).

Much more impressive sums are bandied about in Jesus' parable of the talents. In Jesus' time, a talent was no longer just a chunk of bullion of a given weight, but a gold coin that was worth six thousand drachmas—somewhere in the neighborhood of five thousand dollars. In the parable, a master entrusts three of his servants with one, two, and five talents, respectively. The first servant buries his talent in the ground, for which his master roundly rebukes him; the others invest theirs profitably. This is why "talents" have come to mean our natural gifts or capacities—in the parable they are symbolically equivalent to God's gifts to man—and why we speak of someone who has not made the most of his natural abilities as having "buried his talents." The penalty for this in the parable is no less than eternal damnation: "And cast ye the unprofitable servant into outer darkness: there shall be weeping and gnashing of teeth" (Matthew 25:30).

The cubit, with which we have come to be familiar in connection with Noah's ark, Solomon's brazen sea, and other Old Testament artifacts, seems also to have changed its meaning by the time of Jesus. In the passage that the King James translators rendered as

> *Which of you by taking thought can add one cubit unto his stature?*
>
> —MATTHEW 6:27

the word *cubit* probably refers to a unit of time rather than of length, and so the New International Version's

> *Who of you by worrying can add a single hour to his life?*

is probably more accurate, if not as interesting to visualize.

One of the highlights of the Matthew Gospel is the Sermon on the Mount (which also appears in Luke, chapter 6, though in very different form). The author of Matthew sets the scene with a brief prologue that creates the proper mood of expectancy very well:

> *And seeing the multitudes, he went up into a mountain: and when he was set, his disciples came unto him:*
> *And he opened his mouth, and taught them, saying, . . .*
>
> —MATTHEW 5:1–2

In fact, as a comparison with Luke's version of the Sermon on the Mount makes clear, neither of these sermons was delivered on one particular occasion, nor, probably, did Jesus speak those words at any one time to a single group of listeners. The author of Matthew seems to have taken a series of Jesus' ethical precepts, which deal with many different problems in practical morality, and blended them into a coherent text. This passage was probably intended as a kind of model sermon for the early Christian congregations to which the Gospel was addressed.

The last two verses of the Matthew Gospel are an even more concise summary of Jesus' teachings which specifically refer to the crisis of faith in the early Christian church that is thought to have inspired the writing of all the Gospels:

> Go ye therefore, and teach all nations [this phrase, as we have seen, may have been tampered with]. . . .
>
> Teaching them to observe all things whatsoever I have commanded you: and lo, I am with you alway, even unto the end of the world. Amen.

As we have seen, the idea of Jesus' return to earth was an especially sensitive topic. Later translators have been inclined to think that the Greek original was not quite so decisive about "the end of the world" as the King James. Some modern translations have qualified this to read "until the completion [or "the perfection"] of the world," and the New International Version begs the question a little with ". . . to the very end of the age."

> And the unclean spirits went out, and entered into the swine: and the herd . . . ran violently down a steep place into the sea. . . .

> —MARK 5:13

The Gospel According to Saint Mark

As we have seen, Mark is the earliest of the Gospels (circa A.D. 65), as well as the shortest, and quite possibly it is one of the original source documents upon which the other three

Gospel narratives were based. According to tradition, the Mark Gospel itself was said to have been based on Peter's verbal accounts of Jesus' life—it is sometimes referred to as "Peter's Memoirs"—and was supposed to have been written in Rome. Today it seems certain that Peter's companion, the disciple Mark (or John Mark), was not the author of the Gospel.

Whoever the author of Mark might have been, he was probably not as familiar with Jewish culture and with the geography of Palestine as Matthew seems to have been, and he does not refer to the writings of the prophets nearly as often as the other Evangelists do.

On the other hand, this may be because he was writing for an audience of non-Jewish Christians. This is why, for example, he takes the trouble to explain that the Jordan is a river, or that the "two lepta" that Jesus is offered by "a certain poor widow" was worth the same as a quadrans—a lepton ("a mite," the King James says) was a Greek or a Maccabean coin, the hundredth part of a drachma; a quadrans was the smallest Roman copper coin ("a farthing" in the King James). Most of the exotic touches that we find in Matthew are carefully glossed (or omitted) in Mark.

Mark's literary style may be said to have a certain Roman quality, his writing is smooth, vigorous, even exciting at times. Much of the narrative is in the present tense, and he moves quickly from one incident to the next. One of his favorite words is *immediately* (*straightway* in the King James). Part of the freshness and spontaneity of this Gospel comes from the fact that its author was not a highly organized or systematic writer; he seems simply to be writing down the first thing that comes to his mind (which is one reason some conservative scholars continue to believe that this Gospel really was based on the spontaneous off-the-cuff reminiscences of Saint Peter, or dictated to one of his disciples).

Another of Mark's refreshing qualities is that in his Gospel

Jesus' teachings are illustrated by vivid images drawn from everyday life rather than Old Testament quotations. For example, Jesus explains that his teachings really represent a significant departure from the faith of the prophets in these words:

> No man also seweth a piece of new cloth on an old garment: else the new piece that filled it up taketh away from the old, and the rent is made worse.

> —MARK 2:21

In our own era of preshrunk miracle fibers this may require a word or two of explanation. Before a piece of cloth could be sewn into a garment by the tailor, it was taken to a craftsman called a fuller, who soaked the cloth overnight in a mixture of water, lye, and a chalky clay ("fuller's earth"). The wet cloth was stretched out on a stone and pounded with a wooden pestle to bind the individual wool fibers into a feltlike mat. The cloth was then washed and dried again, teased out with burrs, treated with "brimstone" (sulfur), and pressed flat. Naturally the cloth would have shrunk considerably by the time this ordeal was finished, and no one would be foolish enough to patch an old garment with a piece of "new" (unfulled) cloth, because the patch would shrink and tear away and "the rent [be] made worse." The New International Version makes a brave attempt to compress all this curious lore into a single word:

> No one sews a piece of unshrunk cloth on an old garment. If he does, the new piece will pull away from the old, making the tear worse.

Unfortunately, this misses the contrast between "old" and "new," which is the whole point of the comparison. The next verse, at least, deals with a phenomenon with which we moderns are more familiar:

> And no man putteth new wine into old bottles: else the new

330

wine doth burst the bottles, and the wine is spilled, and the bottles will be marred: but new wine must be put into new bottles.

(So much for the Prohibitionists' claim that the "wine" mentioned in the Bible was actually unfermented grape juice.)

All this—even the business about the fulling and unshrunk cloth—was perfectly clear to Mark and his readers in the western Roman Empire, though he seems to have had a certain amount of trouble with other allusions that refer to specifically Jewish customs. For example, after Jesus has healed a man who "was sick of the palsy," he commands him,

. . . *Arise, and take up thy bed, and go thy way into thine house.*

—Mark 2:11

We would prefer not to imagine the poor man staggering back home beneath the weight of the solid wooden four-poster that was used by Greeks and Romans, so various other explanations have naturally been proposed. The usual one is that "bed" is actually "bedding" ("mat" in the New International Version), and that this was some kind of pallet or straw mat, easily portable even by a very shaky convalescent. In fact, it seems that the "fringed garment" (*tallis*) mentioned in the previous chapter served not only as a robe or cloak during the day but as a blanket at night. Poorer Jews slept on the floor with their robes wrapped around them; according to the laws of Moses, a man was permitted to pawn his *tallis*, but only with the proviso that it be returned to him at night (so that he wouldn't have to sleep on the bare floor). In short, what Jesus was probably saying here was just "Get up, get dressed, and go home now."

The fringes (*tzitzis*) on four corners of the *tallis* were a symbolic reminder of God's covenant with Israel, which is why the Pharisees ostentatiously "enlarged the borders of their garments." The author of Mark says that Jesus' followers begged

331

to touch the fringe ("border") of his garment (Mark 6:56), but the word he uses is singular, so he may have been unaware that there were actually four such "borders." (The Jews of Rome dressed much the same way the Romans did and apparently did not wear the *tallis*.)

Jesus' miraculous healing powers are mentioned more often in Mark than in the other Gospels, which can be seen as indirect evidence that the author was writing for an audience of converted pagans rather than Jewish Christians. The Greeks had the famous shrine of Asclepius at Epidaurus, an important pilgrimage site where many miraculous cures had been reported; Mark's purpose was to persuade his readers that Jesus was a greater miracle worker than any of the pagan gods. Walking on water, for example, is an exploit that turns up in a great many of the legends of antiquity. Mark's account of Jesus' walking on the Sea of Galilee (which is adopted almost word for word by Matthew) provides a small example of the author's profoundly Roman outlook:

> . . . *and about the fourth watch of the night he cometh unto them, walking upon the sea, and would have passed by them.*

> —MARK 6:48

This was the way time was reckoned by the Roman legionnaires: the night was divided into four watches; the third began at midnight and ran till three, the fourth from three until six.

Of all the miracles recounted in this Gospel, certainly the strangest and the least "Christian" is the story of the Gadarene swine. What happens is this. Jesus is approached by a violent madwoman who is possessed by demons. When the demons realize that it is useless to resist Jesus' power, they humbly request "that he would not send them away out of the country." (We will get back to this point in a moment.)

Now there was there nigh unto the mountains a great herd of
swine feeding.

And all the devils besought him saying, Send us into the swine,
that we may enter them.

And forthwith Jesus gave them leave. And the unclean spirits
went out, and entered into the swine: and the herd ran violently
down a steep place into the sea, (they were about two thousand)
and were choked in the sea.

—MARK 5:11–13

Matthew and Luke both give an abbreviated account of this incident; John omits it entirely. For one thing, it is said to take place on the east coast of the Sea of Galilee, near the Greek city of Gadara, which makes this one of Jesus' rare forays into the heathen border regions of Galilee. More than that, it is very possible that this was originally a pagan folktale of some kind, which was said to take place in Gadara to provide a plausible backdrop for the swine, which would never be found in Judea and are obviously essential to the story.

According to pagan tradition, the worst punishment the demons could expect would be to be sent back to the underworld, which is why they plead with Jesus not to be sent "out of the country." (Luke makes this more explicit: "that he would not command them to go out into the deep," namely, the Abyss.) Mark does not have to explain this, because his readers know perfectly well what is going on: the demons would naturally prefer to remain in the world of men.

Of the thirty-five different miracles mentioned in the New Testament, twenty-one are recounted in the Mark Gospel. *Miracle* is a word that immediately polarizes readers into two warring camps, but before the battle is joined, we should bear in mind that in the Old Testament the concept of a miracle does not really exist. Moses and his people regarded the crossing of

333

the Red Sea and the other miraculous events of the Exodus as "signs" of the power of God, just as the New Testament sometimes speaks of "signs and wonders."

It would be interesting to take a survey to find out how many people still believe in miracles, in the sense of inexplicable, supernatural occurrences, incidents in which the ordinary laws of nature seem to be suspended. This would probably represent a much larger percentage of the sampling than those who believe that the biblical accounts of miracles are true. (The really interesting part of this survey would be trying to find out why this is so.)

Nothing is easier than picking apart biblical miracles, because if they could be explained rationally, they would be neither "wonders" nor "signs." This is not the only reason biblical scholars' tireless attempts to provide such explanations are ultimately as senseless and futile as chasing after the rainbow. Jesus' teachings would not be any more profound if he had worked a hundred more miracles, nor would they lose one particle of their meaning if he had not worked any miracles at all. Goethe once remarked that "It is a poor religion that has a miracle for its favorite son," but the philosopher Rousseau probably came closer to the spirit of our own times with the remarkable observation "Take the miracles out of the Bible, and the entire world would fall at Jesus' feet."

As we have seen, the pagan gods of antiquity were credited with all sorts of supernatural exploits, and Mark was obliged to follow suit with his own account of miraculous works of healing that Jesus had performed. This was simply a way of presenting Jesus' message in a context that would be familiar to his Hellenistic readers and would enable them to conceive of the grandeur of the Son of God in terms they could understand. (The concept of the Messiah was unknown to the Greeks.) This was all the more essential, because so much in this new doctrine was revolutionary and unfamiliar, particularly the details involving Jewish customs that must have seemed both outlandish and incomprehensible. This is why Mark has to explain carefully that

. . . the Pharisees, and all the Jews, except they wash their hands off, eat not, holding the tradition of the elders.

—MARK 7:3

This, of course, is not merely a hygienic precaution, though knives and forks were unknown, and even the Pharisees ate with their fingers. This was one of the 613 commandments that all pious Jews were expected to observe in Jesus' time. Even the correct technique was prescribed by the Law; not just "one hand washes the other," but one hand is vigorously massaged with a clenched fist. Still, the early Christian church had already adopted a great many Jewish practices, and Mark had no need to explain, for example, that Jesus was greeted with cries of "Hosanna in the highest" when he rode into Jerusalem. The Hebrew word *hoshaniah* (which means something like "Lord, help us now") was the cry that greeted every faithful worshiper as he entered the Temple; it first occurs in Psalm 118, a hymn of praise that was sung in the Temple during certain festivals.

The last chapter of Mark ends with this verse:

And they went forth, and preached every where, the Lord working with them, and confirming the word with signs following ["and confirmed the word with the signs that accompanied it" *is the New International Version*]. *Amen.*

—MARK 16:20

This style does not correspond very closely to the blunt simplicity of the Gospel's opening sentence, "The beginning of the Gospel of Jesus Christ . . ." The last eleven verses, which describe Jesus' Resurrection, do not appear in the very earliest manuscripts of the Mark Gospel and were apparently added later.

335

These original versions of the Gospel end abruptly with the discovery of Jesus' empty tomb by three women (including Mary Magdalene) who have come to anoint his body with spices:

And they went out quickly, and fled from the sepulchre; for they trembled and were amazed: neither said they any thing to any man; for they were afraid.

—MARK 16:8

It is clear enough why they were afraid; they had just seen "a young man . . . clothed in a long white garment," who said to them, "Ye seek Jesus of Nazareth, which was crucified: he is risen; he is not here . . ."

But whether this author really intended his story to end like this we shall never know. Perhaps the manuscript was left unfinished at his death, or perhaps he was arrested by the Romans while he was still writing the last chapter.

On the other hand, this terse, suspenseful conclusion seems to be exactly what we might expect from this particular author, who was apparently a straightforward, trustworthy observer who simply wrote down what he had heard and left the embellishments and interpretations to others. It hardly seems fair that his Gospel has been overshadowed, as far as modern readers' tastes are concerned, by a later, more elegant work, the Gospel According to Saint Luke.

Which now of these three, thinkest thou, was neighbour unto him that fell among thieves?

—LUKE 10:36

336

The Gospel According to Saint Luke

Forasmuch as many have taken in hand to set forth in order a declaration of those things which are most surely believed among us,

Even as they delivered them unto us, which from the beginning were eyewitnesses, and ministers of the word;

It seemed good to me also, having had perfect understanding of all things from the very first, to write unto thee in order, most excellent Theophilus,

That thou mightest know the certainty of those things, wherein thou hast been instructed.

—LUKE 1:1–4

This smoothly written prologue to the third Gospel tells us three things: that Luke was not one of Jesus' original disciples "which from the beginning were eyewitnesses," that the Gospel was addressed to a certain Theophilus, and that Luke was a man who really knew how to write.

The author of the Gospel was traditionally identified with the physician called Luke, who accompanied Paul on his travels and was said to have been Greek by birth. This may or may not be true; all that we can say for certain is that the Gospel was written after the destruction of the Temple, probably between A.D. 85 and 90, in fluent literary Greek, not the dialect called Koine which was commonly spoken as a second language in Palestine and all over the eastern Roman world. We also have no idea who the "most excellent Theophilus" might have been, nor is it certain that he really existed; presenting a historical account or a fictional memoir as a letter to an imaginary correspondent was a common literary device in the ancient world.

Like the Mark Gospel, Luke was written for Gentile Christians; there are very few quotations from the prophets and many indications that the setting the author imagined for his story could not have been Palestine. Luke's version of the story of the paralytic who takes up his "couch" and walks describes how his friends tried to bring him closer to Jesus, but because they were blocked by the crowd,

> . . . *they went upon the housetop, and let him down through the tiling with his couch into the midst before Jesus.*

—LUKE 5:19

Houses with tile roofs were common enough in Athens and Rome, but houses in Galilee were simple, one-room structures with a thatch of reeds and hemps laid over the rafters. As in the case of Mark, it is not entirely clear whether the author was really unaware of such things or was simply trying to make his story more accessible to his readers.

Just as Mark uses the Roman system of reckoning time—"the fourth watch of the night"—Luke uses the Greek system of counting the days of the week when he writes, "And Jesus came unto Capernaum on the second day." This doesn't mean that he was on the road for two days, but that he arrived on a Monday, which is still called "the second day" in modern Greek.

In the story of the woman of Capernaum who washes Jesus' feet, we are told that she "stood at his feet behind him" while "Jesus sat at meat in the Pharisee's house." This is not easy to visualize, unless we imagine—as the author clearly does—that Jesus was not sitting in a chair but reclining on a couch, as the Greeks did, with his legs stretched out behind him (away from the banquet table). In fact what the author actually says is "Jesus lay down at the table," not "Jesus sat at meat," though the King James translators preferred to think of Jesus sitting upright like a proper Englishman.

In an earlier episode that deals with the birth of John the Baptist, John's family is discussing what name they should give him. Some of his relatives suggest that he be called Zacharias, after his father, but in a Jewish household to name a child after a living relative would have been considered an unmistakable invitation to disaster. Zacharias himself is unable to express his opinion out loud (he has been struck dumb by an angel):

And he asked for a writing table, and wrote, saying, His name is John.

—LUKE 1:63

Whereas a wax tablet (which could be written on with a pointed stylus and erased by scraping off the top layer of wax) would have been a common enough household object in Greece, it would have been a rare and expensive luxury in Palestine.

Luke, who seems to have been familiar with both earlier Gospels, has a tendency to polish and expand Jesus' sayings as they are reported in Matthew and Mark. Sometimes he just smooths off the rough edges; sometimes he clarifies a point or adds an extra embellishment of his own. For example, he adds an extra verse to the parable of the new wine in old bottles which does not appear in either Matthew or Mark:

No man also having drunk old wine straightway desireth new: for he saith, The old is better.

—LUKE 5:39

The author seems to have a special fondness for this kind of indirect, metaphysical language, and his Gospel includes seventeen of the thirty-nine parables found in the New Testament, including three of the most famous ones: Lazarus, the Prodigal Son, and the Good Samaritan.

The last of these, certainly one of the most vivid and immediately accessible of Jesus' parables, is a reliable old standard in Sunday school and confirmation classes. In addition, for all its simplicity, it is also a small masterpiece of literary craftsmanship and artful persuasion.

First of all, like many of Jesus' other parables, the story of the Good Samaritan is presented as an improvisation on a set theme. A "lawyer"—a professional interpreter of the Law—refers to the commandment "Love thy neighbour as thyself" and asks Jesus, "And who is my neighbour?" This is really a rhetorical question. The author tells us that he was "tempting" Jesus—trying to draw him out, in other words, in the hope that his interpretation of the commandment would contradict the Law. As a pious, observant Jew, the lawyer knew perfectly well that his neighbor is another pious Jew and no one else. He has good reason to suspect what Jesus' answer is likely to be: your neighbor is anyone who is in need. Jesus anticipates the trap, and his answer, which seems at first to be simply evasive, turns out to be a brilliantly executed counterattack:

> A certain man went down from Jerusalem to Jericho, and fell among thieves, which stripped him of his raiment, and wounded him, and departed, leaving him half dead.
>
> And by chance there came down a certain priest that way: and when he saw him, he passed by on the other side.
>
> And likewise a Levite, when he was at the place, came and looked on him, and passed by on the other side.
>
> But a certain Samaritan, as he journeyed, came where he was: and when he saw him, he had compassion on him.
>
> And went to him, and bound up his wounds, pouring in oil and wine, and set him on his own beast, and brought him to an inn, and took care of him.

—LUKE 10:30–34

First the reader's (or listener's) attention is completely distracted from the lawyer's original question. Even when retold in the stately language of the King James, pacing and rhythm are Luke's hallmarks as a literary craftsman. The story continues with a rapid flurry of events, and the pace is relaxed only when the Samaritan "came where he was," "saw him," and "had compassion," and finally "bound up his wounds." The story continues for one more leisurely paragraph, and then the psychological moment has arrived:

> *Which now of these three, thinkest thou, was neighbour unto him that fell among the thieves?*

—LUKE 10:36

Jesus has shown that the lawyer's original question is invalid and has forced his adversary to supply the moral to the parable, and thus to endorse his heretical teachings:

> *And he said, He that shewed mercy on him. Then said Jesus unto him, Go, and do thou likewise.*

—LUKE 10:37

(Incidentally, Luke himself seems to have shared Jesus' sympathies for the despised Samaritans more than any of the other Evangelists did and in general seems to have the most highly developed social conscience of the four.)

It may seem that Luke's literary instincts have deserted him by the time he reaches the last verse of his Gospel; his account of Jesus' Resurrection ends abruptly and unremarkably with

> *And [the disciples] were continually in the temple, praising and blessing God. Amen.*

—LUKE 24:53

In fact, Luke had planned from the outset to write a two-volume account of Jesus' life and the founding of the Christian church. The second volume, the Acts of the Apostles, follows the Gospel According to Saint John and (after a few words of introduction,

addressed to the "most excellent Theophilus") picks up immediately where the first volume left off, with the disciples' return
to Jerusalem.

The crucial question of when the Messiah would establish his
kingdom on earth is the very first point to be addressed in the
Acts of the Apostles:

> *Lord, wilt thou at this time restore again the kingdom to Israel?*
> *And he said unto them, It is not for you to know the times or*
> *the seasons, which the Father hath put in his power.*
>
> —ACTS 1:6–7

The Gospels were written to provide the young communities
of the early Church with what Luke calls "infallible proofs" that
Jesus was the Messiah and that he had truly risen from the dead.
The Acts of the Apostles was intended to fulfill the same purpose
and to resolve this critical conflict between faith and disillusion-
ment by reminding them of the works and teachings of the
founders of their church: Peter, "in Jerusalem, in all Judea, and
in Samaria," and Paul, who brought Jesus' message to the
Hellenistic world. And because Luke's history of the apostles is
intended primarily as a work of persuasion, he gives us a highly
colored, idealized account of what those early Christian—
perhaps we should say early early Christian—communities were
like.

Still, an occasional hint emerges that all of Jesus' original
followers were perhaps not quite as noble and cooperative, as
brave and self-sacrificing, as the author would have liked them to
be. For example, chapter 2 offers an idyllic description of the
apostles, living in perfect harmony in Jerusalem and practicing
what would later come to be called "pure communism":

> *And all that believed were together, and had all things*
> *common;*

And sold their possessions and goods, and parted them to all men, as every man had need.

Praising God, and having favour with all the people. And the Lord added to the church daily such as should be saved.

—ACTS 2: 44–45, 47

This experiment in the total redistribution of wealth seems to have worked out very nicely at first, but by chapter 6 the system is already beginning to show signs of strain:

And in those days, when the number of the disciples was multiplied, there arose a murmuring of the Grecians against the Hebrews, because their widows were neglected in the daily ministration.

—ACTS 6:1

Or in modern political jargon, ethnic favoritism, threats of a party split. The situation is critical, but the disciples are unwilling to devote their full attention to the problem—"to neglect the ministry of God in order to wait on table" (New International Version, Acts 6:2). Instead, they decide to appoint a committee of seven men of honest report, "full of faith and of the Holy Ghost," to take immediate action. The disciples may have been inspired by the teachings of Jesus, but they still had a lot to learn.

The evidence that the author of the Luke Gospel and the Acts of the Apostles was the "beloved physician" Luke who is mentioned in Paul's letters is interesting but inconclusive.

Paul refers to Luke as his "fellow-labourer" and most faithful companion, and part of the account of Paul's travels in Acts is written in the first person—"And entering into a ship of Adramyttium, we launched, meaning to sail by the coasts of

Asia . . ." This may be taken to mean that the author actually did accompany Paul on some of his journeys or it may just have been a stylistic device (like the two prologues addressed to Theophilus) to give the narrative a more personal flavor. (Many Greek writers of this period seem to have switched back and forth between the first and third persons more or less arbitrarily.)

We would tend to assume that Luke the physician, Paul's closest colleague, would have been intimately familiar with Paul's letters (in one of them Luke "sends greetings" to the Christians of Colossae). The author of the Gospel and Acts, however, never quotes from them or refers to them, and some evidence leads scholars to suspect that he had never even read them.

You may have heard that Luke, besides being a physician, a missionary, and (perhaps) a distinguished author, was also a painter. This is merely a legend, though a highly stylized portrait of Jesus in the Greek monastery of Lavra is attributed to Luke (at least by the local tour guides).

Leaving aside the various ancient legends, and the various modern theories and scholarly disputes, all we are left with is a remarkable piece of writing—no less remarkable as an anonymous manuscript than as the Gospel According to Saint Luke. In this case it might be best to refer to George Bernard Shaw, who provides a very simple solution to a similar controversy by announcing, "Shakespeare's plays were not written by Shakespeare but by an unknown writer of the same name."

And he had in his right hand seven stars: and out of his mouth went a sharp twoedged sword: and his countenance was as the sun shineth in his strength.

—REVELATION 1:16

344

The Gospel According to Saint John and the Book of Revelation

Matthew, Mark, and Luke are called the Synoptic Gospels, which means that they share a common point of view. John is the odd man out.

His account of the life of Jesus is very different from the other three, and he has the reputation of being not only the most profound but also the most difficult and inaccessible of the Evangelists. (We have already seen how the discovery of the Qumran texts has largely dispelled the idea that he was a kind of Greek philosopher in Christian guise.) Although John was certainly a mystic, he was a very logical mystic, and his writing is not nearly as difficult as it might appear at first glance. Take the majestic opening verse of his Gospel:

> *In the beginning was the Word, and the Word was with God, and the Word was God.*

> —JOHN 1:1

Substitute "wisdom" for "the Word" (the Greek *logos* means both), and the meaning is very clear: God's wisdom created all things and God existed even before "the beginning" in which the heavens and earth were created. John carries this original idea much further:

> *And the Word was made flesh, and dwelt among us . . .*

> —JOHN 1:14

This is a poetic way of announcing (or proving) that Jesus was the Son of God—mystical perhaps, but certainly not incomprehensible.

John seems to have been the best Old Testament scholar of all the Evangelists. He also seems not to have been familiar with any of the earlier Gospels, though it now appears likely that his

345

Gospel was written only a decade or so after those of Luke or Matthew, perhaps as early as A.D. 90. This conclusion was inspired by the discovery of Papyrus 52 (circa A.D. 125), the oldest of any of the Gospel writings. Fifty years later, copies of John's Gospels may well have been dispersed all over the Roman Empire because extant manuscripts from Carthage, Smyrna, and even Lyon are dated to about A.D. 175.

The traditional identification (still widely accepted) of the author of the Gospel with John, "the disciple whom Jesus loved," seems to be borne out by at least two passages in the Gospel itself:

> *And he that saw it bare record, and his record is true: and he knoweth that he saith true.*

—JOHN 19:35

> *This is the disciple which testifieth of these things, and wrote these things: and we know that his testimony is true.*

—JOHN 21:24

But, first of all, the author (though he switches into the first person in the last verse) never explicitly identifies himself with the Apostle John. All he seems to be saying here is that his report of Jesus' life is based on eyewitness testimony, perhaps even a written or oral account supplied by the apostle himself. More important, it now seems likely (as we shall see) that the last chapter of the Gospel was added by a later writer, so that even this highly ambiguous evidence was not contributed by the original author. As we have already seen, he seems to have been influenced by the teachings of the Essenes. It may be worth noting here that a passage in the Gospel implies that John was originally a disciple of John the Baptist (John 1:35–39), and the author of the Gospel emphasizes the role of John the Baptist as Jesus' precursor much more strongly than any of the other Evangelists.

The basic organizing principle of this Gospel also sets it apart from the others. The only events that the author chooses to recount are those that have a clear symbolic meaning. Only seven miracles (which the author calls "signs") are mentioned, and in this Gospel they are not presented simply as spectacular proofs of Jesus' divinity (or his superiority over the pagan gods) but simply as illustrations of an underlying spiritual truth. For example, at the marriage feast at Cana, Jesus changes water into wine (just as men's lives will be transformed and enriched by his teachings). A lame man is made to walk and a blind man to see (Jesus' message will inspire men to seek God and recognize his greatness). Lazarus rises from the dead (but Jesus himself must die if such things are to be possible).

Even the Crucifixion takes on a special symbolic meaning which is present only in this Gospel. The other Evangelists describe how "the veil of the temple was rent" by an earthquake, how the ground shook and the sun was blotted out. In John's Gospel the Crucifixion takes place in brilliant sunshine—a symbol of the victory of the power of Light over the power of Darkness and (quite possibly) another application of the symbolic language of the Essenes.

And for John, as well as the other Evangelists, the primary symbolic meaning of Jesus' miracles is that they could have been accomplished only by the Messiah, as the prophets had foretold. The miracles of the feeding of the multitudes, for example, and the healing of the blind man are both connected with the prophecies of Isaiah:

> *And in this mountain shall the* LORD *of hosts make unto all people a feast of fat things . . . of wines on the lees well refined.*

—Isaiah 25:6

> *Then the eyes of the blind man shall be opened. . . .*

—Isaiah 35:5

347

John's adroit interpretations of Jesus' teachings have made him a particular favorite of theologians, perhaps because they think of him as one of their own (or perhaps because he has saved them so much work). Luther, for example, clearly thought that John was far and away the most admirable of the Gospels:

> *Because only John writes so little about Christ's works and so much about his preachings, and contrariwise the other evangelists give us so many of Christ's works and so few of his words, for this reason John is the chiefest and the finest of the evangelists, and meet to be set far above and as the foremost of the others.*

As a writer, though, John simply can't hold a candle to Luke. His vocabulary is limited, his style is heavily dependent on repetition, and he often uses a very questionable literary device to put across his own interpretations of Jesus' teachings: in John's Gospel the disciples are a fairly sorry lot who never seem to grasp what Jesus tells them the first time around, so everything has to be explained to them all over again.

John seems to have been thoroughly conversant with everyday Jewish customs and ritual practices, and he does not make any special effort to explain them (or explain them away). He is much closer to Matthew in this respect than to Luke or Mark. For example, the water that is turned into wine at Cana is poured into

> *. . . six waterpots of stone, after the manner of the purifying of the Jews, containing two or three firkins apiece.*

> —JOHN 2:6

This "firkin" is the Hebrew *bath*, so the total output of Jesus' first miracle was at least ninety gallons. The water that was used for the ritual washing of the hands was kept in these stone jars, because the porous clay pots that were used for ordinary purposes could not be scrubbed clean enough to be considered "clean" in the religious sense.

In the story of the "man which was blind from his birth" in chapter 9, the author describes how Jesus combined his miraculous gift of healing with a common ancient folk remedy:

> . . . *he spat on the ground, and made clay of the spittle, and he anointed the eyes of the blind man with the clay.*

> —JOHN 9:6

Both "spittle" and clay poultices were thought to have healing properties, though this treatment undoubtedly had never been as spectacularly successful as in this case—the blind man's sight is restored as soon as he washes himself in the pool of Siloam (which was the outlet of the underground aqueduct built by King Hezekiah). The blind man's parents refuse to acknowledge Jesus' miracle, however,

> . . . *because they feared the Jews; for the Jews had agreed already, that if any man did confess that he [Jesus] was Christ ["the anointed," that is, the Messiah], he should be put out of the synagogue.*

> —JOHN 9:22

This is a slight historical lapse on the part of the author, for although this was true in his own time, the policy of summary "excommunication" had not yet been adopted during Jesus' lifetime, or even in the time of Paul, some twenty years later.

All this provides interesting local color, but certainly not so much as to obscure the point of the story. In an earlier chapter, John tells a story whose point depends entirely on a rather sophisticated knowledge of Jewish idiom. Philip, who has already been chosen as one of Jesus' disciples, is trying to persuade a friend of his, Nathanael, that Jesus is truly the Messiah:

We have found him, of whom Moses in the law, and the prophets, did write, Jesus of Nazareth, the son of Joseph.

—JOHN 1:45

Nathanael, however, is skeptical:

Can there any good thing come out of Nazareth? . . .

—JOHN 1:46

But he agrees to go with Philip to see his master; Jesus greets him with these words:

Before that Philip called thee, when thou wast under the fig tree, I saw thee.

—JOHN 1:48

The dialogue between Philip and Nathanael seems to imply that Nathanael has never seen Jesus, though Jesus apparently has seen Nathanael. Nathanael's astonished reaction to this announcement makes it very clear that this could not have been just a chance encounter that has slipped his mind or that he was totally unaware of at the time:

Rabbi, thou art the Son of God; thou art the King of Israel[!].

—JOHN 1:49

Not to prolong this mystery, the fig tree under which Nathanael was sitting was not an actual fig tree but the metaphorical tree of righteousness. "To be under the fig tree" was a rabbinical expression that meant "to study Torah"; the fig tree appears in the Old Testament as a symbol of the righteousness of Israel.* Nathanael is a former rabbinical student, then,

* In the prophetic books the phrase "every man shall sit under his own fig tree" refers to the ideal state of man, in which he keeps God's commandments and enjoys his favor. "The fig tree shall not blossom" (Habbakuk 3:17; compare

and in John's Gospel Jesus' ability to read the stories of people's past lives in their faces—what we would call clairvoyance—is presented as another infallible proof that he was the Messiah. The Samaritan woman that Jesus met at the well is similarly convinced of this when he tells her, more straightforwardly this time, that "thou hast had five husbands; and he whom thou now hast is not thy husband." "Sir," she replies, "I perceive that thou art a prophet" (John 4:18–19).

Later, in chapter 13, John reports another of Jesus' prophecies that is expressed in equally cryptic language. At the Last Supper, after Jesus has washed the feet of the disciples, he explains that he has "chosen" one of his disciples to betray him so

> . . . *that the scripture may be fulfilled, He that eateth bread with me hath lifted up his heel against me.*

—JOHN 13:18

This in turn is a quotation from the Psalms:

> *Yea, mine own familiar friend, in whom I trusted, which did eat of my bread, hath lifted up his heel against me.*

—PSALMS 41:9

"Lifted up his heel" is not, as far as we know, a Hebrew (or Greek or Aramaic) idiom. A few years ago, when scholars decided to take a closer look at the original manuscripts, they discovered that this mysterious phrase must have been the result of a typographical (or rather scribal) error. In Hebrew, strangely enough, the phrases "betrayed me" and "lifted up his heel against me" are identical except for one letter; and what the

---

Jeremiah 8:13) means that God has turned against Israel because the people have abandoned righteousness. Both Matthew and Luke relate an incident in which Jesus curses a fig tree that does not bear fruit, which may originally have been a reference to the same idea, though the Gospels supply an entirely different interpretation (Mark, chapter 11; Matthew, chapter 21).

psalmist must have originally written was "he that ate bread with me, betrayed me." (This correction has found its way only into the most recent translations of the Bible.)

The scene in which Jesus washes the disciples' feet appears only in this Gospel. Apart from serving as a dramatic introduction to Jesus' announcement that one of his disciples will betray him—"ye are not," he says, "not all"—it also has, as we might expect, a symbolic meaning. In Matthew this is made explicit in one of Jesus' sermons to his disciples:

> *But he that is greatest among you shall be your servant*
> *. . . and he that shall humble himself shall be exalted.*

> —MATTHEW 23:11–12

Because this was a service that was ordinarily performed by slaves, Peter objects at first:

> *Thou shalt never wash my feet. Jesus answered him, If I wash*
> *thee not, thou hast no part with me.*

> —JOHN 13:8

Two passages in this Gospel are not included in the most reliable ancient manuscripts, and stylistic analysis confirms that they were added by another writer.

The first of these describes Jesus' encounter with the woman taken in adultery. Because she was caught "in the very act," the Pharisees insist that she be immediately subjected to the penalty prescribed by the Law: death by stoning. Jesus at first pretends to pay no attention—he "stooped down, and with his finger wrote on the ground"; then he finally disperses the crowd with the famous rebuke, "He that is without sin among you, let him cast a stone at her." Both in content and in style, this seems much more reminiscent of the author of Luke, who takes such pleasure in portraying Jesus discomfiting his "tempters" with a few well-chosen words. In fact, this episode was sometimes also included at the end of chapter 21 of the Luke Gospel in early manuscripts of the Bible.

And, as mentioned earlier, the last chapter of the Gospel, which describes Jesus' third meeting with his disciples after the Resurrection, also seems to have been written by someone else. The original text was clearly intended to end with the last verse of chapter 20:

> But these are written, that ye might believe that Jesus is the Christ, the Son of God; and that believing ye might have life through his name.

> —JOHN 20:31

By contrast, the following chapter ends much less impressively, with a commonplace and faintly apologetic observation:

> And there are also many other things which Jesus did, the which, if they should be written every one, I suppose that even the world itself could not contain the books that should be written. Amen.

> —JOHN 21:25

Revelation

The last and the most unusual book of the New Testament (and of the entire Bible, for that matter) is the Book of Revelation. The author refers to himself as John, the servant of Jesus Christ, but this book is so very different in style and content that it is unlikely to have been written by the same author. Its late date of composition (shortly after A.D. 100) makes it even more unlikely that it could have been written by John the Apostle himself.

353

Revelation is the only apocalyptic book of the New Testament. Today we generally associate the word *apocalypse* with a vision of universal destruction—with the end of the world, in short. Certainly the author of Revelation has a great deal to say about this subject, and such well-known artistic treatments of this theme as Dürer's *The Four Horsemen of the Apocalypse* have also contributed to this interpretation. Actually, the Greek word *apokalypsis* simply means "revelation," though what the author intends to reveal is that now Christians of "the Seven Churches of Asia" can prepare themselves for the forthcoming end of the world, which is described in great detail.

The Book of Revelation, of course, is the original "sealed book." This expression is a reference to the "book with seven seals" which the Lamb of God opens after "no man was found worthy to open and to read the book, neither to look thereon" (Revelation 5:4).

This is a very apt description of the Book of Revelation itself; the mystical number seven is invoked repeatedly—seven churches, seven plagues, seven angels with seven trumpets, seven "vials of the wrath"—and its contents are almost as mysterious and inaccessible as those of the "book with seven seals." Many passages in the Book of Revelation have so many possible meanings that they come very close to having no meaning at all.

Many early authorities considered this book to be apocryphal, and it was accepted only very grudgingly by the Eastern Church. The Book of Revelation gives the reader the suspicion that the entire contents of a particularly well-stocked occult bookstore have somehow been compacted into a single volume—astrology, numerology, cabalism, and all sorts of esoteric and obscurantist wisdom are here in abundance. The number of verses that seem to have a clear, unequivocal meaning can be counted on the fingers of one hand. Of course, the use of symbolic language can be poetic and highly evocative, as long as the author and the reader share a common fund of symbols. The problem with the Book of Revelations is that its symbols may be drawn from any one of at least four sources:

1. The prophetic books of the Old Testament, especially historical prophecies in the Book of Daniel. The Book of Revelation bears a greater resemblance to these than to any other book of the New Testament.

2. The early Christian symbolism of the Last Days and the Second Advent of the Messiah, which does not necessarily correspond to the symbolic language of the later Christian church.

3. Hellenistic religious, mystical, and pseudoscientific writings.

4. Allusions to contemporary politics, primarily the persecution of the early Church by the Romans—so that the mystical seven can stand for the seven hills of Rome or the seven Caesars who reigned between Augustus and the beginning of the second century.

For example, in chapter 9, we are warned of a plague of enormous locusts that are sent to torment

> . . . *only those men which have not the seal of God in their foreheads.* . . . *that they should be tormented five months.*
>
> —REVELATION 9:4–5

Why did the author choose locusts? There are several possibilities. Locusts were the last of the plagues of Egypt which destroyed the harvest (this seems likely because the author of Revelations refers to "the seven last plagues"). They are also used by the prophet Joel as a symbol of the "great army" that Jahweh will send to chastise Israel (which also seems likely, because the locusts in Revelation are said to wear breastplates of iron and the sound of their wings was "like the noise of chariots"). Finally, there are the locusts that John the Baptist fed on, like most poor people of Palestine; this doesn't seem very likely but shouldn't be ruled out as a possibility.

And why do the locusts have faces like men, and hair like women? And why are their victims to be tormented for five months? As for the last question, at least, there are several possible answers: because five months is roughly the life expectancy of an ordinary locust, or because the Flood lasted for five months, or because five in ancient numerology was a particularly unlucky number.

At least we should have an easier time with a phrase like "[they] have washed their robes, and made them white in the blood of the Lamb" (Revelation 7:14), which clearly refers to the preeminent Christian symbol of Jesus as the sacrificial lamb, who has spilled his blood to free mankind from sin. But with a verse like this one, we are plunged back into obscurity again:

> To him that overcometh will I give . . . a white stone, and in
> [on] the stone a new name written, which no man knoweth saving
> that he receiveth it.

—REVELATION 2:17

First of all, the Greeks used a stone or a potsherd with someone's name scratched on it as a kind of primitive credit card, identity card, and admission voucher (to a theater, for example). Second, white, in Jewish mysticism, was the color of joy and of victory. Third, in Asia Minor (and elsewhere) it was commonly believed that someone who knew a man's real name thereby gained a kind of power over him. In this case, no one will know the possessor of the stone's "new name" except God, who has bestowed this new name on him, inscribed on a white stone, which is in itself a token of victory and rejoicing.

In both Hebrew and ancient Greek, letters were also used as numbers, which meant that in deliberately cryptic or mystical writings, every word could also be assigned a numerical value.

The classic example of this in Revelation is the number 666, which is mentioned, though of course not explained, in this passage:

> *Here is wisdom. Let him that hath understanding count the number of the beast: for it is the number of a man; and his number is Six hundred threescore and six.*

—REVELATION 13:18

This beast, as we learn in the preceding passage, is an evil beast with horns who is the archdeceiver of mankind. The number of the beast should also tell us the name of the man, if we have "understanding" enough to know the proper correspondences between numbers and letters (remember that vowels are not written down in Hebrew). Thus, 666 is

50	+	200	+	6	+	50	100	+	60	+	200
N	(E)	R		O		N	K	(E)	S	(A)	R

—"Nero Caesar." (Written without the *n*, as it would be in Latin, the numerical value is 616, which also appears as an alternative in some early manuscripts.) This is not the historical Nero, who had died about forty years earlier, but a future emperor whose wickedness would be one of the last great tribulations that the faithful would have to endure. There is no guarantee that any of these interpretations is correct, but the last of these carefully hidden secrets should give us a clue as to why the Book of Revelation was written in this elaborate secret code.

It was Nero who had launched the first systematic persecution of the Christian church. At the time the Book of Revelation was written, Christianity was still an outlaw religion, barely tolerated at best. The Christian communities of Asia Minor were at the mercy of paid informers and hostile Roman officials. To clear themselves of the suspicion of engaging in treasonous correspondence (which, of course, from the point of view of the Romans, they were), they were forced to adopt a cryptic symbolic language derived from various occult and mystical traditions of the ancient world. As we shall see in a later chapter, this exchange of inspirational and interpretive writings was especially important in binding together these isolated communities in an age of political oppression and spiritual crisis. Here, the essential message of the Gospels—that Jesus' kingdom would soon be established on earth, though no man could foresee the day or the hour—is blended with an equally welcome political prophecy, reminiscent of the prophetic books of the Old Testament: that the power of Rome, the new Babylon, the oppressor of Jesus' people, would soon be overthrown.

. . . They have taken the Lord out of the sepulchre, and we know not where they have laid him.

—JOHN 20:2

PART V

THE LAST DAYS OF JESUS

The first fact in the history of Christendom is a number of people who say they have seen the Resurrection. If they had died without making anyone believe this "gospel," no gospels would ever have been written.

—C.S. LEWIS

Perhaps the most convincing proof of the historical existence of Jesus is the Crucifixion. Even if the Evangelists had wanted to contrive an unnatural death for their protagonist, they certainly would never have chosen crucifixion, a punishment that was never prescribed in ancient Israel and is never mentioned in any of the prophecies concerning the Messiah, or in the Old Testament at all. (The Old Testament merely speaks of a kind of posthumous exposure in the stocks, in which the bodies of executed criminals were displayed on an upright post or gibbet— women with their faces turned toward the wooden crosspiece, by the way).

The Sanhedrin, the Jewish high court, originally had jurisdiction in capital cases, but in Jesus' time this was the exclusive prerogative of the Roman occupation authorities—which made it much more difficult for Jesus' sectarian enemies to bring their campaign against him to a successful conclusion.

Jesus had come to Jerusalem to celebrate Passover, the most important of the pilgrim festivals. It was the duty of every pious Jew, beginning at age twelve, to observe the Passover "in the place which the LORD shall choose" (Deuteronomy 16:2). Jerusalem was thronged with pilgrims during Passover week; Josephus tells us that three million people came to Jerusalem in one year, and this figure may not be as wildly exaggerated as it might seem. In A.D. 62 Nero ordered his officials to make an exact count of the number of lambs sacrificed in Jerusalem; they arrived at the impressive total of 256,000. Considering that poorer families (like Mary and Joseph) could afford to sacrifice only a pair of doves, and allowing one lamb for a family of five, we arrive at a very rough estimate of at least two million pilgrims and permanent inhabitants. (The sacrificial lamb was later roasted and eaten, again as prescribed by Deuteronomy 16:7. Our grandmothers' pious belief that there was something vaguely sacrilegious about cutting bread instead of "breaking" it also can be traced back to this chapter of Deuteronomy, by way of the Last Supper—though of course the "bread" that is referred to here is not ordinary leavened bread but matzoh.)

During Passover week all routine business was suspended (including the business of the courts). Rather than postpone the pressing matter of Jesus' arrest and trial, the high priest Caiaphas apparently preferred to have him arraigned by the Sanhedrin before the beginning of the holiday. There were at least two excellent reasons for this.

First, the people of Jerusalem were notoriously unruly during Passover week. The city was overcrowded and swarming with provincials—"the people of the land"—who had many reasons to be discontented; the Romans always reinforced their garrison during Passover week.

Second, delaying the trial would only increase the danger that Jesus' followers would be able to organize some sort of resistance and perhaps influence its outcome.

According to the testimony of the Gospels, this well-planned exercise in judicial murder was carried out overnight, with a total elapsed time of twelve hours between Jesus' arrest and execution. This included his first appearance before the Sanhedrin, preliminary examination by the procurator Pontius Pilate, an additional appearance before Herod Antipas (according to Luke, at least), sentencing by Pilate, scourging, and crucifixion. Remember that all this took place in a Roman protectorate, where Roman authority, and Roman law, was supreme—either Caiaphas was a political wire puller of almost supernatural ability, or things must have actually happened a little differently.

In any case Caiaphas clearly had a gift for calculating the odds very closely; of the three articles of the indictment against Jesus, only the third was a capital offense under Roman law:

1. Jesus had threatened to destroy the Temple.
2. He had claimed to be the Son of God.
3. He had claimed to be the king of the Jews.

And a death sentence, of course, was exactly what Caiaphas had in mind from the outset:

Ye know nothing at all [he tells the chief priests and the Pharisees],

Nor consider that it is expedient for us, that one man should die for the people, and that the whole nation perish not.

—JOHN 11:49–50; compare 18:14

Though this decision, John tells us, was based on a kind of strange Messianic prophecy (see John 11:51–52), Caiaphas is nothing if not a pure political pragmatist from that moment on.

John also tells us that Jesus was crucified on "the preparation of the passover" (that is, Friday, the day before Passover). The other Evangelists, however, are all agreed that it was the day of preparation for the *Sabbath* (hence, Good Friday) but that Passover—"the feast of the unleavened bread"—had begun the previous day, on Thursday, which is when Jesus and his disciples came to Jerusalem to celebrate the last Passover feast together (the Last Supper). Unfortunately, this seems to contradict Matthew's and Mark's report that Caiaphas and the other high priests had agreed to have Jesus executed *before* the beginning of Passover week "lest there be an uproar among the people."

363

Some scholars believe that Jesus' arrest and crucifixion really took place sometime before (or even after) Passover week, but that the Evangelists were reluctant to deprive themselves of the powerful symbol of Jesus as the paschal (Passover) lamb. Actually, it is John who emphasizes this most strongly, when he tells us that the Crucifixion took place on the eve of Passover.

Another theory, which we have already encountered in a different guise, maintains that Jesus and his disciples celebrated Passover on a different day from the Pharisees, the Sadducees, and the "multitude." According to the Jewish lunar calendar, the first day of Passover falls on the fourteenth day of Nisan (which roughly corresponds to our April), the date of the first full moon in spring. But as we know, one Jewish sect had its own calendar, based on the cycle of Sabbaths—namely, the Essenes.

If Jesus and his disciples celebrated Passover on the date prescribed by the Essene calendar, the Last Supper might well have been held on a Thursday. And because the official holiday did not begin until Saturday, Jesus could have been tried and executed on a Friday—in accordance with the Christian tradition, which is based on the reports of the other Evangelists.

The Gospels supply another piece of indirect evidence for this. We know that Jesus had some female disciples, and that men and women customarily sat down together at the same table to partake of the Passover lamb. Among the Essenes, however, this was presumably not the case, and none of Jesus' women followers were present at the Last Supper.

Jesus' appearance before the Sanhedrin seems to have been a typical political show trial, conducted along lines that have become very familiar in our century. All the Gospels report that Jesus was beaten, mocked, and abused before and after the trial:

Then did they spit in his face, and buffeted him; and others smote him with the palms of their hands.

> *Saying, Prophesy unto us, thou Christ, Who is he that smote thee?*

> —MATTHEW 26:67–68

His disciples had been intimidated into silence. In fact, they "forsook him, and fled" when he was arrested. Only Peter, we are told, was outside, awaiting the outcome of the trial, and he went as far as to deny that he had ever been a disciple of "Jesus of Galilee." Matthew and Mark both report that "false witnesses" were induced to testify against him. According to Mark, their testimony was contradictory and inconclusive; according to Matthew, two of them finally testified that Jesus had boasted that he was "able to destroy the temple of God, and to build it in three days."

As far as the Sanhedrin was concerned, the crucial point in this sham trial was count number two: that Jesus claimed he was the Son of God. This was sufficient under Jewish law to convict him of "blasphemy," but not, as we have seen, a punishable offense under Roman law. Three of the Evangelists record Jesus' answer to this accusation:

> *"I am."*

> —MARK 14:62

> *"Thou sayest."*

> —MATTHEW 27:11

> *"Ye say that I am."*

> —LUKE 22:70

Only the first of these replies seems to be an unqualified "yes" to us. The others seem more like what modern lawyers would call a plea of *nolo contendere,* in which the accused neither contests nor admits to his guilt. (This in itself, of course, has generated an enormous amount of commentary and controversy.) Other writings from the time of Jesus, however, have made it clear that to answer such an important question with a simple yes or no was considered rude or insolent. Instead, it was customary to reply with some polite formula like "You have said that this is true [and it is]," so that all three of Jesus' reported replies are really the equivalent of "Yes, I am."

This admission is enough to justify a guilty verdict, and Jesus is brought before Pilate for sentencing. Note that when Caiaphas reports the original indictment to the Roman procurator, he refers only to the third count, that Jesus had proclaimed himself "king of the Jews," thus fomenting a rebellion against the Romans, although this charge is barely mentioned during the trial itself.

Pontius Pilate was later canonized by the Coptic Church because he could "find no fault" with Jesus. He does not seem to have had any other saintly qualities, though he did conduct this second phase of the trial with scrupulous fairness—up to a point at least—especially considering that he himself was merely a time-serving Roman bureaucrat who must have grown very tired of Jewish sectarian squabbles. Unfortunately, Pilate lost his chance to win a more widely recognized immortality by jotting down a brief memorandum of these proceedings, which would have been the most important single document in the history of the world and would have made him the most celebrated state's witness of all times.

We know a little more about Pilate's life from other sources (primarily Josephus), because Pilate himself, like Caiaphas, was unmistakably a historical figure. He was originally a protégé of Sejanus, the sinister lieutenant of the Emperor Tiberius, and he had even married into the imperial family. (His wife was Claudia Procula, a granddaughter of the Emperor Augustus, who, according to Matthew at least, seems to have accompanied him to Jerusalem.) He was abruptly recalled to Rome in disgrace several years later, after a band of inoffensive Samaritans had been massacred on his orders. Apparently he had mistaken those participants in some sort of religious gathering for the ringleaders of a rebellion against Rome. According to one tradition, he lived out the rest of his life in obscurity, in France or possibly somewhere in the Alps; according to another, he committed suicide at the request of the Emperor Caligula.

In the Gospels, Pilate is described as behaving quite correctly. He tries repeatedly to dismiss the charges against Jesus and is dissuaded only by the blackmail threats of Caiaphas and the Sadducees, who have already succeeded in stirring up a convincing "uproar among the people." In the interim Pilate still takes the trouble to try to engage his prisoner in a philosophical discussion. After Jesus tells him that "Every one that is of the truth heareth my voice," Pilate does not immediately dismiss this as Jewish mystical claptrap, but instead asks, "What is truth?" (John 18:38).

As for Matthew's report that Pilate "took water, and washed his hands," we may be inclined to doubt that Pilate was familiar with the text of the Twenty-sixth or the Seventy-third Psalm (see page 254). It is possible that the Evangelists made Pilate into much more of a noble Roman and Caiaphas into much more of a vicious demagogue than they really were; writers of this period did have a tendency to view history exclusively in terms of heroes and villains.

(Although Jesus clearly regarded the trial as merely part of the fulfillment of his destiny, at least two attempts have been made to reopen the proceedings against him in our own century. The first of these belated appeals, which was submitted to the Israeli supreme court in 1972, was dismissed because the official records of the original trial were no longer in existence. The second was rejected because the court felt it did not have jurisdiction over what was essentially a historical rather than a judicial problem.)

As soon as the sentence was handed down, the machinery of swift Roman justice was set in motion. The condemned man was flogged, precisely 720 lashes, no more and no less. Then he was led off to the place of execution, proceeded by a placard inscribed with his name and the crime for which he had been condemned. This was actually a plaque made out of plaster, not the parchment scroll that is usually shown in paintings. In Jesus' case this "superscription," written by Pilate himself, according to John, simply read: JESUS OF NAZARETH THE KING OF THE JEWS (John 19:19–22).

For centuries pilgrims from all over the world have retraced Jesus' steps on the way to Calvary along the Via Dolorosa in Jerusalem. Jesus himself, however, could not have walked along this "Way of Sorrows," a narrow, twisting lane that in his time was part of the northern wall of the city. (In addition, the street level of modern Jerusalem has since risen at least twenty-five feet, on the rubble and accumulated debris of nineteen centuries.)

It was also customary for the condemned man to carry the wooden crosspiece, not the entire cross, to the place of execution outside the city, where the crosspiece was nailed to the vertical post that was already in place. Then the condemned man was nailed or tied to the cross. Medieval and Renaissance paintings of the Crucifixion show the three crosses towering over the heads of the soldiers and the onlookers; this is pure artistic license, because the cross itself was apparently only four or five feet taller than the height of a man. John supplies an indirect demonstration of this when he writes:

> . . . they filled a spunge with vinegar, and put it upon hyssop, and put it to his mouth.

> —JOHN 19:29

(A hyssop bush is not much more than three feet tall.) Most of the paintings correctly show Jesus' ankles transfixed by a single nail, but, as is fairly well known by now, the other nails were thrust through the bones of the forearm, not through the palms of the hands (which are too fragile to support a man's full weight). The upper body was often supported by a narrow wooden ledge called the *cornu* ("horn"), which was fixed to the cross at about waist height; this was merely an added refinement to prolong the victim's sufferings.

Crucifixion, certainly one of the cruelest punishments that has ever been devised, was inflicted only on slaves and non-Roman citizens. It was often a matter of days before the condemned man finally died, usually of heart failure. Although his sufferings were thought to have an exemplary effect on others, if he managed to survive for too long, the *cornu* was removed and his legs were broken; the ensuing strain on the heart was invariably fatal. The two thieves who were crucified on either side of Jesus had to be dispatched in this manner; Jesus himself was found to be already dead.

However, this may well have been one of those instances in which the Evangelists were more concerned with introducing additional proof that Jesus was the Messiah than what we would call objective historical reporting. According to them, the two thieves represent the fulfillment of Isaiah's prophecy that the Messiah would be "numbered with the transgressors" (Isaiah 53:12). The Thirty-fourth Psalm says explicitly that

> He [the righteous man] keepeth all his bones: not one of them is broken.
>
> —PSALMS 34:20

This passage, which is quoted in John's account of the Crucifixion, refers in turn to the original "ordinance of the Passover," which requires that the bones of the sacrificial lamb should not be broken (Exodus 12:46).

369

Matthew, Mark, and Luke all mention that Jesus died during "the ninth hour," about three o'clock in the afternoon. ("The first hour" was six o'clock in the morning, the first hour after sunrise.) All the events that take place during this last hour of Jesus' life are portrayed (at least in the Synoptic Gospels) as the fulfillment of the Messianic prophecies of the Old Testament, even though they may be reported differently and subject to different interpretations. Three of the Evangelists tell us that Jesus "cried out in a loud voice":

My God, my God, why hast thou forsaken me?

—MATTHEW 27:46; MARK 15:34

Father, into thy hands I commend my spirit.

—LUKE 23:46

Both versions of Jesus' last words on the cross, as you may recall, are quotations from the Psalms. John tells us that his last words were "It is finished" (John 19:30), which seems to refer back instead to Jesus' prayer in the Garden of Gethsemane: "I have finished the work which thou gavest me to do" (John 17:4).

This provides us with three different perspectives on the meaning of Jesus' life and works. Matthew and Mark seem to reflect the early Christians' despair that Jesus, who had worked so many miracles, could not work one more and save himself from death. Luke gives us a more hopeful interpretation: the Son of God has been reunited with his Father. John, as we might expect, works out a kind of synthesis of these two ideas: Jesus has no need to perform any further miracles; the task that his Father has sent him to carry out on earth is finished. John interprets Jesus' death as the fulfillment of his life on earth, as the final victory of light over darkness.

The catastrophic earthquake described by Matthew— ". . . the vail of the temple was rent in twain . . . and the earth

370

did quake" (MATTHEW 27:51)—and the "darkness over all the earth until the ninth hour" described by Luke and Mark are equally symbolic, though their meanings are very different. First of all, we can be quite certain that "the darkness over all the earth" does not refer to an actual solar eclipse. There can never be an eclipse of the sun during the full moon, and the first day of Passover was, by definition, the time of the full moon. Virgil describes similar phenomena that accompanied the death of Emperor Augustus, and neither Virgil nor the Evangelists intended these metaphysical passages to be taken literally. For Virgil, however, it was merely a literary convention that "the heavens themselves blaze forth the death of princes." For the Evangelists, these events represent the fulfillment of a prophecy:

> *Shall not the land tremble for this, and every one mourn that dwelleth therein. . . .*
>
> *And it shall come to pass in that day, saith the Lord GOD, that I will cause the sun to go down at noon, and I will darken the earth in the clear day.*
>
> —AMOS 8:8–9

With Jesus' death Roman justice had been done, and though the usual policy was to leave criminals' bodies exposed on the cross as a further warning to others, the Romans did not insist on this in Judea, out of deference to Jewish burial customs. Because his disciples were apparently still in hiding, Jesus' body was claimed by Joseph of Arimathaea, one of his clandestine followers (who was also a member of the Sanhedrin, at least according to Mark and Luke). Both coffins and cemeteries were unknown in Judea. The dead were prepared for burial—washed, embalmed, and wrapped in a linen shroud over twenty feet long—and entombed in "sepulchres," burial vaults hollowed out of a cliffside on the outskirts of the city. According to John, the "spices" with which Jesus' body was embalmed were provided by

371

another of his clandestine followers, a Pharisee called Nicodemus—"a mixture of myrrh and aloes, about an hundred [troy] pound weight" (about sixty-three pounds avoirdupois).

A linen shroud of this kind, imprinted with the faint outline of a human body, has been preserved as a relic in the Turin Cathedral since the sixteenth century. The Turin shroud has been subjected to repeated scientific testing since the turn of the century (not always, unfortunately, by the most exacting methods). Some tests appear to demonstrate that the shroud was woven at about the time of Jesus and that its fibers contain grains of pollen from plants that are found only in Palestine. Ultraviolet photographs reveal that the man who was originally wrapped in this shroud had been flogged shortly before his death; there are distinct traces of blood, sweat, and sputum, as well as nail holes in the forearms and ankles. But all this does not mean that this was the identical shroud in which Joseph of Arimathaea and Nicodemus wrapped Jesus' body. Crucifixion was all too common in first-century Judea—during Titus's siege of Jerusalem in A.D. 70 there was not enough wood to make crosses for all the captured rebels who had been condemned to death. Two additional points, however, cannot be so easily disposed of:

1. The dead man's scalp and forehead seem to have been lacerated in a way that certainly suggests the Crown of Thorns, which was not a routine punishment by any means.

2. There are no traces of decomposition, which means that the shroud must have been unwrapped from the body shortly after death, which would have been difficult to explain—unless this was indeed the shroud Peter discovered in the empty tomb after the Resurrection (John 20:6).

The Turin shroud has been the object of intensive study by a special papal commission, headed by Monsignor Ricci, for the past thirty years. More recently, a team of American scientists were permitted to examine the shroud and to subject it to a whole battery of rigorous scientific tests, using the most advanced equipment. (The results of this investigation were inconclusive, but some scientists involved have independently announced that they believe the shroud to be authentic.) True believers feel that the authenticity of the shroud proves that the Gospels' account of the Crucifixion is historically accurate (and vice versa—the Gospels prove that the shroud is authentic). Skeptics reply that the reference in the Gospels to the shroud in the empty tomb was too much of a temptation for some medieval forger, who made it his business to "rediscover" this relic in order to provide tangible proof that the Resurrection actually occurred.

Both sides are likely to be disappointed as the investigation continues. It seems fairly clear already that the fabrication of such a relic would have severely overtaxed the abilities of even the most sophisticated forger. On the other hand, it is doubtful that any scientific proofs of the shroud's authenticity will ever tell us much more than that it was the authentic burial cloth of a first-century Palestinian who died on a cross—but not necessarily the Cross.

O death, where is thy sting?
O grave, where is thy victory?

—I Corinthians 15:55

PART VI

THE APOSTLE PAUL

Isn't it curious that men should be so willing to
fight for their religions and so unwilling to live
by their precepts?

— GEORG CHRISTOPH LICHTENBERG

The King James translators must have felt uneasy about including seven Catholic letters in their Protestant Bible, so they rebaptized them "general epistles." This was fair enough, because *Catholic* means "general," in this context at least, and the Catholic letters were originally so called (almost fourteen hundred years earlier) because they were addressed to the entire Church, not just to a particular community or congregation. There is one more thing they have in common: "Not a single one of them was written by the author whose name appears on the title page."

Comparisons of style and modern critical dating methods have enabled scholars (in the case of the quotation above, the Protestant Bible scholar Willy Marksen) to make such claims— which would easily have been enough to get them thrown out of their churches a hundred years ago. Sometimes questions of authorship are not as abstruse and technical as they might sound. For example, it does seem unlikely that Peter, the fisherman of Galilee, could have written the two letters that are credited to him in such a remarkably polished Greek; or that the

377

Apostle Jude, who may have been Jesus' brother or cousin, survived to write his epistle shortly after A.D. 100.

Originally there were many more than seven of these open letters to the early Church (it should not be too difficult to imagine why that particular number was chosen), and several of those that were eventually excluded as apocryphal are just as much worth reading as the lucky seven that were chosen by the Fathers of the early Church. Together with the fourteen letters traditionally ascribed to Paul, the Catholic letters make up about a third of the New Testament.

Even in very early times, it was recognized that this division was somewhat artificial. Though the Letter to the Hebrews, for example, was treated officially as a Pauline letter, the Church Fathers had serious doubts that it was actually written by Paul: "As to who was the author of the epistle," wrote Origen in the fourth century, "God alone knows." Today the Letter to the Hebrews (which is probably so called because it deals exclusively with Old Testament themes rather than because it was actually addressed to the Jewish Christians) is frequently classified with the Catholic letters, which brings Paul's total down to thirteen (and this is only the beginning, as we shall see).

Several centuries ago Bible scholars worked out a separate classification system for the Pauline letters, including such categories as "pastoral letters" (three in number, written to the pastors of particular congregations rather than to an entire community of the faithful) and "captivity epistles," or "prison letters" (written while Paul was imprisoned, or under house arrest actually, in Rome.)

Modern scholars have been more concerned with two more fundamental categories: spurious and authentic. The present consensus is that four of the Pauline letters (including Hebrews) were definitely not written by Paul—a discovery that caused something of a sensation when it was announced. The more rigorous critics are inclined to accept only seven of the remaining ten as genuine. These are First and Second Corinthians, Romans, Galatians (the Galatians were distant relatives of the Gauls, a Celtic people who settled in what is now northwestern Turkey in the third century B.C.), Philippians, First Thessalonians, and Philemon (a private letter to a Greek Christian in Asia Minor which deals with the emancipation of a runaway slave). First Thessalonians (addressed to the Christians of Salonika) is the oldest of the Pauline letters and thus the earliest book of the New Testament; it can be reliably dated at A.D. 50 or 51.

To make up for this savage onslaught on the extant Pauline letters, modern textual critics can offer persuasive evidence that at least three authentic letters have not come down to us. If they should ever turn up, this will at least help make up the deficit.

Because Paul was that much closer to the actual events of Jesus' life than the authors of the Gospel, it is all the more surprising that so many of the important themes and personalities of the Gospels are only briefly mentioned (Judas Iscariot, the Virgin Mary) or not mentioned at all (the Lord's Prayer, for example). The central theme of all of Paul's letters is the Resurrection and the grace—Paul's favorite word—that mankind acquired through Jesus' sacrifice.

Paul is not supposed to have been much of an orator, though this is hard to believe after reading his letters and the later account of his ministry in the Acts of the Apostles. Paul seems to have tried to sense the temper of his audience and, unlike many more recent missionaries, to have taken particular pains to adapt his message accordingly. In Athens, for example, which he found to be "wholly given to idolatry," he disputed in the marketplace like Socrates and tried to engage the sympathies of the Athenians with the audacious philosophical proposition that they were already worshiping the Christian God without even being aware of it:

> *For as I passed by, and beheld your devotions, I found an altar with this inscription, TO THE UNKNOWN GOD. Whom therefore ye ignorantly worship, him declare I unto you.*

—ACTS 17:23

Unfortunately, the "philosophers of the Epicureans, and of the Stoicks" begin to lose interest when Paul informs them that the son of this unknown god had risen from the dead.

In his Letter to the Romans, as he says, "I speak to them that know the law." He draws a neat legalistic analogy between Roman family law—in which a wife was released from all obligations to her husband on his death—and the Mosaic law—from which, he assures his readers, all men are released by the death of Jesus:

> *Wherefore, my brethren, ye also are become dead to the law by the body of Christ; that ye should be married to another, even to him that is raised from the dead, that we should bring forth fruit unto God.*

—ROMANS 7:4

A better-known metaphor from Paul's Letter to the Romans is often quoted, but not usually in the sense that Paul intended:

> *Therefore if thine enemy hunger, feed him; if he thirst, give him drink: for in so doing thou shalt heap coals of fire on his head.*

—ROMANS 12:20

Paul is supposed to be counseling his readers against trying to avenge themselves on their enemies ("I will repay, saith the Lord"), but here it sounds as if Paul is just recommending a new technique: inflict pain and suffering on your enemies ("coals of fire") by treating them with Christian generosity and forbearance. In fact, this is an allusion to the Book of Proverbs

380

(25:22), with which his readers (who used the Septuagint in their services because the New Testament had not yet been written) were presumably quite familiar. This apparently refers originally to an Egyptian mourning custom in which recent widows carried braziers full of glowing coals balanced on their heads as a sign of mourning and repentance. *Repentance*, then, is the key word here—treat your enemies with Christian charity, and you will cause them, not to suffer, but to repent.

Paul's personal contacts with the other apostles were infrequent—and not always cordial, it seems. In his Letter to the Galatians, a community that had been strongly influenced by Jewish Christian missionaries, he describes a serious doctrinal dispute between himself and Peter (who is called by his Aramaic name, Cephas). The subject of this controversy was circumcision—in particular, whether it was necessary for Gentile converts to Christianity to be circumcised. This seems to be the least of the problems that the early Christian would have had to worry about, but of course the real issue was whether it was necessary for Christians to obey the laws of Moses. As we know already, Paul believed that it was not, and his opinion was confirmed (with respect to circumcision at least) by an apostolic conference that was held in Jerusalem in A.D. 49. Still, a powerful faction of Jewish Christians resisted this decision, and Peter, the leader of the Christian community in Antioch, seems to have come under their influence. By about A.D. 56 Peter had apparently yielded completely to the separatist tendencies of "them which were of the circumcision." Paul reproaches him for this—

> *If thou, being a Jew, livest after the manner of Gentiles, and not as do the Jews, why compellest thou the Gentiles to live as do the Jews?*
>
> —GALATIANS 2:14

—before he arrives at the crucial point:

*Knowing that a man is not justified by the words of the law,
but by the faith of Jesus Christ. . . .*

—Galatians 2:16

An essential part of Paul's doctrine of the risen Christ (which
does not always correspond to the teachings of Jesus himself)
seems in our era to be a kind of grim asceticism that flatly
contradicts human nature and what we are accustomed to think
of as the natural order of things. His remarks on marriage, sex,
and women in particular seem to provide irrefutable evidence
not only that Paul was an enemy of the human passions but also,
as many of his critics have pointed out, that he exerted a sinister
and unwholesome influence on the doctrines of the Christian
church:

It is good for a man not to touch a woman.
*Nevertheless to avoid fornication, let every man have his own
wife, and let every woman have her own husband.*

—I Corinthians 7:1–2

*I say therefore to the unmarried and widows, It is good for them
if they abide even as I.*
*But if they cannot contain, let them marry: for it is better to
marry than to burn.*

—I Corinthians 7:8–9

First of all, these lines are not quoted out of context, they
mean exactly what they say. Before we dismiss Paul as a hopeless
misogynist, however, we have to remember one thing. Paul
expected that the end of the world might arrive literally at any
moment. Consequently, he recommends against forming any
attachments in this world—marrying and begetting children in
particular—when we should be preparing ourselves for a new life
in the world to come.

Also important to bear in mind is that this letter is addressed to the Corinthian Christians, and that Corinth was a wide-open town where temple prostitution was a major local industry. So the temptation for Paul's fellow Christians to form less permanent attachments was present night and day. The Greeks, of course, had a more concise way of saying this, and the verb *korinthiazesthai*, which literally means "to carry on like a Corinthian," actually meant something more like "to lead a life of total sexual depravity."

A related charge that has been leveled against Paul is that he was an unabashed male chauvinist, or to use the more current terminology, a typical representative of male-dominated patriarchal religion:

> But every woman that prayeth or prophesieth with her head uncovered dishonoureth her head; for that is even all one as if she were shaven.
>
> For the man is not of the woman; but the woman of the man;
>
> Neither was the man created for the woman; but the woman for the man.
>
> For this cause ought the woman to have power [that is, a token of her husband's power over her] on her head because of the angels.

> —I CORINTHIANS 11:5, 8–10

The phrase "because of the angels" seems reminiscent of the monastic rule of Qumran, where women were forbidden to share the communal meal "so as not to drive away the angels."

Paul was very clear about how the heavenly and earthly hierarchy was arranged: "the head of the woman is the man," and woman is subordinate to man, just as men are subordinate to Christ, and Christ is subordinate to God. The "power" that Paul instructs women to wear on their heads is the origin of the Roman Catholic custom that requires women to cover their heads with a scarf or a mantilla in church. However, this ambiguous verse has been given an interesting new interpretation in a recent German edition of the Bible, where it appears as

> . . . and woman should wear the sign of her power upon her head, out of respect for the angels.

In particular, the translators explain, the power that Paul is referring to—and that he has explicitly granted to woman—is the power to prophesy, to lead the congregation in prayer, and to engage in the kind of inspired charismatic preaching that was favored by the early Church.

Whether you prefer to imagine Paul as a cold-blooded woman hater or a pioneering champion of equal opportunity, it is important to bear in mind that his brief sermon on this subject in First Corinthians finally resolves on a note of reconciliation and harmony:

> Nevertheless neither is the man without the woman, neither the woman without the man, in the Lord.
> For as the woman is of the man, even so is the man also by the woman; but all things of God.
>
> —I CORINTHIANS 11:11–12

In his Letter to the Galatians Paul reminds his readers that before his conversion, "I persecuted the church of God, and wasted it." A far more detailed and dramatic account of Paul's conversion is recounted in the Acts of the Apostles: Saul was employed as a kind of grand inquisitor by the high priest in Jerusalem until Christ appeared to him in a blinding vision on the road to Damascus, at which point, as you probably recall from Sunday school, Saul became Paul the Apostle. This last part of the story is untrue, by the way; Saul was simply his Hebrew name, by which he was more commonly known in the Gentile world. (Both names are used interchangeably in the Acts of the Apostles.)

Paul is otherwise not very forthcoming about his own life in his letters, and we know very little about him. He was born in Tarsus on the south coast of Anatolia, which was an important commercial center in Roman times, though today it is just a sleepy Turkish provincial town.

Paul's parents were Jews; his father worked as a tent maker, which meant that he was either a tanner who sewed tents out of hides or a weaver who worked at a loom and wove tent material out of goat hair. Paul's father was also a Roman citizen, and both his inherited trade and his Roman citizenship stood Paul in good stead in later life. His trade enabled him to support himself as an itinerant craftsman. His Roman citizenship saved him from summary execution in Jerusalem when he fell afoul of the Sanhedrin.

During his last visit to Jerusalem, near the end of his career as a missionary, Paul was accused, among other things, of having "gone about to profane the temple" by bringing a Gentile into the inner sanctuary. Because he was a Roman citizen, Paul was taken into protective custody and detained by the Roman governor for two years before he requested, as was every citizen's right, that his case be brought before the emperor.

Paul is sent off to Rome, under guard; Acts tells us that he lived there for several years, under a nominal kind of house arrest that still allowed a certain amount of freedom. And that is the last we hear of him in the New Testament, though most scholars think that the traditional story is probably accurate—that he was beheaded during Nero's persecutions.

Some scholars suspect that the account of Paul's life in Acts breaks off so abruptly because the author of Luke himself was rounded up during a later persecution and his second volume was simply left unfinished. It is also possible that, as far as the author was concerned, his story had already been brought to a very satisfactory conclusion:

And Paul dwelt two whole years in his own hired house, and received all that came in unto him,

Preaching the kingdom of God, and teaching those things which concern the Lord Jesus Christ, with all confidence, no man forbidding him.

—Acts 28:30–31

Luke is not writing a biography of Paul as a kind of sequel to the life of Jesus, but an account of how the Jewish Messiah was transformed into the Savior of all mankind. His story begins in Bethlehem and it ends in Rome, when Paul brings Jesus' Gospel to the capital of a great world empire. Paul's active career as a missionary is over, and the author may well have felt that even the briefest postscript describing his last years and his martyrdom would have marred the dramatic unity of his great history of the Christian church.

Paul himself clearly felt that his only importance was as a messenger of Jesus's Gospel. Though he does take a certain pride in recalling how his great theological rivals, the Christians of Judea, "praised God because of me" (New International Version, Galatians 1:24), his definitive statement on the subject is surely this:

Though I speak with the tongues of men and of angels, and have not charity, I am become as sounding brass, or a tinkling cymbal.

—I Corinthians 13:1

("Sounding brass" is "a resounding gong," the New International tells us, and "charity" is the Greek *agape*, the love between God and man.)

Paul spent about thirty years as a traveling missionary, in Arabia, Judea, and Syria, Asia Minor, Greece, and Macedonia, and on his final harrowing sea voyage from the coast of Judea to

386

Rome. The Acts of the Apostles reports that there were 216 passengers on board, and after the ship strikes a rock in the Adriatic Paul narrowly escapes drowning and is stranded on the desolate isle of Malta for three months. Paul's earlier journeys by land may have taken him over twenty-five thousand miles altogether; he traveled by coach (the vehicle itself was more like a wagon), which was probably no less comfortable than in Dickens's time.

But as we have seen, in very few cities did Paul find a very inspiring welcome. Of the two examples we have seen so far, certainly the murderous hostility that greeted his appearance in Jerusalem was far more typical than the bland indifference of the Athenians. The Jews despised him as a renegade and a heretic, and many Christians apparently were skeptical about the sincerity of his conversion. His own struggle against what he regarded as heresy among his fellow Christians created more enemies for him within the Church itself. In pagan communities that took their religion more seriously than the Athenians did, "there arose no small stir about that way," as we read in the King James account of Paul's mission to Ephesus (Acts 19:23).

Ephesus was the capital of the Roman province of Asia and, more important, the site of the Temple of Artemis, one of the seven wonders of the ancient world and a great pilgrimage center. The statue of Ephesian Diana (as the Romans called her), the many-breasted goddess of fertility and of the hunt, was said to have fallen from heaven. She was the object of particular veneration, the basis of a flourishing trade in amulets and silver souvenir replicas "which brought no small gain unto the craftsmen." Paul has driven away too many of their customers by preaching several sermons with the theme "they be no gods, which are made with hands."

The next time he arrives in Ephesus, the silversmiths give the rallying cry—"Great is Diana of the Ephesians"—and stage a mass indignation meeting in the great amphitheater (which could accommodate twenty-four thousand people). Charac-teristically, it is only with great difficulty that Paul's disciples dissuade him from confronting the indignant pagans in the amphitheater. And as soon as the disturbance has died down, he sets off on his travels again, this time for Macedonia.

It may be tempting to find the moral for this story in a modern Christian shrine like Lourdes, where the streets that lead to the basilica are lined with tawdry souvenir stands selling egg timers that bear the likeness of Saint Bernadette, Lourdes water in tablet form for the convenience of air travelers, and where the modern Diana of the Ephesians is provided with a luminous plastic halo. But it is difficult to keep these obvious ironies in mind when we read a passage such as this one, in which Paul describes the hardships that he willingly endured as a messenger—and as an interpreter—of the Gospel:

> . . . thrice I suffered shipwreck, a night and a day have I been in the deep;
>
> In journeying often, in perils of waters, in perils of robbers, in perils by mine own countrymen, in perils by the heathen, in perils in the city, in perils in the wilderness, in perils in the sea, in perils among false brethren;
>
> In weariness and painfulness, in watchings often, in cold and nakedness.
>
> If I must needs glory, I will glory of the things which concern mine infirmities.
>
> —II CORINTHIANS 11:25–27, 30

APPENDICES

MIRACLES PERFORMED BY JESUS

	Matthew	Mark	Luke	John
Miraculous Healing				
A leper	8,2–3	1,40–42	5,12–13	
Centurian's servant	8,5–13		7,1–10	
Peter's wife's mother	8,14–15	1,30–31	4,38–39	
Two madmen near Gadara	8,28–34	5,1–15	8,26–35	
A lame man	9,2–7	2,3–12	5,18–25	
Woman with an issue of blood	9,20–22	5,25–29	8,43–48	
Two blind men	9,27–31			
A dumb man possessed by the devil	9,32–33			
A man with one withered hand	12,10–13	3,1–5	6,6–10	
A blind and dumb man	12,22		11,14	
The Canaanite woman's daughter	15,21–28	7,24–30		
An epileptic boy	17,14–18	9,17–29	9,38–43	
Bartimaus and another blind man	20,29–34	10,46–52	18,35–43	
A deaf mute		7,31–37		
A madman in the synagogue		1,23–26	4,33–35	
A blind man at Bethsaida		8,22–26		
A crippled woman			13,11–13	

	Matthew	Mark	Luke	John
A man afflicted with dropsy			14,1–4	
Ten lepers			17,11–19	
Caiaphas' servant Malchus			22,50–51	
A nobleman's son in Capernaum				4,46–54
A lame man at the Pool of Bethesda				5,1–9
A blind beggar				9,1–41
Power over the Forces of Nature				
Stills the storm	8,23–27	4,37–41	8,22–25	
Walks on water	14,25	6,48–51		6,19–21
Feeds 5000	14,15–21	6,35–44	9,12–17	6,5–13
Feeds 4000	15,32–38	8,1–9		
The tribute money	17,24–27			
Withers the fig tree	21,18–22	11,12–14 20–26		
Miraculous draught of fishes			5,1–11	
Turns water into wine				2,1–11
Second draught of fishes				21,1–11
Raising the Dead				
Jairus' daughter	9,18–19 23–25	5,22–24 38–42	8,41–42 49–56	
Widow's son at Nain			7,11–15	
Lazarus				11,1–44

Source: *Handbuch zur Bibel and Unger's Bible Dictionary*

PARABLES OF JESUS

	Matthew	Mark	Luke
Light under a bushel	5,14–15	4,21–22	8,16; 11,33
House built upon sand	7,24–27		6,47–49
Put new patch onto old garment	9,16	2,21	5,36
Put new wine into old bottles	9,17	2,22	5,37–38
The sower	13,3–8	4,3–8	8,5–8
The mustard seed	13,31–32	4,30–32	13,18–19
The tares	13,24–30		
The leaven	13,33		13,20–21
The "hid treasure"	13,44		
The pearl of great price	13,45–46		
The drag net	13,47–50		
The lost sheep	18,12–15		15,4–7
The unmerciful servant	18,23–35		
The vineyard	20,1–16		
The two sons	21,28–32		
The wicked husbandman	21,33–46	12,1–12	20,9–19
The wedding of the king's son	22,2–14		
The fig tree of summer	24,32–33	13,28–29	21,29–32

Parable	Matthew	Mark	Luke
The wise and foolish virgins	25,1–13		
The talents (Matthew); The pounds (Luke)	25,14–30		19,12–27
The Last Judgement	25,31–36		
The seed growing secretly		4,26–29	
The two debtors			7,41–43
The Good Samaritan			10,30–37
The friend at midnight			11,5–8
The foolish rich man			12,15–21
The watchful servants			12,35–40
The faithful and wise servants			12,42–48
The barren fig tree			13,6–9
The wedding and the feast			14,7–14
The great supper			14,16–24
The tower and the king			14,28–33
The piece of money			15,8–10
The Prodigal Son			15,11–32
The unjust steward			16,1–9
The rich man and Lazarus			16,19–31
The unprofitable servants			17,7–10
The widow and the judge			18,1–8
The Pharisees and the publican			18,10–14

Source: *Handbuch zur Bibel and Unger's Bible Dictionary*

HISTORICAL—BIBLICAL CHRONOLOGY

The chronological table points out the relationship between political events and accounts in the Bible.

BABYLONIA	SUMER	YEAR	BIBLE	EGYPT
		B.C.		
		4000		
	3500 Sumer's heyday Introduction of writing, Gilgamesh epic	3500		
			(uncertain) between **3000** and **1500** The Age of Abraham	**2600** Cheops builds the Great Pyramid
		3000		
		2500		
		2000		
				1700 Invasion of the Hyksos by horseback
		1500	about **1400** Joseph in Egypt	**1367** Pharaoh Akhnaton and the Cult of Aton

GREECE and ROME

1250 Destruction of Troy

1750 Hammurabi's Code
1686 Babylonian Empire falls after Hammurabi's death

about **1220** Exodus from Egypt under Moses; Settlement of Canaan under Joshua, the beginning of judicial law

1050 Saul becomes the first king of Israel

PHILISTINE

1175 Philistines occupy Canaan

950 Under Hiram Tyre (Phoenicia) becomes great

920 Egypt conquers Jerusalem

1000 David conquers Jerusalem
950 Solomon builds his temple
922 After Solomon's death, the kingdom splits—Israel in the north and Judea in the south

587 Babylonian captivity

275 The Jews carry into Alexandria the Old Testament in Greek

167 Maccabee revolt against the Seleucids

150 Establishment of the Essene cult at Qumran

1000

500

400

300

200

100

800 Etruscans wander into Italy
776 The first Olympic games
753 The establishment of Rome
750 Homer writes the Odyssey and the Iliad

334 Alexander the Great conquers Persia, occupies Jerusalem

218 Hannibal penetrates as far as Rome

587 Nebuchadnezzar destroys Jerusalem, leads the people into the Babylonian exile

BABYLONIA	GREECE and ROME	YEAR	BIBLE	EGYPT
	49 Caesar crosses the Rubicon	B.C.		
	44 Caesar's assassination			
	40			
	27 Augustus: First Roman Emperor		10-4(?) Birth of Jesus	
		0		
		A.D.		
			c. 27 John the Baptist	
			c. 29–30 Crucifixion of Jesus	
			c. 35 Conversion of Paul	
			45 First missionary journey of Paul	
		50	50 or 51 Paul's letters to the Thessalonians	
			c. 55 The Thomas Gospel	
			c. 65 Gospel According to Mark	
	70 Destruction of Jerusalem by Titus' legion		c. 80 Gospel according to Matthew	
			c. 85–90 Gospel according to Luke	
			c. 90–95 Gospel according to John	
		100	c. 90–100 Revelation	

SELECTED BIBLIOGRAPHY

A. BIBLE TRANSLATIONS AND REFERENCE WORKS

Archäologisches Lexikon zur Bibel. Abraham Negev, ed., München, n.d.
Atlas zur Bibel. M. Rowley. Wuppertal, 1965.
Die Bibel nach der übersetzung Dr. Martin Luthers. Berlin, 1908.
Biblisches Lexikon für Jung und Alt. Cecil Northcoll. Konstanz, 1973.
Einheitsübersetzung der Heiligen Schrift. Das Neue Testament. Stuttgart, 1979.
Handbuch zur Bibel. David and Pat Alexander, eds. Wuppertal, 1974.
The Holy Bible . . . Commonly Known as the Authorized or King James Version. New York, n.d.
Kleines Bibellexikon. Konstanz, 1972.
Lexikon der ägyptischen Kultur. Georges Posener. Wiesbaden, 1960.
The New Testament. New International Version. New York, 1973.
Praktisches Bibellexikon. Freiburg im Breisgau, 1969.
Das Sachbuch zur Bibel. Josef Scharbert. Aschaffenburg, 1965.
Unger's Bible Dictionary. Merrill F. Unger. Chicago, 1965.

B. GENERAL WORKS

Anfanasjew, Georg. *Moses ist an allem schuld.* München, 1972.
Albright, William F. *From the Stone Age to Christianity.* Baltimore, 1957.
Allegro, John M. *The Dead Sea Scrolls.* Baltimore, 1956.
Arenhoevel, Diego. *So wurde Bibel.* Stuttgart, 1974.
Augstein, Rudolf. *Jesus Menschensohn.* München, 1972.
Bailey, Albert E. *Daily Life in Bible Times.* New York, 1943.
Bamm, Peter. *Frühe Statten der Christenheit.* München, 1955.
————. *Welten des Glaubens.* München, 1959.

Bauer, Hans, and Leander, Pontus. *Kurtzgefasste biblischaramäische Grammatik* . . . Halle, 1929.

Ben-Chorin, Schalom. *Bruder Jesus.* 3rd ed. München, 1970.

Blinzler, Josef. *Der Prozess Jesu.* 4th ed. Regensburg, 1969.

Böttcher, Helmuth. *Gott hat viele Namen.* München, 1964.

Bornmann, Günther. *Jesus von Nazareth.* Stuttgart, 1972.

Bruin, Paul. *Steht das wirklich in der Bibel?* Luzern, 1978.

Budge, E. A. W. *The Babylonian Story of the Deluge and the Epic of Gilgamesh.* London, 1920.

Burrows, Millar. *The Dead Sea Scrolls.* New York, 1955.

———. *More Light on the Dead Sea Scrolls.* New York, 1958.

Canu, Jean. *Religious Orders of Men.* New York, 1960.

Craveri, Marcello. *The Life of Jesus.* New York, 1967.

DeCamp, L. Sprague, and Catherine C. *Great Cities of the Ancient World.* Garden City, 1964.

Dimier, Catherine. *The Old Testament Apocrypha.* New York, 1964.

Frischauer, Paul. *Es steht geschrieben.* Zürich, 1967.

Garden, Ernest. *Sagt die Bibel die Wahrheit?* Lüneburg, 1957.

Haemmerling, Konrad. *Die fünf Weltreligionen.* Berlin, 1947.

Hennecke, Edgar. *Neutestamentliche Aprokryphen.* Tübingen, 1959.

Herrge, Paul. *Die Bibel-Korrektur.* Stuttgart, 1979.

Hinker, Wolfgang, and Speidel, Kurt. *Wenn die Bibel recht hätte.* Stuttgart, 1970.

Holl, Adolf. *Jesus in schlechter Gesellschaft.* Stuttgart, 1971.

Huxley, Julian. *From an Antique Land.* London, 1954.

Josephus, Flavius. *Antiquities of the Jews.* Cambridge, MA, 1929.

———. *History of the Jewish War.* Cambridge, MA, 1929.

Kaufmann, C. M. *Handbuch der Christlichen Archäologio.* n.p., 1922.

Keller, Werner. *The Bible as History.* 2d rev. ed. New York, 1981.

———. *Da aber staunte Herodot.* Dusseldorf, 1972.

Kleist, Heinrich von. *Die Erzählungen und kleinere Schriften.* Berlin, 1935.

Koenigswaldt, Hans. *Lebendige Vergangenheit.* München, 1974.

Koldewey, Robert. *Das wieder erstehende Babylon.* Leipzig, 1913.

Kühner, Otto Heinrich. *Das Jahr Null und die Bibel.* n.p., 1962.

Langewiesche, Marianne. *Spüren in der Wüste.* n.p., 1970.

Selected Bibliography

Lehmann, Johannes. *Die Jesus GmbH*. Düsseldorf, 1972.
————. *Jesus Report*. Düsseldorf, 1970.
Lissner, Jvar. *So habt ihr gelebt*. Freiburg, 1955.
Marxsen, Willi. *Einleitung in das Neue Testament*. Gütersloh, 1964.
Morison, Frank. *Who Moved the Stone?* New York, 1930.
Morton, H. V. *In the Steps of the Master*. New York, 1953.
Pritchard, J. M. *Solomon and Sheba*. London, 1974.
Rehork, Joachim. *Archäologie und biblisches Leben*. Bergisch-Gladbach, 1972.
Schierse, Franz Joseph. *Patmos—Synopse*. Düsseldorf, 1968.
Schneider, Wolf. *Überall ist Babylon*. Düsseldorf, 1960.
Schott, Albert. *Das Gilgamesh-Epos*. n.p., 1934.
Schubart, Walter. *Religion und Eros*. München, 1966.
Sizoo, Alexander. *Die antike Welt und das Neue Testament*. Konstanz, 1955.
Stählin, Wilhelm. *Auch darin hat die Bibel recht*. Stuttgart, 1964.
Uhlig, Helmut. *Die Sumerer*. München, 1976.
Weiser, Alfons. *Was die Bibel Wunder nennt*. Stuttgart, 1975.
Wellhausen, Julius. *Israelitische und jüdische Geschichte*. n.p., 1921.
Yadin, Yigael. *Hazor*. London, 1976.
Zink, Jörg. *Die Wahrheit lässt sich finden*. Stuttgart, 1972.

INDEX

Aaron, 110–111, 125
Abimelech, 146
Abishag, 174, 175, 176
Abraham, 13, 63–87, 120
  character of, 79–82
  in Christian theology, 64
  chronology of, 65, 68, 74–75, 78–79
  in conversation with God, 79–81
  as Eblaite, 76–77
  historical existence of, 63, 65, 67, 77, 82
  language difficulties in story of, 82–83
  Mitanni society and, 71–74
  significance of name, 64
Acts of the Apostles, 292, 341–342, 379, 384, 385, 387
  quoted, 342–343, 380, 386, 387
Adam, meaning of, 42
Adam and Eve, 40–43
"Adam's apple," origin of, 41
adonai, 28
Adonijah, 174–176
afterlife concepts, in Egypt, 100, 102–103
agape, in New Testament, 317, 386
age, of patriarchs, 129
Agur, Proverbs and, 255
Ahab, king of Israel, 195–197, 217–218
Ahasuerus, 238–240
Akhenaten, 30–31, 95, 121
Akkadians, 46, 47
Alexander the Great, 61, 65, 123
Alexandria, Library of, 20
Allah, 28

Allegro, John M., 278
alphabet, invention of, 137
Amen, meaning of, 233
Ammon, 123
Ammonite people, 147
Amos, prophet, quoted, 371
Andreas edition, of the Bible, 138
Andrew, Apostle, 315
angels, Old Testament, 140–141
Annals (Tacitus), 298–299
Antipater, 56, 57
apocalyptic books:
  Daniel as, 271
  meaning of, 354
  Revelation as, 353–358
apple, of Tree of Knowledge, 40–41, 42
Aramaic, 229, 309
Ararat, Mount, 52–53
archaeological research, 41–42, 45–47, 61, 65, 66, 70, 118–119, 123, 130, 136, 137, 142–143, 159, 162, 177–179, 186, 190–191, 221, 277–288, 293, 297
  clarifications due to, 13–14
  clay tablets found in, 37, 67, 68, 71–73, 75–77, 85, 162, 218, 227
  historical verifications by, 31–32
Aristotle, 264
ark, Noah's, 49–50, 51–53
Ark of the Covenant, 124–126, 173
Arnold, Matthew, 150–151
Assurbanipal, library of, 37
Assyria, 37, 45–48
  armies of, 218–220
  bas-reliefs, 219, 224

Assyria (cont.)
  cuneiform tablets relating to, 218
  as God's scourge, 218, 223
  Israel and Judah attacked by,
    218–226
  Messiah concept in, 267
  see also Nineveh
Aten, 31
Athanasius of Alexandria, Bishop, 292

Baal, 123, 133, 137, 139–140, 141,
  197–218, 232
Babel, 57, 58, 63
Babylon, 57–61, 227–228
Babylonia, 221–222, 225–226
  clay tablets in, 227
  sagas of, 35, 46–48
  written Old Testament begun in, 229
Babylonian Captivity, 57, 78, 226–227,
  229, 249
  return from, 220–221, 230–231, 267
Bamm, Peter, 44
baptism, Essenes and, 279, 281, 283,
  286–287
Bar Kokhba revolt, 151
Bartholomew, Apostle, 315
Baruch, Book of, 266
Bathsheba, 133, 166, 169–170, 175
Benjamin, tribe of, 153–154, 164
Bethlehem, 271, 302
Beuron, Benedictine cloister of, 23
Bible:
  apocryphal texts in, 16, 124, 192,
    234–240, 251–265, 292, 354, 378
  authenticity issue on, 32
  authorship of, 14, 28, 31, 33–34
  as best-seller, 11–12
  canonical texts in, 16
  Catholic version of, see Roman
    Catholic Church; Vulgate Bible
  chronological scope of, 14, 28, 34
  as collectors' item, 21, 22–23
  Dead Sea Scrolls and, see Dead Sea
    Scrolls
  division of Old and New Testaments
    in, 28
  early Latin manuscripts of, 15
  "ecumenical" edition of, 17, 23

errors in, 15, 18, 38, 112, 122, 123,
    178, 267, 273, 293, 294–295,
    351–352
  Jewish version of, see Old Testament;
    Septuagint
  literary language of, 11–12, 14
  medieval interpretations of, 42, 43,
    123, 125, 141, 192
  original source of elements in, 14,
    29–31, 37, 40–42, 46–55, 71, 78,
    105, 119–120, 134–135, 141–142,
    148, 152, 163, 235, 238, 261,
    332, 333, 355
  original texts of, 14–15, 17
  Protestant version of, see German
    Bible, Luther's; King James Ver-
    sion; New English Bible; New
    International Version
  rationalists' attempts to discredit, 32,
    34, 35–36, 48
  retroactive tampering with, 36,
    77–78, 161, 172, 180, 258–259,
    296–297, 321
  selection process of texts in, 16, 33
  translations of, 11–16
  as Word of God, 14, 31, 32
  written transmission of, 19–23
  see also New Testament; Old
    Testament
Bible As History, The (Keller), 162
Big Bang theory, 36
Boaz, as "redeemer," 156–158
Book of the Dead, 120
Botta, Paul-Émile, 46
Brecht, Bertolt, 9
Brockhaus-Bilderlexikon, 189
Buchert Institute, 249
burning bush, 108–110

Caiaphas, 312, 362, 366, 367
Calvary, 368
Canaan, conquest of, 129–137, 138,
  139
Canticle of Canticles, see Song of
  Solomon
Capernaum, woman of, 338
Catholic letters, 377–378
census taking, 171–172, 302

Index

Chaldea (Sumer), 66–67
chariot cities, Solomon's, 177–178
children, in New Testament, 322–323
Christianity:
  Abraham's place in, 64
  Daniel's place in, 271–272
  Elijah's place in, 199–217
  Essene doctrine vs., 282–285
  founding of, 341–342
  Greek philosophy and, 264, 285,
    379–380
  Jacob's place in, 86
  Jephthah's place in, 147
  Maccabees' place in, 246–247
  Moses' place in, 200
  Old Testament prophecy and, see
    prophets
  Osiris cult and, 100–101
  Passover and, 111, 364
  Psalms' place in, 253–254
  Ruth's place in, 155
  secret language during early persecu-
    tions of, 357–358
  Wisdom of Solomon's place in,
    264–265
Chronicles, Book of, 161, 172, 177,
  234, 246
  Book I, quoted, 179, 180
  Book II, quoted, 177, 183
Cid, El, 196
circumcision, ritual, 77–78, 381
clairvoyance, 350
Codex Vaticanus and Codex
  Sinaiaticus, 293
Columbus, Christopher, 39
communion, Essene vs. Christian prac-
  tice of, 283
Constantine, Emperor, 304
Coptic Church, 366
Coptic manuscripts, 16, 300
Corinthians, Letters to the, 379,
  382–384
  Letter I, quoted, 375, 382, 383, 384,
    386
  Letter II, quoted, 388
cosmetics, Egyptian, 89–90
Creation myths, 29, 33–63, 76
Crown of Thorns, 372

Crucifixion, of Jesus, 254, 362,
  363–364, 368–371
  symbolic meaning of, 347, 361
cubit, meaning of, 327
Cyrus, king of Persia, 229
  religious toleration decreed by,
    229–230, 231, 232

Daniel, Additions to, 16
Daniel, Book of, 16, 271–273, 355
Daniel, prophet, 272
David, House of, 158, 271, 302, 306
David, King, 158–172, 254
  crimes of, 171–172
  Goliath and, 159–162
  historical evidence and, 159–162
  as king, 169–170, 171, 172–173,
    174, 179–180
  Saul and, 166–168, 170–171
  as soldier of fortune, 167, 168–169
  Solomon's Temple and, 180
  succession issue and, 174–176
  women and, 169–170
davidum, meaning of, 162
Dead Sea Scrolls, 236, 277–288
  contents of, 280–281
  Jesus and the Essenes in, see Jesus
  physical condition of, 18, 278, 279
  site of, 278, 279
  verifications of texts by, 15
Deborah, 143, 144–145
Deisler, Adolf, 29
Delilah, 148–149
Denin, Avinoam, 116
Descartes, René, 55
Deuteronomy, Book of, 126, 127
  quoted, 127–128, 140, 184–185,
    189, 362
Dheilly, Joseph, 138
Dirne, meaning of, 15–16
disciples, of Jesus, 313–318, 323, 348
  feet of, washed by Jesus, 284, 352
  female, 315–317, 364
  as symbol of twelve tribes of Israel,
    284
  twelve, as apostles, 314–315
  "undesirables" among, 314, 315,
    342–343

disciples, of Jesus (cont.)
 writings by, see Gospels; specific
  disciples
divination, in Egypt, 98–99
dowsing, 117
dream interpretation, 92–93
Duino Elegies (Rilke), 250

earthquake, at Crucifixion, 370–371
Ebla, 37, 65, 75
 "Eblaite" tablets of, 75–77
Ebrum, King, 76–77
Ecclesiastes, Book of, 192, 251,
  258–260
 authorship of, 258
 quoted, 258, 259, 260
Ecclesiasticus, Book of (Book of Jesus
  Son of Sirach), 192, 251, 262–264
 quoted, 263
economic system, in Egypt, 101–102
Eddas, 54–55
Eden, 33, 34, 36, 37–40
 location of, 38–39
eden, meaning of, 37
Eglon, king of Moab, 141–142
Egypt, 181–182, 306
 in alliances with Judah, 221–222,
  225, 226
 daily life and customs in, 89–104
 Hebrew refugees from, 112–114
 Hebrew slaves in, 104–107
 New Kingdom, 30–31
Ehud, son of Gera, Elgon and,
  142–143
El, 28, 140, 186
Elhanan, Goliath and, 161
Elijah, prophet, 195, 197–217
 holy war by, 198
 miracles performed by, 200, 217
 on Sinai, 198–199, 217
Elisha, prophet, 197, 199–200,
  217–218
Elohim, 28
embalming, 102–103, 371–372
Encyclopaedia Britannica, 49
Enki, in Sumerian myth, 37
Enlil, 53–54
Ephesus, 387–388

ephod, meaning of, 145–146
Epic of Gilgamesh, The, 45–46, 50, 52,
  54
epistles, of New Testament, 285, 292
 authorship of, 377–378
 of Paul, 343, 344, 378–388
Ernst, Max, 299–300
Essenes, 279–288, 312, 346, 347, 364
 Gospels and, 284–286
 Jesus and, 274, 279, 283–284, 286,
  287, 288, 310
 as militant order, 281
 organization of, 281–282
 Qumran community of, 279, 280,
  281–282, 313
 teachings of, 282–285, 286–287
Esther, Additions to, 263
Esther, Book of, 238–240
 quoted, 239, 240
Euphrates, 67
evangelist, meaning of, 291–292
Exodus, Book of, 104–126, 127
 quoted, 104, 110, 112, 113, 114,
  116, 118, 119, 121, 122, 124, 125
Exodus, events of, 112–118, 130
Ezekiel, Book of, 269
Ezra, Book of, 230, 231, 233–234
 quoted, 230, 231
Ezra, prophet, 230, 231, 232

faith, revelation vs. interpretation and,
  274
Faust (Goethe), 249
Fertile Crescent, 29, 37, 39–40, 41
fig tree, as symbol, 350n–351n
Flood, story of, 29, 33, 44–55, 76
forty, as mystical number, 18
Four Horsemen of the Apocalypse, The
  (Dürer), 354
fraxinella plant (Dictamnus alba),
  109–110
Frederick the Great, 275, 282
Freud, Sigmund, 31
Fundamentalists, 14, 172, 249

Gadarene swine, Jesus and, 332–333
Galatians, Letter to the, 379, 381, 384
 quoted, 382

Index

Galilee, Galileans, 307, 311, 333
Gan Eden, 37–40
Garden of the Hesperides, 41
Genesis, Book of, 33–63, 126
  quoted, 13, 37–38, 40, 43, 44, 49,
    52, 54, 55, 58–59, 62, 63–64,
    68–69, 71, 73, 74, 77, 78, 79,
    80–81, 82, 83, 84, 86, 87, 88, 91,
    92, 93, 95–96, 97, 98, 99, 100,
    101, 102, 103
  two accounts of Creation in, 33–35
German Bible, Luther's, 12–13, 15, 59,
    74, 82, 83, 84, 109, 122,
    196–197, 252, 257, 258, 295
  recent edition of, 384
German Requiem (Brahms), 270
Gibeah:
  old man of, 151–153
  Saul's capital at, 161, 165–166
Gibeon, siege of, 133–134
Gideon, 145
Gilboa (el Jib), 135
Gnostic Gospels, 16
God, evolution of idea of:
  Elijah and, 199, 250
  Greek philosophy and, 264, 379–380
  in human affairs, 137–138, 234
  Job and, 250
  Moses and, 121, 250
  Nehemiah and, 250
God, names of, 28–29
Goethe, J. W. von, 249, 334
gold, Solomon's, 179, 180, 181–183
Goliath, 159–162
Good Samaritan, parable of, 221,
    339–341
Goshen (Wadi Tumilat), 107, 112
Gospels, 254–255, 270, 292, 318–353
  authorship questions in, 286, 292,
    329, 337, 343–344, 346, 352–353
  chronology of, 292, 318, 337, 346, 353
  Essene texts and, 284–286, 288, 347
  intent of, 301, 309–310, 342
  meaning of word, 291
  order of, 319
  parables in, 339–341
  Paul's letters and, 379
  selection of texts in, 16

Synoptic, 345
  two-source theory of, 302
  variations among, 301–308, 318,
    320, 321, 327, 333, 339, 362,
    363, 370
grace, Paul's concept of, 379
"Grateful Dead, The," 235
Greece:
  rebellious provinces of, 241–247
  speculative philosophy in, 264, 285
  Tree of Knowledge myth in, 40–41
Gutenberg (Gensfleisch), Johannes,
    22–23

Hagar, 73
Haile Selassie, emperor of Ethiopia,
    190
Hammurabi's Code, 118–120
Handbook of the Bible, 138–139, 261
Hanging Gardens of Babylon, 228
Hannibal, 115
Haran, 69–70, 74
Harnack, Adolf, 27
Hatshepsut, Queen, 181–182
Havilah, 38
Hazor, conquest of, 136
heavenly reward, concept of, 264
Hebbel, Friedrich, 237
Hebrew, biblical, 18, 229, 267, 309
Hebrews, Letter to the, 378
Heisinger, Werner, 36
Helios (Baal), 139
Herbinius, 39
Herod, King, 287, 302, 306, 362
Herodotus, 60–61, 89, 102
Hezekiah, king of Judah, 221–226
Hiram, king of Tyre, 181, 182–184,
    187–188
historical investigations, 14, 34, 48–49,
    61, 108, 159–162, 185–186, 225,
    246, 258, 297
Hittites, 139, 149
Holofernes, 236–237
Hor, 39–40
Horeb (Sinai), Mount (rock of), 117,
    198
horns, power and, 122–123
hosanna, meaning of, 335

Hosea, Book of, 306
Huth, Ricarda, 12, 13
"Hymn to the Sun," 30–31

incense, use and disuse of, 191
incunabula, 23
infant heroes, 105
International Bible Society, 17
Iraq (Shinar), 58–59
Isaac, 64, 78
Isaiah, Book of, 270
  quoted, 227, 265, 269–270, 347, 369
Isaiah, prophet, 225–226, 269
Ishmael, 73
Islam, 73, 77
  Abraham's place in, 64–65
Israel, *see* Jacob
Israel (ancient state), 194, 231
  Baal worship in, 197–218, 232
  Samaritans vs. returned exiles in,
    220–221, 231
  "wicked kings" of, 218
Israel (word), 28
Israel and Judah, dual kingdom of,
  172–194
  destruction of, 218
  as empire, 176–177
  prophets in, 198, 266

Jacob, 62, 64, 83–86, 87, 95–96, 100,
  102–103
  angel and, 86
  Rachel and, 83–85
Jael, Sisera and, 143–145
Jahweh, 29, 107, 111, 118, 126, 137,
  173, 252
  Baal vs., 139, 197–218, 232
James, Apostle, 315
James, "brother" of Jesus, 308
Jamnia, Council of, 16
Jasher, book of (Book of the Righteous),
  134–135
Jaspars, Karl, 62
Jebusite tribe, 172, 173
Jehovah, 28
Jehu, King, 197–198, 217–218
Jephthah, 146
Jeremiah, Book of, 269
  quoted, 187

Jeremiah, prophet, 125
Jericho, 132
  walls of, 35, 131
Jeroboam, king of Israel, 194
Jerome, Saint, Latin Vulgate Bible of,
  122, 123, 295
Jerusalem, 271, 304, 361–362, 385,
  387
  Assyrian siege of, 221, 222–225
  as David and Solomon's capital,
    161–162, 172–173, 176
  Hellenized Jews in, 242–243
  restoration of, 230–231, 232–233
  sacking of, 125, 185, 187, 226, 313
  Syrian pillage of, 245
Jerusalem Bible, 236
Jesus, 87, 221, 291, 297, 298–313
  allusions to Psalms and, 253–255,
    367, 369, 370
  ancestry of, 64, 133, 302, 306
  biographical information on,
    299–313
  burial of, 371–372
  Crucifixion of, 254, 347, 361, 362,
    363–364, 368–371
  date of birth of, 298, 302–306
  disciples of, 313–318
  Elijah and Elisha as parallels of,
    199–217
  Essenes and, 274, 279, 283–284,
    286, 287, 288, 310
  healing powers of, 321, 332, 349
  historical, 298–299, 301, 307, 361
  Isaiah as parallel of, 269–270, 347
  Last Supper of, 362, 363, 364
  on laws of Moses, 284
  as Messiah, 274, 288, 299, 302, 306,
    319, 321, 347, 361, 369–370, 371
  miracles and, 200–217, 299,
    332–334, 347, 370
  Moses story and, 105, 306
  as Nazarene or Nazarite, 307
  original Hebrew text on, 16
  personality of, 301
  "portraits" of, 310, 344
  Resurrection of, 335–336, 341, 359,
    379, 382
  as sacrificial lamb, 111, 356, 364,
    369

Index

Second Coming of, 301, 328
teachings of, 281, 300–301, 311,
  312, 317, 320, 322–323, 327–328,
  330, 340–341, 352
Ten Commandments and, 121
trial of, 361, 362–368
Jesus Son of Sirach, Book of (Book of
  Ecclesiasticus), 192, 251, 262–264
Jewish rebellions (A.D. 66–73), 281,
  282, 313
Jezebel, Queen, 195, 197–198, 218
Jirku, Anton, 159
Job, Book of, 248–251
  quoted, 247, 250, 251
  Satan in, 248–249
John, Apostle, 284–285, 315, 346, 353
  as mystic, 345
John, Saint, Gospel According to, 254,
  292, 293, 311, 316, 320, 345–353
  author of, 346, 348, 352–353
  Essenes and, 284–285, 345, 346, 347
  last days of Jesus and, 363, 364, 367,
    369, 370, 371–372
  later additions to, 352–353
  quoted, 9, 221, 285, 297–298, 345,
    346, 348, 349, 350, 351, 352,
    353, 359, 363, 368, 370
  symbolic intent in, 347
John Paul II, Pope, 265
John the Baptist, 286–288, 315,
  338–339, 346
  quoted, 269
Joseph, 87–104
  chronology of, 95
  dream interpretation by, 92–93
  grave of, 103–104
  historical existence of, 88
  Jacob and, 96–97, 101
  in prison, 91–93
Joseph and His Brothers (Mann), 87
Joseph of Arimathaea, 371, 372
Josephus, 282, 286, 287, 299, 302,
  361, 366
Joshua, 129, 139
  as composite hero, 130
  miracles at Gibeon and, 134–135
Joshua, Book of, 129–138
  chronology of, 130, 131, 136, 137
  as heroic saga, 130

historical validity of, 130
Jahweh and, 137
literary allusion in, 134–135
quoted, 129, 131, 132, 136
Judah, kingdom of, 172, 194, 218, 221
  destruction of, 218
  exiles' return to, 230
  Hezekiah's rebellion and, 221–226
  as vassal of Babylon, 226–227
Judah Maccabee, 241–247, 267
Judas Iscariot, Apostle, 313, 315, 379
Jude, Apostle, 378
Judea, 232, 241–247
  Hellenized culture in, 241–243
Judges, Book of, 138–154
  chronology of, 151
  derived tale in, 151–152
  executive decisions in, 138
  quoted, 138, 141–142, 143–145,
    147, 148, 152, 153, 154
  tribal chieftains in, 141
Judith, Book of, 236–238, 263
  quoted, 237
  story of, 236–237
Judith of Bethulia (Hebbel), 237

Kant, Immanuel, 11
Keller, Werner, 162
Kepler, Johannes, 303
Kierkegaard, Sören, 300
King James Apocrypha, 236, 241, 263,
  272
King James Version (Authorized Ver-
  sion), 12n, 13, 14, 15, 74, 82–83,
  84, 122, 123, 142, 145, 156, 178,
  196, 200, 217, 234, 257, 258,
  295, 327, 328, 329, 338, 377
Kings, Books of, 174–227
  Book I, quoted, 173–174, 178, 180,
    182, 183, 184, 185, 186, 188,
    189, 190, 191, 193, 194, 195,
    196, 199, 200
  Book II, quoted, 197, 199, 217, 220,
    222, 223, 224, 225, 226, 227
King Solomon's Mines (Rider Haggard),
  179, 181
Kleist, Heinrich von, 43–44
Kohelet, Words of, 258–260
Koine dialect, 337

Koldewey, Robert, 227
Koran, Holy, 65
kyrios, meaning of, 29

Laban, 83, 85
Lagash, 47
Laodicea, Council of, 16
Last Judgment, concept of, 264
Last Supper, of Jesus, 362, 363, 364
laws:
  in Egypt, 92, 93–94
  of Hammurabi, 118–120
  of Moses, 118–122, 127, 139–140,
    231, 244, 274, 284, 308, 312,
    380, 381–382
Layard, Sir Austen Henry, 46
Lazarus, 86–87
Leah, 83–84
Lebanon, cedars of, 184
Lemuel, King, Proverbs and, 255, 256,
  258
Levites, 126
Leviticus, Book of, 126–127, 155
  quoted, 121
Lewis, C. S., 359
Liberius, Pope, 16, 305
Lichtenberg, Georg Christoph, 377
locusts, as symbol, 355–356
London *Daily Telegraph*, 45–46
Lord Sabaoth, 29
Lord's Prayer, 296, 379
Lot, 72–73, 80, 81, 152
Lourdes, shrine of, 388
Luke, Saint, Gospel According to, 64,
    292, 295, 302, 306, 313, 316,
    317, 327, 333, 336, 337–344, 345,
    352–353
  audience intended for, 337–338, 342
  author of, 337, 343–344, 385–386
  last days of Jesus and, 362, 370, 371
  quoted, 86–87, 254, 300, 301, 305,
    308, 314, 315, 317, 336, 337,
    338, 339, 340, 341, 365
  second volume of, *see* Acts of the
    Apostles
Luther, Martin, 12–13, 40, 237, 348
  see also German Bible, Luther's

Maccabees, 241–247, 274

Maccabees, Books of the, 241–247
  Book I, quoted, 240–241, 242, 243,
    244–245
  Book II, quoted, 243, 246, 247
  cultural conflict in, 242–243
  excluded books from, 241
  resurrection concept in, 246, 247
Madan people, 39–40
Malachi, Book of, 273–274
"Malachi," prophet, 273–274
Mamre, 82
mandrakes, 84
Mann, Thomas, 86
manna, *Hammada salicornica* and, 116
Manual of Instruction, Qumran text,
  285
Marah lake, 114
Mari, cuneiform tablets at, 68, 71, 162
Mark, Saint, Gospel According to, 292,
    307, 318, 321, 328–336, 345, 371
  audience intended for, 330, 331–332,
    334–335
  last days of Jesus and, 363, 365, 370,
    371
  later additions to, 335–336
  literary style of, 329
  quoted, 255, 288, 289, 296, 301,
    308, 312, 328, 330, 331, 332,
    333, 335, 336, 365, 370
  as source document, 328–329
Marksen, Willy, 377
marriage, Mosaic laws on, 156,
    231–232
Mary Magdalene, 315–317, 336
Mary of Bethany, 316
Masada, stronghold of, 281, 313
Masoretes, 15
Massacre of the Innocents, 319
Matthew, Apostle, 314–315
  biographical information on, 319
Matthew, Saint, Gospel According to,
    64, 132–133, 200, 281, 284, 292,
    302–303, 304–305, 306, 318–328,
    345
  last days of Jesus and, 363, 365, 367,
    370–371
  as propaganda for Jewish Christians,
    319–325
  quoted, 121, 254, 287, 307, 308,

313, 320, 321, 322, 323, 324, 325, 326, 327, 352, 364–365, 370
menorahs, 35
Mercury, Olympian, 141
Messiah:
  concept of, 267
  Essene idea of, 281
  false, 274
  House of David and, 271, 302, 306
  Jesus as, 274, 288, 299, 302, 306, 319, 321, 347, 361, 369–370, 371
  John the Baptist as, 287
  in prophecy, 267, 274, 281, 288, 302, 306, 319, 321, 347, 361, 369–370, 371
Messiah (Handel), 270
Micah, Book of, quoted, 270–271
Micah, prophet, 270–271
Michelangelo, 122, 129, 168
miracles:
  Elijah and, 199–200, 217
  Elisha and, 200, 217
  Gideon and, 145
  Jesus and, 200–217, 299, 332–334, 347
  Joshua and, 134–135
  Moses and, 108–110, 113–118, 217
  Old vs. New Testament views of, 333–334
Mitanni:
  Abraham and, 65, 69–74
  cuneiform legal tablets of, 71–73, 85
monotheism, idea of, 29–31, 95
Moses, 104–129, 171, 199, 217
  ascription of five books to, 123–124
  Exodus and, 112–118
  historical existence of, 108
  horns of, 122–123
  last days of, 127–128
  laws of, 118–122, 127, 139–140, 198, 231, 244, 274, 284, 308, 312, 380, 381–382
  Midianite religion and, 107
  monotheism and, 31
  oppression of Hebrews and, 104–105, 106–107
Moussa, Professor, 103
Muhammad, 64
Muller, Herbert J., 291

Nathan, prophet, 175
Nazarites, 148–149
Nebo, Mount, 128, 130
Nebuchadnezzar, king of Babylon, 187, 236
Nebuchadnezzar II, king of Babylon, 226, 227–229
Nefertiti, 30
Nehemiah, Book of, 230, 233–234
  chronology and authorship of, 234
  quoted, 232, 233
Nehemiah, prophet, 230, 231–232
Nero, Emperor, 361–362, 385
  in Revelation, 357
New English Bible, 236, 241
New International Version (New Testament), 295, 314, 323, 325, 327, 328, 330, 331, 335, 343, 386
New Testament, 28, 29, 291–358
  Aramaic words in, 309
  authorship of, 292, 377–378
  chronology of, 280, 292
  contents of, 292
  Dead Sea Scrolls and, 280–281
  language of, 292, 294–297
  Old Testament references and quotations in, 200, 253–255, 269–270, 292–293, 367, 369, 370
  as postscript to Essene scrolls, 283, 284–285, 286
  selection of texts in, 16, 292
  surviving texts of, 293–294
  Thomas Gospel and, 300–301
  variant readings in, 294–295
  see also Acts of the Apostles; Bible; epistles; Gospels; Revelation, Book of
Nicodemus, 372
Nineveh, 37, 45–46, 218, 268–269
Nisir mountain, 52
Noah, 49, 54, 64
  see also Flood, story of
Numbers, Book of, 126, 127
  quoted, 125, 304
numbers, mystical, 356–357
  see also seven, as mystical number
Nuzu-Guzur, 69, 71
  cuneiform tablets at, 71–73

Oetlinger, Friedrich Carl, 297
Old Testament, 16, 27–274, 291, 361
  ancient Hebrew versions of, 15, 18
  chronological sequence in, 27
  Dead Sea Scrolls and, 15, 280
  disputed passages in, 17
  earliest surviving copies of, 17–18
  first written texts of, 19
  Greek translation of, see Septuagint
  International Bible Society project
    on, 17
  Masoretic manuscripts of, 15, 234,
    280
  numbering in, 18
  omissions from, 16, 234, 238, 266,
    272
  oral tradition as basis of, 14–15, 18
  translations of, 11–16
  see also Bible; Septuagint; specific
    books
Omri, king of Israel, 194–195, 197
Ophir, land of, 180–183
Oppert, Jules, 66
Orthodox Jews, 86
Osiris cult, 100–101
Oxyrhynchus, 293

Palestine, origin of name, 151
palimpsests, 21
paper, 21–22
papyrus, 20
  texts on, 18, 19
Papyrus 52, 293, 346
Papyrus 5501, 91
Paradise, Eden and, 37–40
parallel ancient texts and sources, 14,
    29–31, 37, 40–42, 46–55, 71, 76,
    78, 105, 119–120, 134–135,
    141–142, 148, 152, 163, 235, 238,
    261, 332, 333, 355
parchment, 20–21
  monks' handwritten texts on, 21
Parrot, André, 61
Passover (Pesach):
  calendar reckoning of, 364
  Jesus and, 361–364, 369
  origin of, 111
Paul, Apostle, 292, 342, 343–344, 378,
    379–388

  Acts of Apostles and, 292, 341–342,
    379, 384, 385, 387
  biographical information on, 385,
    386–387
  Mosaic law and, 380, 381–382
Paul, Jean, 44
Paul, letters of, 343, 344, 378–388
  authenticity of, 378–379
  chronology of, 379
  quoted, see specific letters
Pentateuch, 19, 126
Persia, 229–230, 231, 232, 238–240
  Messiah concept in, 267
  religion of, 249–250
Peter (Simon Peter), Apostle, 307, 315,
    329, 342, 365, 372, 377, 381
Petinato, Giovanni, 76
Pharisees, 311, 312, 315, 316–317,
    324, 326
Philemon, Letter to, 379
Philip, Apostle, 315, 349–350
Philippians, Letter to the, 379
Philistines, 137, 149–151, 159–165
  etymological spin-offs of, 150–151
  as Vikings, 137, 150
Philo, 32
philology, philologists, 48
  Beuron project of, 17, 23
  function of, 23, 34, 35
Phoenicians, 181–184, 187–188
phylacteries, 324
pillar of fire, 114
Pines, Professor, 16
Pison river, 38–39
Pithom, 107, 108, 112
Plato, 264, 293
Pontius Pilate, 254, 298, 362, 366–367,
    368
Potiphar, Potiphar's wife, 87, 88, 91
"Preacher, Book of the," 258
priests:
  Jesus' vs. Essene view of, 284
  Leviticus and, 126–127
printing, of Bible, 22–23
Promised Land, 128–129
prophets, 265–274
  in holy wars, 198–218
  "Malachi" as last of, 274
  Messiah theme of, 267, 274, 288,

302, 306, 319, 321, 347, 361, 369–370, 371
"minor," 266–267
Old Testament meaning of, 266
unity of faith and, 274
women as, 384
prostitution, attitudes toward, 132–133, 139–140, 257, 383
Protestant Bible, 16
 see also German Bible, Luther's; King James Version; New English Bible; New International Version
Proverbs, Book of, 251, 255–258, 263, 380–381
authorship of, 255
quoted, 255, 256, 257
Psalms, Book of, 170, 173, 251, 252–255
authorship of, 252–253
in Christian allegory, 253–255, 367, 369, 370
quoted, 30–31, 229, 251, 252, 253, 254, 255, 305, 351, 369
pseudepigraphical texts, 241
Ptolemy V (Epiphanes), 20
Purim, 238, 239, 240

Q-document, 302
Qumran, Essene community at, 18, 279, 280, 281–282, 313, 345, 346, 347, 383
Qumran Texts, quoted, 281, 285

Raamses, 106–107, 108, 112
Rachel, 83–85
Rahab, the harlot, 132–133
rainbow, covenant and, 54–55
"Rainbow Bibles," 21
Ramses II, Pharaoh, 106, 108
Ramses III, Pharaoh, 150
Raphael, angel, 235–236
Ras Shamra, excavations at, 137
Rebekah, 73
Red Sea, 113–114
Reformation, paper and, 22
Rembrandt, 122, 129, 236
resurrection, concept of, 246, 247, 264
Resurrection, of Jesus, 335–336, 341, 359, 379, 382

Revelation, Book of, 271, 292, 353–358
apocryphal origin of, 354
author of, 353
political prophecy in, 358
quoted, 344, 354, 355
symbolic language of, 354–355, 356–358
Rider Haggard, H., 179
Rilke, Rainer Maria, 250
Roman Catholic Church, 64, 288
Maccabee martyrs in, 247
Satan in, 249
version of Bible, 16, 234, 236, 238, 241, 246, 252, 263, 266, 272
Romans, Letter to the, 379, 380
quoted, 380
Rome, persecutions by, 281, 312–313, 357–358, 361–371, 385
Rosicrucians, 109
Rousseau, Jean Jacques, 334
Ruth, Book of, 155–158, 280
quoted, 155, 156, 157, 200

Saba (Sheba), 190–192
Sabbath, ritual, 36
Sadducees, 311–312, 367
Sakkara, 103
Salome, 287
salt, spilling of, 146
Samaria, Samaritans, 194, 195, 218, 220–221, 231, 320
Samson, exploits of, 148–149
Samuel, Books of, 159–173
Book I, quoted, 159–160, 164, 165, 167, 168, 171
Book II, quoted, 159, 160–161, 169, 170, 171
chronology of, 161–162
Samuel, prophet, 163–164, 167
Sanhedrin, 371, 385
modern Israeli review sought of, 367
trial of Jesus by, 312, 361, 362, 364–365
Sarah, 71–72, 73, 80
Sargon, king of Akkad, 105
Satan, 172, 248–249
Saul, King, 161, 163–166
character of, 165, 166, 167, 171
science, religion vs., 265

scientific investigations, 32, 34, 36, 48–49, 52–53, 109–110, 115–118, 181, 265, 303, 372–373
see also archaeological research
Sea of Reeds, 113–114
Seleucids, 241
Sennacherib, king of Assyria, 222–225, 226
Septuagint, 19, 234, 236, 238, 241, 293, 302, 381
Sermon on the Mount, 281, 327–328
serpent, 111
Tree of Knowledge and, 40–42, 43
seven, as mystical number, 18, 35, 56, 246, 314, 354, 378
Seven Wonders of the World, 35, 36, 387
sex, 90–91
Paul on, 382–383
as sin, 43
Shaddai, 28
Shakespeare, W., 251, 262, 344
Shaw, George Bernard, 344
Sheba, Queen of, 190–191
Shechem, 146
shibboleth, as stratagem, 147–148
Shinar (Mesopotamia), 58–61, 66
siege towers, Assyrian, 219
Siloam, tunnel of, 221
Simon Zelotes, Apostle, 313, 315
sin, of Adam and Eve, 42–43
Sinai (Horeb), Mount, 117–118, 198
Singer, Isaac Bashevis, 235
Sinuhe, 69–70
666, as mystical number, 357
Smith, George, 37, 45
Sodom and Gomorrah, 72–73, 76, 80–81
soham, meaning of, 38
Solomon, King, 170, 173–194, 305
army created by, 177–178, 193
cultural legacy of, 176, 192
Ecclesiastes attributed to, 258
as king, 175–177, 193–194
merchant naval projects of, 180, 182–183
Proverbs attributed to, 255–257

in struggle for the throne, 173, 174–175
Temple built by, *see* Temple, Solomon's
wisdom of, 192, 193
Wisdom of Solomon text attributed to, 263
women and, 188–192
"Solomon's mines" (Wadi Timnah), 178–179
Solomon's Seventh Seal, 192
"Solomon's stables," 178
Soncino, Gershon ben Moshe, 13
Song of Solomon (Canticle of Canticles), 192, 253, 261–262, 263
erotic love vs. religious metaphor in, 261
quoted, 90, 261, 262
Star of Bethlehem, 303–304
Stevens, Robert, 292
Strauss, Richard, 287
Suetonius, 299
Sumer, Sumerians, 58–61, 65, 66–67
cuneiform tablets of, 37, 67, 68, 75
cylinder seals in, 39, 41–42, 141
sagas of, 46n, 47, 51, 53–54, 78
Susanna and the Elders, 16, 272
quoted, 272–273
synagogues, in Babylon, 229
Synoptic Gospels, 345

Tacitus, 36, 298–299
talents, meaning of, 326–327
Tale of Sinuhe, 70
tallis, 324, 331–332
Talmud, 86, 299, 307
Tamar, 133
Teacher of Righteousness, 282, 283–284, 288
Tel Mardiqu, 75
Temple, Solomon's, 180, 183–187
brass basin in, 186–187
Dead Sea Scrolls and, 277–278
description of, 185–187
destruction of (A.D. 70), 313
Phoenicians and, 183–184, 186–187
rebuilding of, 230–231

Index

sack of, 125, 185, 187, 226
Samaritan obstructionists and, 231
Zeus's altar installed in, 242
"Temptation Cylinder Seal," 42
Ten Commandments, 118, 120–122
Ten Lost Tribes of Israel, 226
testament, meaning of, 27–28
Testament of Solomon, 192
textual criticism, function of, 13–14,
  297
Theophilus, 337, 342, 344
theraphim, 85
Thessalonians, Letters to the, 379
Thomas Gospel, 16, 300–301
Three Wise Men, 304–305, 306
Tilmun, as Sumerian paradise, 37, 42
tithes, justification of, 78
Tobias, 235–236
Tobit, Book of, 234–236, 280
  quoted, 234
  story of, 235–236
Torah, 126
Tower of Babel, 56–63
Transfiguration, 200
Tree of Knowledge, 40–44
tribute money, as temple tax, 325–326
tulli, 70
Turin shroud, 372–373
twelve disciples, Essene vs. Christian,
  282, 283
two-source theory of Gospels, 302

Ugarit, 137
Ur, 47–48, 66–67, 68
  ziggurat of, 60, 61–62, 66
Urartu, 53
ushabti, 100
Utnapishtim, 50–51, 54

Vedas, 55
Virgil, 371
Virgin Mary, 379
*Virgin Spanks the Christ Child in the
  Presence of Three Witnesses, The*
  (Ernst), 299–300

Vogelweide, Walter von der, 262
Voltaire, 282
von Däniken, Erich, 125
Vulgate Bible, 122, 123, 295

Wailing Wall, 185
walking on water, miracle of, 200, 332
War of Jenkins's Ear, 153
Wellhausen, Julius, 34, 35
Wilde, Oscar, 287
Wisdom Literature, 251–265
Wisdom of Solomon, 192, 251,
  262–265
  Greek philosophy and, 264
  quoted, 262
Woolley, Sir Charles Leonard, 47
women:
  in Egypt, 89–91, 94–95
  in Essene community, 283
  in Greece, 89
  Jesus and, 312, 315–317, 364
  in Mitanni, 72–73
  Paul and, 382–384
  in Persia, 239
  in Proverbs, 256–258
Württemberg State Library, 23

Xerxes, 61
Xerxes I, king of Persia, 238

Yadin, Yigael, 136, 177–178
Yahweh (YHWH), 28, 29

Zealots, 313
Zerubbabel, 267
ziggurats, 60–62, 66, 228
Zimbabwe, 181
Zimri, 197
Zion, Mount, 173
Zipporah, 107
Ziusudra, 47, 51, 54
Zoroaster, prophet, 250
Zulu mythology, 55